FASHION ON TELEVISION

Identity and Celebrity Culture

HELEN WARNER

B L O O M S B U R Y
LONDON · NEW DELHI · NEW YORK · SYDNEY

Bloomsbury Academic

An imprint of Bloomsbury Publishing Plc

50 Bedford Square
London
WC1B 3DP
UK

1385 Broadway
New York
NY 10018
USA

www.bloomsbury.com

Bloomsbury is a registered trademark of Bloomsbury Publishing Plc

First published 2014

British Library Cataloguing-in-Publication Data
A catalogue record for this book is available from the British Library.

ISBN: HB: 978-0-8578-5440-7
PB: 978-0-8578-5441-4
ePDF: 978-1-4725-6745-1
ePub: 978-1-4725-6746-8

Library of Congress Cataloging-in-Publication Data
A catalog record for this book is available from the Library of Congress.

Typeset by Apex CoVantage, LLC, Madison, WI, USA
Printed and bound in India

CONTENTS

LIST OF ILLUSTRATIONS

FOREWORD

Pamela Church Gibson

The film *American Gigolo* (Paul Schrader, US) appeared in 1980, a fitting start to what some would christen 'the designer decade'. In the most memorable scene, which became the subject of detailed academic scrutiny, Richard Gere famously prepared for a date by fanning out his colour-coordinated Armani shirts and ties on his bed to help with difficult decisions as to his final outfit. Richard Martin, head of fashion at the Metropolitan Museum of Modern Art in New York, described this scene as 'a seminal moment in the history of menswear'. It was certainly a seminal moment for Giorgio Armani, who became synonymous with what was now called 'unstructured tailoring'; many people outside fashion's inner circles were starting to become very familiar not only with designer names but also with their characteristic styles. Armani and his former employer, Nino Cerruti, soon garnered contracts to dress the stars of cinema both on- and off-screen. But, thirty years later, it could be argued that that it was perhaps the television of the period that had more impact on the popular imagination of the time—and certainly on the buying habits of the general public.

The popular CBS series *Dallas* was already running when the decade opened. A year later ABC created *Dynasty*, a similar saga of a dysfunctional family involved in the oil business. But whereas the Ewings of *Dallas* lived on a ranch, their televisual rivals owned a massive redbrick mansion, complete with a Georgian portico flanked by heraldic lions. *Dallas* executives responded speedily, hiring veteran Hollywood designer William Travilla. He had dressed Marilyn Monroe throughout her career, creating not only the white dress that so memorably shoots skywards in *The Seven Year Itch* (Billy Wilder, US, 1955) but also the hot-pink ballgown and long evening gloves worn as she sang 'Diamonds Are a Girl's Best Friend'. Travilla was adept at creating exactly the kind of 'spectacular' costume that features in the pages of this book; for Sue Ellen Ewing, he designed the ferocious shoulder pads which were copied everywhere and which came to define women's wear of the period.

In contrast, the costume designer for *Dynasty*, Nolan Miller, had no experience at all. Nevertheless, it was his extraordinary outfits for stars Joan Collins and Lynda Evans that made the series so successful and inspired commercial tie-ins rather than simple emulation. Miller created a '*Dynasty*' collection and later a men's fashion line. Soon there were more affordable goods on sale—lingerie, '*Dynasty*' bed linen and towels and even '*Dynasty*' paper patterns for those with sewing skills. The two stars endorsed their own fragrances, while their images were featured in magazines at every market level; all this commercial activity, so reminiscent of Hollywood in its heyday, was novel for television. Fast forward to 2010 and the series *Gossip Girl*, discussed in these pages, has orchestrated things so that a fan might, with a mouse-click, assure herself that an acceptable copy of what Blake Lively wore onscreen would arrive on her doorstep the very next day.

This book is the first foray into that increasingly complex relationship between television and fashion. In a new millennium increasingly dominated by the symbiotic relationship between celebrity culture and the fashion industry, television has a central role in the circulation of fashionable images and the creation of demand. Yet so far, this has not been discussed within the area of television studies; this book seeks to put the relationship between television, costuming, celebrity and fashion on the academic agenda.

Most scholarship on screen fashion has focused on cinema, but it is television which perhaps has more to do with the way in which fashion circulates today. It is now several years since Sarah Street called for more academic enquiry into television costume, but so far there has been little response. This book is a welcome intervention and provides the basis for future debate and the opening up of discussion. It adopts an interdisciplinary approach, and unlike much work on screen costume, the author does not neglect questions of production. She uses the trade press to examine the changing working conditions of the costume designer.

'Stardom' is now so interwoven with celebrity culture that the fashion industry and its activities are impossible to understand without looking right across the spectrum of visual culture; this book deploys that same sideways glance and will, I trust, generate activity within the academy.

ACKNOWLEDGEMENTS

There are a number of people whose input has been invaluable throughout the process of writing this book. I wish to thank Pamela Church Gibson and Sarah Gilligan for providing much stimulating conversation and encouragement. I am also indebted to my colleagues (past and present) and friends at the University of East Anglia—in particular Eylem Atakav, Tori Cann, Hannah Ellison, Su Holmes, Sanna Inthorn, Melanie Kennedy, Richard McCulloch, Brett Mills, Liz Powell, Tom Phillips, Heather Savigny, Kate Seaman and John Street. Special thanks go to Professor Mark Jancovich for being a fantastic mentor and an even better friend. At Bloomsbury, Anna Wright, Emily Roessler and Hannah Crump have been a strong source of support throughout the project, for which I'm truly grateful. I also wish to thank Lewis Swift for being incredibly patient, supportive and inspirational. Finally, I am grateful to my family: Mitchell and Jasper Cooper for providing welcome distractions; my Labrador dogs, Will and George, for their silent sympathy (particular thanks to George who chewed through my laptop cable during the early stages of writing); and lastly, Lynne Warner and Jenny Cooper, whose influence can be found on every page—this book is dedicated to you with so much love.

1
INTRODUCTION: APPROACHING FASHION, IDENTITY AND CELEBRITY CULTURE

Pilot episode *Sex and the City*, June 1998:

The camera reveals Carrie. Seated at her writing desk, in a pale-blue casual shirt, she welcomes viewers to the 'age of *un*-innocence'. Cut to the busy streets of Manhattan, Carrie—dressed in an oversized raincoat—is surrounded *only* by well-dressed New York women and observes that: 'There are thousands, maybe tens of thousands of women like this in the city. We all know them and we all agree they're great. They travel, they pay taxes, they'll spend four hundred dollars on a pair of Manolo Blahnik strappy sandals. And they're alone.'

In his pilot script, Darren Star imagines his quirky protagonist Carrie Bradshaw as 'Heather Locklear gorgeous cursed with the brain of Dorothy Parker' (Star 1996: 6). Bradshaw is vivified by Sarah Jessica Parker and the pilot's costume designer, Ellen Lutter. Parker's star body gives existence to her costuming, and together the character is made to *mean*. Star's adaptation of Candace Bushnell's popular newspaper column would become a landmark series within television history, noted for its unique sartorial display. His pilot script hints at the importance of fashion, not only as costume but also as an independent 'aesthetic discourse' (Gaines 1990). The specific namecheck of Manolo Blahnik in the prologue signals, to a self-selecting fan base, the premium which would ultimately be placed on fashion within the narrative.

Following the success of *Sex and the City* (1998–2004), the number of shows with fashion at their centres has grown considerably and led to the development of a discursive category identified in the trade press as 'fashion programming'.[1] This category of programming marks a departure from so-called traditional Hollywood costuming in which wardrobe *serves* character and narrative. While the costumer must interpret and translate the script, there is no unequal relationship where fashion is subservient to narrative demands. The clothes are given meaning and audiences are encouraged to take pleasure in deciphering and appropriating that meaning. This book is about that process.

Using a number of case studies (including *Sex and the City*, *Ugly Betty* (2006–2010), *Gossip Girl* (2007–2012), *The O.C.* (2003–2007), *Mad Men* (2007–) and *Boardwalk Empire* (2010–)), this book considers the following: first, it examines the ways in which certain meanings become attached to the texts and the fashion on display within them. Second, it explores the role of cultural workers—in the form of costume designers and celebrities—in securing these meanings. Finally, it traces the representative trajectory of those meanings from beyond the text into wider contextual apparatuses (in the form of celebrity and fashion inter-text). Thus, the impetus behind this book is to respond to calls for academic enquiry into costume in television programming (Street 2002) and to gain an understanding of the precise ways in which onscreen fashion develops into a semiotic language that audiences and consumers may assimilate and appropriate in order to express and negotiate cultural identities.

Such an endeavour demands a truly interdisciplinary approach; thus this introductory chapter pursues the related work of contextualizing this book within relevant academic debate and outlining its parameters. What follows, then, is a brief outline of key debates within fashion theory, media/cultural studies and celebrity studies. Since the majority of existing scholarship regarding onscreen clothing is informed to some degree by fashion theory, it provides a useful starting point for thinking through the complex relationship between fashion and costume.

Fashion and Popular Culture

Most introductory anthologies on fashion begin with an attempt to answer the following question: what is fashion? This seemingly simple question lacks a simple answer. The meaning and significance of the term has altered over time, and therefore it can be difficult to offer an exact definition. This is compounded by the fact that certain terms are often used interchangeably: e.g. clothing and fashion. This project adheres to the school of thought which, to put it simply, conceives of fashion as a symbolic product, as opposed to a material one (Kawamura 2005). This distinction is important because it reminds us that fashion is imbued with meaning that is absent from clothes (the raw materials). For Deborah Nadoolman Landis this distinction is crucial and has implications for the way in which we define fashion and costume—which she also considers to be separate. For Landis (2003: 8), 'Fashion and costumes are not synonymous; they are antithetical.' However, such taxonomy does not stand up to intense scrutiny, particularly if one is to comprehend the use of fashion *as* costume in a show like *Sex and the City* or its contemporaries. Within the texts examined here, garments are invested within meaning that exists both within and outside of the diegetic context, and therefore it is necessary to employ a more fluid definition.

The ambiguity of the term 'fashion' has had not only implications for its study, and the ways in which it has developed as a discipline, but also implications for the discourses of value attached to the term. Fashion, as Pierre Bourdieu (1993b: 185) notes, 'is a very prestigious subject in the sociological tradition, at the same time as being apparently rather frivolous'. Similarly, in their introduction to *Fashion Cultures*, Stella Bruzzi and Pamela Church Gibson (2000: 2) posit that '[p]art of the perceived problem with fashion has been that academics in particular have not always known with what tone to approach and write about it—it's too trivial to theorise, too serious to ignore.' Indeed, this understanding emerges out of a longstanding reluctance to take popular culture (particularly that which is coded as 'feminine') seriously. As such, scholars have attempted to 'explain away' Western culture's preoccupation with fashion from two very different academic perspectives (E. Wilson 1985: 47).

Art historians initially called for the legitimization of fashion as an area of study. However, their interest was limited to haute couture, and consequently work on fashion within an art history tradition focused exclusively on the conservative (and inherently masculine) notions of production and authorship.[2] Given that the notion of the author was, and remains still, central to the construction of value judgements within art and culture more generally, high fashion (that which has a designated author) was accepted within the field of art history as a serious object of study.[3] This resulted in a division between academic approaches to high fashion and 'everyday' fashion. Mass-produced everyday fashion (often perceived as 'feminine') was not considered a legitimate area of study in its own right, but rather served as evidence of mass culture's manipulation of 'passive' consumers within moralist critiques of consumer capitalism. In her influential book *Adorned in Dreams*, Elizabeth Wilson comments on this development and notes that '[i]t was easy to believe that the function of fashion stemmed from capitalism's need for perpetual expansion, which encouraged consumption. At its crudest, this kind of explanation assumes that changes in fashion are foisted upon us, especially women, in a conspiracy to consume far more than we "need" to' (1985: 4). As such, fashion was (and in some cases is) viewed as excessive and unnecessary, and those (women) who participated in its consumption were perceived as cultural dupes.[4] This negative view of fashion (as wasteful, trivial and narcissistic) informed early feminist writing on fashion consumption and the performance of femininity. For example in the 1850s, American women's rights advocate Amelia Bloomer considered certain apparel such as the corset as a form of 'bondage', responsible for the physical incapacitation of women (Bloomer 1895/1975). Similarly, feminists in the 1970s and 1980s struggled to view fashion as anything other than a tool in the oppression and exploitation of women (see Baker 1984; Brownmiller 1984; Coward 1984; Oakley 1981). Joanne Hollows (2000) observes that this 'functionalist' feminist critique of fashion generated two anti-fashion responses. While some rejected feminine clothes in favour of 'masculine' apparel, others favoured the 'natural' self. However, in rejecting feminine dress, anti-fashion feminists were arguably privileging masculinity and masculine values over femininity and feminine values. Similarly, those seeking to reclaim the 'natural' self privileged the 'natural' over the 'artificial'. Not only does this dichotomy fail to acknowledge the constructedness of a 'natural' identity, thereby confusing the term 'natural' with 'authentic', but it also problematically associates 'artifice' and 'performativity' with 'passivity'.

While second-wave feminism sought to condemn fashion as trivial and inconsequential, more recent feminist criticism seeks to rescue fashion from this status and to consider its pleasures and radical potential. This book reflects the more recent feminist agenda and adopts the position put forth by Elizabeth Wilson (1985), that fashion should be considered as a 'performance art'. Traditionally, those who privilege the 'natural' form of dress argue that fashion should—as Llewellyn Negrin (1999: 99) observes—'reveal the body for what it [is]'. However, as Joanne Entwistle (2000) has argued, there are problems with the notion that fashion can be used to simply 'interpret' a person's identity. She writes: 'On the one hand the clothes we choose to wear can be expressive of identity, telling others something about our gender, class status and so on; on the other, our clothes cannot always be "read", since they do not straightforwardly "speak" and can therefore be open to misinterpretation' (112). Therefore Entwistle and Wilson, along with other postmodern fashion theorists, have rejected the notion of a 'natural' form of dress, adopting the post-structuralist position that the 'natural' is a cultural construct (see Mascia-Lees and Sharpe 1992). They contend that the functionalist rejection of 'ornate' clothing has 'denied the legitimacy of the aesthetic pleasures derived from dress' (Negrin 1999: 107). Such a position disturbs second-wave feminism's disparaging understandings of 'artifice' and 'performativity'. Indeed, Wilson's and others' work can be regarded as part of a broader shift in which consumers are viewed as more 'active' than in previous accounts. For example Angela Partington's (1992: 156) study of fashion in post-war Britain presents the construction of the 'artificial' feminine identity as that which requires 'an *active* gaze to decode, utilize and identify with those images' (my emphasis). According to Partington's research, women demonstrated increasingly sophisticated consumer competences and appropriated fashion in order to articulate class identities, thereby challenging early feminist writing which relied on the assumption that fashion (and culture in general) was 'a mere expression of socio-economic relations rather than as a site of the active production of consumers' (149). Indeed, this process required a specific set of consumer competences in order to create and disrupt class identities. Significantly, as Partington acknowledges, this reveals a resistance to 'proper' consumer practices supposedly imposed upon women through advertising and, perhaps most importantly, through cinema and the 'woman's film'.[5]

The women's films of the 1940s sought to address women as consumers in order to regulate and secure the economy (previously jeopardized by the Great Depression). That is the woman's film was intended to educate women in consumer competences and to encourage the consumption of fashion and beauty products (see Doane 1987; LaPlace 1987; Partington 1992; Stacey 1994). Thus, it is my contention that parallels can be drawn between these texts and fashion programming, as I argue that one of its primary functions is to educate and to allow viewers to practice sophisticated consumer competences in reading fashion.

In *The Desire to Desire*, Mary Ann Doane (1987: 26) suggests that the 1940s woman's film was designed to position the female spectator as consumer. In a rather bleak account of women's relationship with film, she describes how cinema marketed 'a certain feminine self-image', achieved through the consumption of the fashion and beauty products advertised onscreen. In so doing, she argues that the female spectator is encouraged to consume and commodify herself (i.e. become a desirable object for a man). She argues that when presented with the image of a glamorous female star, the female spectator is 'invited to witness her own commodification and, furthermore to buy an image of herself insofar as the female star is proposed as the ideal for feminine beauty' (24). I would argue that Doane's work is underpinned by a view of fashion that is homogenous and simplistic, and as such discounts the myriad ways in which audiences could engage with onscreen fashion and consumer practices. This somewhat pessimistic view of the audience is typical of psychoanalytic theory which suggests that, within patriarchal society, all female desires and pleasures are ultimately passive. However, it is important not to dismiss psychoanalytic film theory entirely. For one thing, it has a great purchase on some of the early writing on costume and cinema.

Informed by psychoanalytic theory, Jane Gaines's (1990: 181) influential article 'Costume and Narrative', argues, in relation to classical realist cinema, that all aspects of mise en scène were designed to serve 'the higher purpose of narrative'. She claims that costume in the classical era was motivated by characterization, and was essentially required to remain 'subservient' to narrative demands. Failure to do so could 'distract the viewer from the narrative' (193). Underpinning this argument is Laura Mulvey's well-known concept of 'the gaze'. Just as Mulvey (1975/1989: 19) has argued that '[t]he presence of woman [onscreen] . . . tends to work against the development of a story-line [and] freeze the flow of action', Gaines (1990: 193) asserts that costume which is not adequately motivated by character could also result in a disruption of narrative, 'breaking the illusion and the spell of realism'. Within this formulation, fashion acts primarily as 'spectacle' and a 'distraction', thus disrupting the economy of narrative flow.

For the most part then, Gaines's article is guided by more traditional screen hierarchies which privilege narrative over mise en scène. Other studies of classical cinema and costume are also informed, to some extent, by this assumption, including Sarah Berry's (2000) *Screen Style*, Sue Harper's (1987) 'Historical Pleasures: Gainsborough Costume Melodrama' and Pam Cook's (1996) *Fashioning the Nation*;[6] and subsequent enquiries into the function of costume in contemporary cinema, such as Sarah Street's (2002) examination of *The Talented Mr. Ripley* (1999) and *The Matrix* (1999) in her book *Costume and Cinema*, and Peter Wollen's (1995) analysis of *Prêt a Porter* (1994) in his article 'Strike a Pose'. While these studies have offered invaluable insights into the examination of film costume, I suggest throughout this book that it might be useful to revisit and revise previous assumptions regarding fashion and costume, and spectacle and narrative, not least of all for the following reasons: first, productive enquiries with regard to action cinema have advanced the discussion of spectacle and narrative insofar as they illustrate that these often '"intermesh" in action sequences' (Romao 2004: 143). In addition, Pearson and Messenger-Davies's (2003) discussion of *Star Trek* in film and television (particularly *Star Trek: The Next Generation* (1987–1998) and *First Contact* (1996)) highlights the importance of the audience in defining discourses of narrative and spectacle, observing that 'the same shot may be seen by some as pure spectacle and by others as having a narrative function' (109). Thus, it is important to remember that analyses of costume and narrative conducted at a textual level are limited by the wider conceptual and methodological problems of purely textual approaches, the most oft-cited of these being the marginalization of the audience and the suggestion of a rather deterministic and homogenous reading of audience response. Thus, within some previous studies of fashion and film, there has been a tendency to overlook the importance of the viewer and more general questions of reception, yet these issues seem integral when making assumptions about the way in which spectacle is interpreted in the text. The notion that spectacle 'disrupts' narrative can surely only be substantiated through reception studies, which requires analysis beyond the text itself.

Second, discussions of spectacle and narrative are rarely taken up in relation to television. This is perhaps in part due to the notion that the televisual image is secondary to the cinematic image. This understanding of the televisual image is informed by the medium's specific conditions of production and consumption. For example television's connection to realism, screen size, picture resolution and domestic setting all contribute to the notion that television and spectacle are antithetical. In addition, the spectacle-as-distraction debate may not have initially seemed applicable to television given that early conceptions of TV-viewing claim that television is always watched in a distracted way or is constantly disrupted by commercial breaks, or both (Ellis 1992; Williams 1975/2003). However, as this assumption has long since been called into question, an investigation into fashion, spectacle and narrative television is overdue.

Finally, we might also review the use value of this screen hierarchy when approaching contemporary film and television on the grounds that considerable social, cultural and political changes have affected every other aspect of film and television forms since the classical period.[7] Perhaps, most significantly, seismic shifts have occurred within celebrity culture which, I suggest, cannot be separated from any discussion of costume. Indeed, it is crucial to this study, for I perceive stars and celebrities to be the organizing principle within fashion television. The star or celebrity provides a momentarily fixed point of meaning for the audience—that is a site in which a garment's meanings are temporarily stabilized within a text. Thus, I draw heavily from the field of star and celebrity studies in order to shed light on the lengthy and varied relationship between the celebrity and fashion industries.

Stardom and Celebrity

In his book *Stars*, Richard Dyer (1979/2004) examines the concept of the film star and its cultural, economic and political function within popular culture. In his analysis of 'stars as images', Dyer gestures towards the importance of fashion in the construction and circulation of the star image. That is to say, star images have long since been used to endorse various fashion and beauty products, and in so doing, they are involved in meaning making processes—that is mediating the symbolic value of products between producers and consumers while simultaneously benefitting from the association with particular brands. For example Dyer's discussion of Gloria Swanson and Chanel demonstrates the ways in which celebrity inter-texts (in this case, fan magazine *Photoplay*) provide a space in which these meaning-making processes can take place (38). Drawing on Dyer, Rachel Moseley (2005b) further explores how fashion and celebrity foster a reciprocal relationship. She writes:

> On the one hand [fashion] is separating and defining; fashion and dress, in relation to stars, can become the supreme marker of their identity—indeed the uniqueness of their persona. It can make them special, unreachable and untouchable. At the same time, however, dress and fashion are also part of the connective tissue of the social, allowing us to make judgments—even sartorial choices—based upon our ability to read their articulations in relation to that identity. (6)

Taking a cue from these assumptions, I devote considerable attention to the ways in which star images function as texts in which our understanding of cultural identity and society at large are embedded. My interest lies specifically in their roles as 'fashion icons' and what this status means in contemporary consumer society.

The importance of stars within consumer society is evident in the earliest writings on fashion and film (see Charles Eckert's (1990) and Linda Mizejewski's (1999) analyses of *Ziegfeld Girl* (1941)). Indeed, in their article 'Puffed Sleeves before Tea-Time: Joan Crawford, Adrian and Women Audiences', Herzog and Gaines (1991) demonstrate how fashion has long since been connected to the construction and reception of the star persona. Their analysis of Joan Crawford and the 'impact' of the 'Letty Lynton' dress (from the film of the same name (1932)) within consumer society suggests that female fans adopted an 'active' role in the processes of consumption. Ultimately, they conclude that 'fashion worked to elicit women's participation in star and screen myth making' (87). In other words, Herzog and Gaines's analysis of 1930s star–fan relationships echoes Moseley's comments cited above, which suggest that fashion facilitates the perception that the star is 'unreachable' yet 'connected' to the audience.

Also seeking to expand upon Dyer's early work, a body of feminist scholarship has emerged which examines the consumption of the star image—which also foregrounds the importance of fashion in the process of making stars *mean*—for indeed, as with film costume, star fashions are a central audience pleasure.[8] This work often concerns itself specifically with female star–fan relationships. For example Jackie Stacey's (1994) book *Star Gazing* offers a feminist critique of the relationship between fans and female stars of the classical era. In so doing, she challenges existing feminist film theory which is primarily concerned with 'images of women' in media, arguing that previous work which seeks to examine how the media socializes women into traditional gender roles (see Haskell 1974/1987; Mulvey 1975/1989) neglects to consider the role of the audience in the meaning-making process. For Stacey, the fan practices of female filmgoers in the classical era complicate previous assumptions regarding the 'woman as image' insofar as female fans often appropriate, and identify with, star images in myriad and complex ways. In her analysis of the identificatory practices of fans, she claims that fans often actively participated in appropriating certain elements of particular star fashions in order to construct their own individual identities.

The specific focus on female stars and their relationship to fashion speaks to the ways in which the cultural function of the star image is informed by gender—and resultantly reminds us of the importance of gender in the star's meaning. In her article 'Re-examining Stardom: Questions of Texts, Bodies and Performance', Christine Geraghty (2007: 106) argues that female stars operate differently from their male counterparts. Geraghty posits that the category of celebrity is most commonly associated with female stars. She writes:

> Women function effectively as spectacle in the press and on television as well as in the cinema. In addition, the common association in popular

culture between women and the private sphere of personal relationships and domesticity fits with the emphasis, in the discourse of celebrity, on the private life and leisure activity of the star. (106)

Similarly, in his analysis of Sandra Bullock, Peter Kramer (2004: 89) suggests that '[w]hile female stars . . . dominate magazine covers and the talk show circuit there are numerous indicators showing that in Hollywood they usually do not amount to much [in terms of box office bankability]'. Inherent within both of these comments is the fact that female stars are often made visible precisely because of their 'to-be-looked-at-ness'. As such, fashion and style are of the utmost importance in determining a star's meaning. Fashion is used to forcefully define the boundaries of cultural identities (i.e. gender, ethnicity, class etc.). Moreover, the function of fashion as a marker of cultural identity is arguably made more apparent given that it is mediated, and made visible through, the circulation of the star image in celebrity inter-texts.

To return once more to Geraghty's comments above, it is important to note that the category of celebrity is bound up with discourses of value. In her article she explores the specificities of stardom and celebrity in an attempt to articulate their (gendered) difference—a difference that has long since been debated within the field. The common assumption is that stardom is reserved exclusively for film actors and relies upon the ability to maintain a 'duality between actor and character' (Allen and Gomery 1985: 11).[9] To use Dyer's initial definition, the star is necessarily contradictory and ambiguous, given that it must simultaneously appear 'ordinary' and 'extraordinary'; they are both like us in their ordinariness and unlike us in their specialness. Conversely, it has been argued that television actors achieve 'celebrity' or 'personality' status. For example John Langer's (1981: 357) essay 'Television's Personality System' argues that the television actors 'exist as more or less stable "identities" within the flow of events, situations and narratives'. In accordance, John Ellis (1992) notes that the television personality is 'too ordinary' and fails to embody the 'ordinary/extraordinary' paradox. However, more recent developments within celebrity culture have obscured these definite taxonomies of fame. This is often attributed to the increase in celebrity magazines, and the increasing speed and saturation of Internet 'gossip' blogs resulting in the 'democratization' of the celebrity culture.[10]

In conjunction with this development in celebrity culture, academic approaches to fame have also shifted. Recent work on stardom and celebrity appears to emphasize the political economy of celebrity (see Turner 2004; Turner, Bonner and Marshall 2000; Evans and Hesmondhalgh 2005) and attempts to explain contemporary categories of fame (Cashmore 2006; King 2003). Joshua Gamson's theory of twentieth-century fame has been widely adopted within contemporary media and cultural studies and informs the final section of this book. In his book *Claims to Fame*, Gamson (1994) suggests that there are two explanations of fame which jostle for dominance within celebrity culture. He argues that in the earlier part of the twentieth century, the star system foregrounded discourses of 'talent', 'star quality' and 'personality' as the dominant explanation for fame. This discourse is not entirely evacuated from contemporary celebrity culture, but rather competes with a 'manufacture' discourse. In the latter part of the twentieth century, the increase in extra-textual material offers 'supposedly unmediated access' to the processes of fame and serves to present the star or celebrity as an 'artificially manufactured' image (10). This, according to Gamson, encourages readers 'to visit the real self behind those images . . . [in so doing, the] public discovers and makes famous certain people because it (with the help of magazines) *sees through* the publicity-generated, artificial self to the real, deserving special self' (39, emphasis in original). This notion of a 'real self' that exists in awkward conjunction with an 'artificial self' is not limited to discourses of stardom, but rather extends to more general discussions of identity performance in contemporary culture. This is perhaps unsurprising given that stardom serves as a location in which our ideas about cultural identity are embedded.

Postmodernity, Television and Identity

Though it has been claimed that identity has long since pivoted on notions of performance (see Goffman 1959/1990), academic work on the subject of selfhood has noted a shift towards a more 'mobile, multiple, personal, self-reflexive [model of identity that is] . . . subject to change and innovation' (Kellner 1992: 141). Indeed, in the contemporary period, the now-familiar claims that identity is increasingly fragmented, unstable and 'artificial' resonates, to varying degrees, with academic and popular discourses on selfhood. However, there remains some disparity over precisely when this move towards a fragmented identity began, and what particular social change (or changes) were responsible for it.

Postmodern theory offers a pervasive (yet, in some ways, problematic) explanation of contemporary identity, which suggests that the 'subject has disintegrated into a flux of euphoric intensities . . . and no longer possesses the depth, substantiality and coherence that was the ideal and occasional achievement of the modern self' (Kellner 1992: 144). Thus, the postmodern model of selfhood suggests that traditional power structures (gender, 'race' and class) no longer shape identity.

While the notion of a postmodern self is, for some, flawed (see Giddens 1992; Kellner 1992), the anxieties it engenders resonate within contemporary celebrity (and consumer) culture (Dunn 1998). Thus, the increasing coverage of celebrity which encourages individuals to reflect upon the construction of the celebrity image, while simultaneously attempting to locate an 'authentic self', can be viewed as symptomatic of this supposed wider shift. Indeed, these shifts have broader implications for the study of fashion and celebrity.

Two studies adjacent to this book sketch out the interdependence of fashion, stardom and identity which I will elaborate on in the final section. In her article 'Sharon Stone in a Gap Turtleneck', Rebecca Epstein (2007) examines how the increase in celebrity literature (and 'fashion reporting') impacts the star's role as a style icon. She argues that, in contrast to those stars of the classical era (who she claims functioned as 'style dictators'), contemporary star styles are subject to increasing scrutiny and criticism by audiences. Similarly, Julie Wilson (2010) introduces the concept of 'star testing' in order to account for the ways in which celebrity magazines encourage readers to evaluate, as opposed to identify, with celebrity images. Thus, according to both Epstein and Wilson, audiences are fully aware of the performative nature of fashion, and are invited to 'deconstruct' the 'styled' celebrity image.[11] The value of their work, for my purposes, not only underscores the importance of celebrity inter-texts in attaching meanings to fashion and the star persona, but also reminds us of the ways in which audiences might organize their sense of self through the consumption of fashion and star images.

I should note here that I approach the subject of postmodernity/ postmodernism with caution, for as Dick Hebdige (2006: 410) among others, notes, 'the postmodern' has become a contemporary 'buzz word'. Moreover, as John Storey (2006) observes, '[i]t has so many different meanings, in so many different debates and discourses, that it is tempting to dismiss it and move on to something with more academic substance' (385). Yet, postmodernism's pervasiveness within the field of fashion, consumer culture, identity and television studies makes it difficult to be ignored by this book. For example it would be foolhardy, as Elizabeth Wilson (1992: 6) asserts, not to recognize its role in 'rescu[ing] the study of dress from its lowly status . . . [for it] has created—or at least *named*—a climate in which any cultural aesthetic object may be taken seriously' (emphasis in original). Thus, two key features of postmodernism in particular have shaped this development: the supposed collapsing of distinctions between high and low art and the increasing value of style for style's sake.

For some, the increasingly blurred boundaries between high art and popular culture are viewed as potentially socially progressive (see Chambers 1986; Huyssen 1986; McRobbie 1994), while others consider the 'flattening of hierarchies' to be 'commercial', 'shallow' and in some way 'immoral' (Bauman 1992: 34). Similarly, the prioritization of the visual also causes this polarization of opinion; while some seek to interrogate the political possibilities of this supposed shift, this particular aspect of postmodernism is often invoked in negative discussions of consumption, identity and media, in which it is often claimed that style and image are privileged above all else (see Gitlin 1987; Grossberg 1987). Mike Featherstone's (2007) work on postmodernism and consumer culture explores the now familiar postmodern assumption that 'we are moving towards a society without fixed status groups in which the adoption of styles of life (manifest in choice of clothes, leisure activities, consumer goods, bodily dispositions) which are fixed to specific groups have been surpassed' (81). Thus, Featherstone examines the ways in which this supposed shift could be perceived as a move towards an 'egalitarian' society (in which previous power structures no longer shape identity) or a move towards a 'flat', 'depthless' society (as described by Jameson 1985). It is not the aim of this book to evaluate these positions, but I mention them here because they inform the narrative content of fashion programming and celebrity inter-texts. I argue that the shows under discussion here negotiate these conflicting philosophies in order to make a comment on and to work through issues of contemporary identity performance.

It is important to note here that television has been afforded a central role within debates about postmodernity and identity. Indeed, as Kellner notes elsewhere, the supposed shift toward an increasingly fragmented identity has resulted in television becoming a primary resource for providing viewers with a meaningful sense of self. If this is the case then, despite its low cultural status, fashion television functions as a reassuringly fictional space in which 'real' identity work can take place. In addition, it has been claimed, that the broader debates regarding the postmodern preoccupation with 'image culture' are thought to have impacted television texts themselves. In his analysis of US TV show *Miami Vice*, Kellner (1995: 235) argues that a common claim in the postmodern era is that the 'television *image* often decentres the importance of narrative' (emphasis in original). Therefore, it could be said that this apparent cultural turn has at most dismantled, or at least problematized, those hierarchies which privilege narrative over costume—and thus calls for its re-examination within the field of fashion, cinema and television studies.

Methodological Approaches to Fashion Television

Historically, television scholars have exercised caution when dealing with purely textual approaches. Emerging as a field in its own right in the 1970s, television studies initially adopted a more sociological approach; focusing primarily on the 'effects' of television rather than the close aesthetic analysis of television 'texts'. Indeed, the very concept of the television text—as scholars John Ellis (1992) and Raymond Williams (1975/2003) have demonstrated—is difficult to isolate, which has led to a lack of textual analysis within television studies (Brunsdon 1991). This is not to suggest that textual analysis was entirely evacuated from television studies, but rather that it has not historically been at its centre. In her article

'Text and Audience', Charlotte Brunsdon (1991: 125) posits that while television studies has traditionally focused on the audience, it is important for scholars working in this area to 'retain a notion of the television text'. Thus, a recent body of work has emerged which seeks to make a case for textual analysis within television studies in order to critically analyse television aesthetics. Scholars including Sarah Cardwell (2006), Glen Creeber (2006) and Jason Jacobs (2001) have recently published articles which call for a renewed interest in textual analysis in order to establish television as a 'legitimate' art form.[12] However, these studies also acknowledge the limitations of textual analysis insofar as they seek to offer less prescriptive accounts of particular programmes. According to Creeber (2006: 85), acknowledging the limitations of purely textual approaches is essential, for '[i]f textual analysis is to survive into the future, then it (like all methodologies) must learn from past mistakes.'

As previously mentioned, the most oft-cited criticism of textual analysis is that it can only provide one possible reading of a text, and as Creeber (2006) illustrates, 'if audiences can read a text in a number of ways then what is the validity and relevance of one textual interpretation?' (82). Furthermore, he suggests that '[t]extual analysis on its own is rarely enough, but when it combines with the wider contextual or extra-textual nature of the subject it can still offer insight and inspiration' (82). Indeed, Brunsdon's (1991) article also demonstrates the importance of contextual readings as she suggests that in order to 'usefully learn from the practices of television itself . . . we have to accept the potentially infinite number/flow of textual sites' (125).

It is pertinent to note here that the debate over the relationship between a text and its extra-textual circulation has equally been waged in the context of genre studies. In particular, Jason Mittell's (2001: 5) work argues that media scholars traditionally considered 'genre primarily as a textual attribute', which often produces a vague and ultimately reductive understanding of genre. Instead, he suggests that 'we need to look beyond the text as the locus for genres and instead locate genres within the complex interrelations among texts, industries, audiences and historical contexts' (7). He claims:

> we should gather as many diverse enunciations of [a] . . . genre from the widest possible range of sources, including corporate documents, press reviews and commentaries, trade journal accounts, parodies, regulatory policies, audience practices, production manuals, other media representations, advertisements and the texts themselves. (9)

This approach is useful for my purposes because, like genre, costume articulated as fashion exists in a framework of discourses that can be located beyond the text. Indeed, reports in the popular press reveal that fashion programming is increasingly reliant on fashion to attract viewers and as such, magazine articles, internet blogs and websites contribute to promoting onscreen fashion outside of the text and can, as Barbara Klinger (1991) argues, affect the reception of the text. In 'Digressions at the Cinema: Commodification and Reception in Mass Culture', Klinger claims that the filmic text operates to encourage the viewer to call upon information obtained from extra-textual material and at times to digress from the unfolding action onscreen. She writes:

> A host of promotional forms such as media stories about the stars, the director and the making of the film, which arm the spectator with background information . . . fall into relation with moments of the film being screened. (119)

While Klinger's concept of digression is discussed with regard to cinema, it demonstrates the value of examining extra-textual material and the way in which it offers productive insights into the spectator-text relationship, which is, of course, integral to contemporary television-viewing practices. Seeking to contribute to this body of work, my own interrogation of onscreen fashion and television acknowledges the importance of the television text and its relationship to various inter-texts.

For this purpose, I examine not only specific examples of fashion programming, but also the production context through the analysis of trade press and also the wider contextual apparatus in the form of celebrity inter-texts. Thus, my somewhat triangulated approach to the study of fashion programming seeks to counteract the deficiencies of purely textual methods. That is to say, I approach the function of onscreen fashion in contemporary US television from several different angles; a process which not only negotiates the limitations associated with specific methods but also renders the relationships between production, text and reception that might have remained invisible visible.

Tracing Patterns: The Structure of the Book

It is the assumption of this book that fashion television, in its current incarnation, emerges out of a specific set of industrial conditions which have informed the ways in which fashion is deployed within them. Thus, it pursues a synchronic approach to fashion television; viewing case studies as the results of an intriguing moment of intersection between fashion, television and contemporary celebrity culture. However, this is not to suggest that contemporary fashion programming is created in a vacuum with no connection to television history. In her monograph on *Sex and the City*, Deborah Jermyn (2009) acknowledges the thematic similarities between the HBO prime-time comedy drama and women-centred comedies from the 1950s through the 1980s, such as *I Love Lucy* (1951–1957),

The Mary Tyler Moore Show (1970–1977), *That Girl* (1966–1971) and *The Golden Girls* (1985–1992). Parallels can, of course, be drawn between *Sex and the City* and some of these female-oriented shows in terms of their narrative focus of a single woman in a city, but they can also be drawn in terms of the shows' impact upon the fashion industry. Indeed, there are similarities between the examples of fashion programming examined here, and historical precursors such as *The Mary Tyler Moore Show* (*The MTM Show*). *The MTM Show* has been identified as an extremely influential show, thought to be responsible for popularizing headscarves, flower print dresses, large necklaces and high-waisted skirts.[13] Similarly, other examples from the 1980s, such as *Dynasty* (1981–1989) and *Dallas* (1978–1991), reintroduced bold-coloured shift dresses, shoulder pads and furs back into popular and high fashion. In terms of male fashion, *Miami Vice* (1984–1989) helped to popularize Giorgio Armani's unconstructed suit; according to Jim Moore (creative director of *GQ*), '[i]t's the first point in fashion history where you can really show a TV having that influence on fashion' (Moore in Trebay 2006). In addition, the *New York Times* recently claimed that *Miami Vice* 'may also have marked the earliest mainstream appearance of that indestructible cultural chimera, the metrosexual' (Trebay 2006). Yet one must exercise caution when considering the relationship between contemporary television and television historiography, lest we create an 'undue proximity' between past and present, erasing important historical differences (Corner 2003: 277). Within the 1990s, there is evidence to suggest that shifts occurred within the fashion market (such as the emergence of off-the-rack designer garments in department stores), consumer culture (individuals' supposed increasing desire for material 'lifestyle' goods (see Featherstone 2007)) and celebrity culture (e.g. the supposed democratization of fame). Equally, media scholars such as Brian L. Ott (2007) and Amanda Lotz (2007) note that the 1990s witnessed extreme economic and cultural changes for the US television industry, such as the emergence of the multichannel/digital era, and, consequently, these contextual factors must be taken into account when critically analysing fashion television.

To fully comprehend fashion television as a cultural phenomenon, and to explore its role in contemporary society, I dedicate individual chapters to specific aspects while attempting to remain sensitive to the overall aims driving this project. Thus, the book is divided into three parts. The first examines the production context within which fashion programming is thought to have emerged. The second focuses on the texts themselves, and the final part examines the wider contextual apparatus in the form of fashion and celebrity inter-texts.

The first section is informed by the persuasive body of work which views the production of culture, and cultures of production, as not only deeply interconnected but also central to furthering our understanding of meaning-making processes (du Gay 1997; Garnham 1995; Hesmondhalgh 2002, 2006b; Hesmondhalgh and Baker 2013; Mayer, Banks and Caldwell 2009; Negus

1992). That is to say, cultural artefacts cannot be understood in isolation from those economic processes which bring them to fruition, however, neither can we conceive of the production of cultural artefacts as motivated by economics alone.

Drawing on the work of those scholars mentioned above, Part 1 examines the industrial discourse surrounding fashion programming and homes in on one trade paper in particular: the *Hollywood Reporter: Fashion in Entertainment* special issues. Of course, as with all methods, it is important to acknowledge limitations, and remember that trade papers serve as a representation of the industry, reliant upon the available testimonies of industry professionals—it is by no means an exhaustive account. Yet, at the same time, we must bear in mind that this material is in no way any more or less 'authentic' than other forms of 'inside information' (e.g. face-to-face interviews with industry professionals). As John Caldwell (2008: 2–3) reminds us, 'insider knowledge is always managed; and because research-practitioner contacts are always marked by symbiotic tensions over authenticity and advantage, media studies must avoid limiting research to a clean menu of disconnected methods; textual analysis, reporting, interviewing, economic analysis, or ethnography.' Thus, the *Hollywood Reporter: Fashion in Entertainment* special issues offer a self-reflexive narrative which centralizes fashion programming and, as such, is worthy of serious attention in its own right. Moreover, as a trade publication—as opposed to popular press— it provides a space for some of the anxieties surrounding the increasing use of fashion onscreen to be voiced, which are often concealed from the public (see Negus 1997). As such, it reveals useful insights into concerns regarding the cultural value of fashion and television which structure attitudes towards fashion programming.

These supplements, which began in 1998, are published annually in October/ November (following the new season premieres in the US) and offer both information about, and a commentary on, the creative and commercial dilemmas faced by both the fashion and screen industries (film and television). The importance of the *Hollywood Reporter* as a trade publication is demonstrated by its readership of industry professionals.[14] In addition, the contributors to the *Hollywood Reporter: Fashion in Entertainment* special issues are made up of both fashion and screen industry commentators (e.g. many write for the fashion trade press, *Women's Wear Daily*). Thus, while it is important to remember that the information presented within the supplements is tailored to a particular audience (and therefore the content is specifically shaped by this specific advertorial discourse), it is also the case that this publication provides an insight into the relationship between the costume designers, the shows and the wider fashion market.

Chapter 2 explores, from a production studies perspective, the relationship between fashion and television as narrated in the trade press. I examine the ways in which the trade publication makes sense of fashion programming, with a particular focus on the strategies employed to manage public perceptions. Chapter 3 continues to explore debates outlined in the previous chapter and examines the representation of television costume designers within the trade press. This in turn contributes to a broader discussion that perpetuates certain assumptions regarding gender, labour and authorship. Underpinning this methodology then, is the argument that an analysis of the trade and popular press can shape our understanding of the cultural and economic functions of costume designers and their work onscreen. In this section I attach critical importance to the understanding of these functions, as they can begin to elucidate the ways in which texts are constructed to mean.

The second part involves close textual analysis of specific case studies. This includes a kind of semiotic analysis insofar as I seek to examine the precise ways in which onscreen fashion operates as a system of signs which require decoding. However, more specifically, the focus is on the use of recurrent tropes that allow a space for issues of identity and consumer culture to be worked through. In other words, this part concerns itself with the precise ways in which the narratives focus on the relationship between character and fashion, and how, to some extent, the characters are defined by their relationship to consumption. This book argues that one of the defining characteristics of fashion programming is the way in which the narratives deal (either explicitly or implicitly) with individuals' relationship to consumption. In particular, the shows are concerned with moral dilemmas about fashion which underpin the narrative. Thus, the characters adopt different positions in relation to appropriate and inappropriate consumption which allows the narrative to work through these moral dilemmas. In this sense, onscreen fashion in contemporary fashion programming proves a troubling case study for previous academic approaches to fashion and costume, which have hitherto presented fashion as either expressive of narrative or excessive and distracting, precisely because it is neither. As this section seeks to demonstrate, the relationship between onscreen fashion, narrative and character is thus much more complex than previous studies of costume and cinema would suggest.

Chapter 4 uses *Sex and the City* (hereafter *SATC*) and *Ugly Betty* as case studies to examine the ways in which fashion as costume can be considered spectacle. There have been many discussions of *SATC* and its relationship with gender and consumer culture (see Arthurs 2003; Jermyn 2004, 2009; Negra 2004), and it has subsequently been identified as 'the most interesting television phenomenon in terms of fashion, celebrity and sales of fashion related products' (Church Gibson 2012: 103). In their article 'Fashion is the Fifth Character: Fashion, Costume and Character in *Sex and the City*', Stella Bruzzi and Pamela Church Gibson (2004: 115) suggest that *SATC* 'inverts the normative relationship between script and costume . . . [where traditionally] costume serves character and action not vice versa'. Building on Bruzzi and Church Gibson, I argue that both *SATC* and *Ugly Betty* do more than this. Not only do they subvert those traditional screen hierarchies which privilege narrative over mise-en-scene, but in some cases reject them entirely; that is to say, moments of spectacle complement, rather than disrupt narrative. Thus, this chapter interrogates specific (but interrelated) debates regarding fashion as both a textual language and a semiotic system within Western society by revisiting (and disturbing) the long-standing assumption that fashion acts primarily as spectacle and a distraction, thus disrupting the economy of narrative flow (Gaines 1990).

Chapter 5 examines the way in which teen shows *The O.C.* and *Gossip Girl* can be understood as seeking to address an audience of potential consumers who have the ability to 'read' fashion. This chapter differs from others in Part 2 as it considers the representation of youth fashion practices and the relationship between fashion and masculine identities within these shows. Indeed, the cultural knowledge and competences necessary to 'read' fashion have long since been considered an implicitly feminine skill, and according to some fashion theorists, the common assumption regarding men's participation in fashion is that it does not exist. However, the men's fashion within the case studies above is often the focus of extra textual discussion. That said, the onscreen male fashion practices depicted are in some ways connected to those 'anti-fashion' (and typically 'masculine') processes associated with subculture and style. As such, I seek to contribute to the current level of knowledge about youth, gender and subcultural style.

Chapter 6 examines the use of period costume in quality US dramas, specifically *Mad Men* and *Boardwalk Empire*. These programmes have been identified in the popular press as fashion-forward, often inspiring contemporary fashion collections and reigniting an interest in 'vintage' fashion. Thus, this chapter continues to revisit existing debates regarding spectacle and narrative, and fashion and costume, in the context of period drama and examines the ways in which we might approach period costume articulated as fashion.

Finally, the book examines the relationship between fashion television and celebrity culture. The fashion industry and celebrity culture have developed an increasingly complex, symbiotic relationship, and this has industrial, cultural and aesthetic implications for fashion television. In order to assess this relationship, this final section examines a selection of celebrity images associated with fashion television. I suggest that by examining the representation of the celebrity image in fashion and celebrity magazines one is offered an insight into the desired role of viewers as consumers. For example it is claimed that 'stars articulate what it is to be human in contemporary society' (Dyer 1986: 10), thus it could be argued that the use of the celebrity image within fashion magazines can articulate what it is to be consumers of fashion in contemporary society.

Chapter 7 focuses on the construction of female fashion icons Sarah Jessica Parker and Blake Lively. It examines US celebrity and high-end fashion magazines and argues that these star images function as 'cultural intermediaries', designed to educate audiences in reading fashion. Moreover, it also examines how discourses of class are foregrounded within these star personae. Thus, it demonstrates how these images are used to reinforce class boundaries in a landscape which has supposedly destabilized the meanings of cultural identities. Chapter 8 explores the relationship between gender, celebrity and consumer culture with a particular focus on masculinity. Drawing on the work of Tim Edwards (1997) and Frank Mort (1988) on masculinity and consumption, the chapter considers the construction and mediation of the male fashion icon. It considers extra textual coverage of male actors from fashion programming (Jon Hamm (*Mad Men*) and Adam Brody (*The O.C.*)), in order to consider the precise ways in which specific notions of heterosexual masculinity are constructed and affirmed within traditionally 'feminine' cultural texts (fashion and celebrity magazines). The final chapter examines the intersection of 'race', fashion and celebrity culture. It uses the circulation of America Ferrera's star image as a lens through which to examine these issues. In particular, it centres on America Ferrera's position as an 'unlikely' fashion icon. Ferrera's physicality and ethnicity fall outside of the dominant ideologies of Western beauty commonly associated with the elite fashion industry. However, the circulation of her star image in US celebrity and fashion magazines construct Ferrera's 'otherness' as a marker of authenticity and 'ordinariness'. Finally, an ongoing and crucial theme within this book is the rejection of the notion that fashion, as it is presented within these texts, is trivial and politically innocent. Throughout this book, I endeavour to foreground the social and cultural significance of onscreen fashion in its televisual context in an attempt to ignite a critical interest in the study of television costume.

PART I

PRODUCTION CULTURES AND INDUSTRY EXPLANATIONS OF CONTEMPORARY FASHION TELEVISION

2

THE PLACE OF FASHION TELEVISION IN CINEMA HISTORY: INDUSTRIAL DISCOURSE AND CULTURAL LEGITIMACY

In the summer of 2000, journalist Merle Ginsberg observed a transformation in fashion communication. The emergence of US 'quality' programming reportedly prompted new promotional opportunities for the fashion market. She writes:

> While everybody's kept busy oohing, ogling and mining movie, pop and hip-hop stars for new fashion trends, it's been the stars of television who have been not only selling clothes and creating buzz at retail, but influencing designers and inciting them to attempts at product placement rarely seen in fashion circles outside of glossy magazines. (Ginsberg 2000)

A prolific writer for fashion and screen trade publications (*Women's Wear Daily* and the *Hollywood Reporter*), Ginsberg's report reflects a tendency within the industry press to view the development of closer links between fashion and television with a certain degree of surprise and bewilderment. The 'unlikely' relationship between the fashion and television industries is presented as something which must be rationalized. Consequently, trade papers began to produce competing histories of popular culture in order to make sense of television's emerging power in contemporary fashion communication. These representative histories undoubtedly served to support certain economic goals; that is to ensure the survival of newly established marketing opportunities by legitimizing the medium of television. However, they also inform attitudes towards fashion programming, attaching cultural meaning to the texts themselves in a way that will be central to the concerns of my argument.

During the late 1990s and early 2000s, fashion programming occupied a precarious position within traditional value systems. Commentators in the fashion trade press suggest that up until this point, television was too 'ordinary' and 'familiar' to serve as an appropriate advertising platform for high fashion. However, developments within celebrity culture, combined with a reorientation of programme content, supposedly improved the status of television and led Ginsberg (2000) to claim that 'television is now a more powerful tool than movies'. The power of cinema had never been questioned within the fashion trade press. In fact, the representational discourses employed go some way to affirming this power, investing deeply in a romanticized view of Hollywood as a 'dream factory'. It delights in cinema's ability to provide audiences with an immersive, personal advertising experience, and simultaneously reproduces the popular mythology surrounding the 'golden age' of Hollywood. Such a representation of the film industry is also activated in screen trade publications, though for different purposes.

Unlike cinema, television's past has to be sanitized and reimagined. To ensure that high-end designer brands were not contaminated by associations with the 'ordinary' and the 'familiar', television was contextualized by the screen trade press within a broader, 'legitimate' history of screen entertainment. Rescuing television from its 'lowly' status assured potential collaborators of the (literal and figurative) value of fashion programming; a strategy which, according to Ginsberg (2000), proved most effective: 'These days, companies as sophisticated as Prada, Tod's, Jimmy Choo and Burberry are falling over themselves to get clothes on *Sex and the City* and other programs.'

The narrativization of the emergence of fashion television within the trade press reveals useful insights into the industry's concerns regarding its cultural value and sheds light on the ways in which fashion programming (as a discursive category) is made to mean. Thus, the *Hollywood Reporter: Fashion in Entertainment* special issues offer a self-reflexive narrative which centralizes fashion programming and, as such, is worthy of serious attention in its own right. As a trade publication—as opposed to the popular press—it provides an (albeit managed) space for some of the anxieties surrounding the increasing use of fashion onscreen to be voiced, which, as the work of Keith Negus (1997) among others demonstrates, are often concealed from the public. Moreover, it makes clear the importance of certain elementary factors of economic and industry power which shape entertainment production. Thus observations about the meaning of fashion television for contemporary audiences must take place within a framework that considers the ways in which these competing discourses may contain or constrain and inform television content and reception.

Macro Approaches to Fashion Onscreen

The 1998 inaugural edition of the *Hollywood Reporter: Fashion in Entertainment* special issue emerged during a time of supposedly increased synergy between the fashion and film industries; yet its title—*Fashion in* Entertainment (my emphasis)—suggests that the trade press anticipated a much more seismic shift which would engulf a number of media and entertainment industries. However, echoing Ginsberg's comments cited above, it was assumed that sport and music would be the most suitable platforms for fashion promotion, as opposed to television. Film, for the moment, remained the most suitable vehicle for fashion promotion. It was believed that fashion retailers could reach a wider audience through the medium of film, while the film industry explored new avenues of promotion.

The opening article in the 1998 special issue, 'Clothing the Deal', sets the tone for subsequent reports, and gestures towards the potential for corporate success in both the fashion and the film industries. It reads:

> High profile fashion and product placement can be more effective than a 10-page advertisement in *Harper's Bazaar* . . . [C]elebrities' clothes are of infinite interest to the general public which translates into unlimited potential for big consumer bucks. And as much as films can galvanize product sales, the product can also buttress the film. The right fashion and product-placement choices can only help; films with thoughtfully prescribed aesthetics, like 'Men in Black' and 'Scream,' frequently become known as much for their unique looks as for their characters and special effects. (Penn 1998: 3)

The economic agenda is foregrounded within the above passage, and tales of corporate success in which the commercial potential is realized therefore dominate the *Hollywood Reporter*; for example the Tommy Hilfiger–Miramax deal. Hilfiger reportedly supplied 85 per cent of the costuming for *The Faculty* (1998), while the films' stars participated in a $10 million promotional campaign involving print advertisements in a number of popular magazines (including *Teen People*, *Spin, Vibe* and *YM*) and a short video commercial.[1] The commercial, which aired on VH1, MTV and Comedy Central throughout the month of December 1998, was launched in conjunction with Hilfiger's 'back-to-school' collection. Such material is worthy of attention in its own right, as it offers an insight into the ways in which the fashion industry seeks to present its relationship with the film industry to both the general public and potentially interested collaborators. In the Hilfiger commercial, the cast are filmed on a fictional set in drab clothes before wardrobe is called in to replace the costumes with clothes that 'work' onscreen: enter

Hilfiger jeans. The commercial ends with the double entendre: 'Tommy Jeans make a scene', meaning on the one hand, of course, that Tommy jeans make 'a statement' for the individual and express an element of their cultural identity, but also that they 'complete' a movie scene.[2] Thus, the Hilfiger short not only serves as an advertisement for Hilfiger's jeans and *The Faculty*, but also makes an appeal to the film industry more generally.

Central to the success of the Hilfiger-Miramax relationship was the geographic expansion of its publicity department. Perhaps foreseeing the opportunities for film and fashion synergy, publicists opened branches on the West Coast, which allowed retailers to forge relationships with Hollywood. This additional change in organizational procedures is identified as a key moment in fashion and film synergy. Indeed, in the mid-1990s public relations departments began to formalize their methods of securing product placement. Clothing retailer Guess?, Inc.—who famously designed Michael J. Fox's jeans in *Back to the Future* (1985)—advertised in the *Costumer's Directory* and had two full-time staff members responsible for 'cold calling' costume designers and senior stylists (Penn 1998). Similarly, major fashion houses (including Prada, Mizarahi, Calvin Klein and Donna Karan) have employed full-time fashion coordinators, tasked with creating relationship with studios. This exponential rise in personnel within this particular area points to the importance of media within contemporary advertising strategies.

The economic benefit of fashion placement is not simply limited to the fashion industries. When filming *Being John Malkovich* (1999) and negotiating a particularly tight budget, costume designer Casey Storm approached Prada, Armani and Versace as potential collaborators. All three fashion houses reportedly donated pieces in exchange for advertising within the film (extras were asked to carry Prada, Armani and Versace shopping bags in crowd scenes). In so doing, Storm was able to shave a considerable 20–30 per cent off his costuming budget. However, despite these notable success stories, there were fundamental problems which impeded the relationship between the fashion and film industries. This has to do with the very nature of film production and exhibition, as the closing paragraph of 'Clothing the Deal' makes clear:

> From the fashion industry's viewpoint, the path to Hollywood success is a minefield. How can long-range promotions be planned when you don't know if Batman is going to fly or if your Reebok scene in 'Jerry Maguire' will be cut? When it does work, oftentimes it's almost by accident. Despite all the product-placement specialists, West Coast publicists, energetic young starts, stylists and houses of haute couture, much of the success of these deals is predicated on an enigmatic fusion of chemistry, timing and luck. (Penn 1998: 9)

The issue of timing is continually raised within the trade press as one of the most challenging aspects of fashion and film fusion due to the fact that projects can be shelved indefinitely.[3] Thus, the systemic problems related to the conditions of production prove detrimental to fashion and film synergy. The film industry is too uncertain to support the economic goals of fashion retailers. Television, by comparison, is much less of a risk as its existing infrastructure better accommodates the needs of the fashion industry. Indeed, commercial television has always accommodated corporate interests. The aesthetics of US drama have been profoundly shaped by commercially motivated scheduling to the extent that serial narratives are structured in such a way as to factor in commercial interruptions. US drama's grounding principle has been to deliver audiences to advertisers, and thus its content is shaped by this ethos (see Gripsrud 1995). It is no surprise then that television is often held up as the ultimate example of commercial cultural production.

Paradoxically, it is precisely this connection to the commercial which initially prevented fashion retailers from collaborating with the television industry. Thus television's notable absence from early issues of the *Hollywood Reporter* serves as evidence of the fact that fashion television emerged as a reactive response to historically specific economic and industrial conditions. It was the invention of necessity—to satisfy the commercial needs of the fashion industry in ways that film could not. To return to the issue of timing, television works to a completely different schedule. The short turnaround time between shooting and broadcasting allows fashion designers the opportunity to exhibit their new designs to potential consumer audiences in a timely fashion. Moreover, this strict shooting regime allows for tighter control over image dissemination. That is to say, fashion houses can plan for more long-term promotional campaigns, as they are certain of release dates. Consequently, it is logistically possible for broadcast dates to coincide with particular seasonal collections.

This arrangement is beneficial not only for the fashion industry. Indeed, the demanding shooting schedules of serial dramas result in costume designers rarely having the time to create and fit garments for an entire cast, as *Ally McBeal* costume designer Rachael Stanley's comments make clear: 'Last week I had seven days to prep, I did 85 outfits from head to toe. We rely heavily on our relationship with stores and designers' (Stanley in Penn 1998: 25). Thus, the relationship is truly symbiotic.

In addition to these practical considerations, there were broader developments occurring within the fashion industry which affirmed television's emerging power in contemporary fashion communication. Writing in the autumn of 2000, Randee Dawn claims that: 'Designers are mass marketing their fashions like never before—with Armani and Prada in department stores for example—and they realize the best way to reach the greatest number of potential consumers is through television' (2000a: 3). To be sure, in the late 1990s the fashion industry witnessed an increase in diffuse designer lines, such as those mentioned in the trade press, and as a consequence television became a platform for the display of not only the ready-to-wear lines but also high fashion, as a way of raising the profile of designer brands.

Indeed, mass-produced designer brands are thought to have been created in order to finance, and thereby ensure the survival of, haute couture (which was and remains incredibly expensive to custom-make). This particular strategy prompted concerns within the fashion industry regarding haute couture's symbolic value, insofar as designers (the producers of symbolic value) were attaching their names to the cheaper mass-produced garments; and as discussed in the introduction to this book, the designer was, and for the most part still is, crucial to maintaining the symbolic value of fashion.

Concerns such as these are not new—whenever industrial, cultural or economic conditions alter within the industry there are claims that fashion is becoming 'democratized'. The phrase 'democratization of fashion' is employed within popular discourse whenever a shift occurs that results in fashion becoming in some way accessible to, or influenced by, the 'masses'. Significantly, the media often plays a central role in the 'democratization' process. For example the phrase was first applied to industrial shifts in the late nineteenth century; specifically, the emergence of ready-cut patterns which enabled the masses to (re)create garments from patterns used by skilled dressmakers. As Margaret Walsh (1979: 301) affirms, it was the print media which first provided an 'impersonal and dispersed audience' with the tools required for dressmaking, and consequently allowed for the lower classes to participate in fashion practices. Similarly, the emergence of 'ready-to-wear' fashion in the first part of the twentieth century also resulted in fashion becoming more accessible to all social classes insofar as it replicated both mass-produced high-fashion designs and, significantly, Hollywood costumes (see Gaines 1990; Eckert 1990) which could be sold at lower prices to the general public.

As with the emergence of ready-to-wear fashion, the increase in designer diffusion lines engineered the widespread adoption of designer garments. Both of these developments raised concerns regarding the symbolic and cultural value of haute couture which relies on its exclusivity in order to justify its high price. However, these concerns were, and continue to be, managed by 'the fashion system'. 'The fashion system' as Kawamura (2005: 73) explains, 'creates symbolic boundaries between what is and what is not fashion and also determines what the legitimate taste is.' Indeed, as Kawamura among others argue, it relies upon these tensions and anxieties in order to sustain itself (see also Crane 2000; Leopold 1992; Steele 1998).

In her examination of the 'fashion system', Ellen Leopold (1992: 113) describes how the fashion industry is often understood as 'being in the grip of forces beyond their control . . . [this is] based on the view that "it is fashion that makes the industry rather than the industry that makes the fashion." ' This belief contributes to the mythology surrounding the fashion industry. That is to say, fashion must be understood as a 'cultural phenomenon' that cannot be forecast, as opposed to a mass-produced, standardized product of industry—though it may of course incorporate aspects of mass production. Indeed, this 'surprise' element is considered to be a characteristic of legitimate 'art' (a point to which I shall return shortly) insofar as it is an object that is unpredictably born out of moments of 'inspiration'. The work of the scholars cited above, then, seeks in some sense to demystify the fashion system, exposing the complex machinations which construct this myth. The concerns which arise in response to the democratization of fashion are considered to be a product of a strategic, institutionalized system; created, or at the very least perpetuated by, the fashion industry for a specific purpose. That is the availability of mass-produced 'ready-to-wear' designer lines encourage a form of 'discrimination' by its sophisticated consumers, and consequently the fashion industry is able to secure the demand for custom-made gowns which are, as Leopold observes, 'presented as one-off style "creations" . . . in a world of increasingly mass-produced goods' (109). Underpinning this understanding of the fashion system then, is Georg Simmel's (1904/1957) concept of 'class differentiation'. Simmel's work centres on the notion that fashion cycles are motivated by processes of 'imitation' and 'differentiation'. He argues that certain styles of dress are adopted by the upper or middle classes and then imitated by the working classes. The upper or middle class then seek to distance themselves from the lower classes by disregarding those initial styles of dress and implementing new ones. Consequently, a self-sustaining fashion cycle is created.

Aspects of the fashion system resonate with all cultural industries insofar as their position as commercial enterprises and producers of 'popular' culture threatens the symbolic value of their product. As such, a careful balance must be maintained between the economic and symbolic value of cultural artefacts (in order for the latter to be converted into the former). To be sure, tales of corporate success dominate the *Hollywood Reporter*, presumably with the intent of encouraging both parties to continue to invest in the relationship. However, discussions of the blatant commerciality of the union threaten to endanger the symbolic value of both cultural industries. Consequently, these threats must be managed and the mythology surrounding both industries restored.

Industry Perceptions of Fashion, Film and Television

As previously discussed, initially film, as opposed to television, was considered the dominant medium for the exhibition of high fashion. Within early editions of the trade press, film is presented as a more 'spectacular' medium with the capacity to have a 'bigger impact' than television. These views arise from wider, historical prejudices surrounding the aesthetic functions of cinema and television and speak to a persistent hierarchy in which film is positioned as more culturally legitimate than television. To be sure, television's connection to the domestic, and by default the 'feminine', has ensured its subordination and contributed to its construction as a passive/pacifying medium (see Petro 1986). In addition, its supposed association with the commercial denies television any claim to legitimate culture.

In *The Field of Cultural Production*, Bourdieu (1993a) reminds us that the value of cultural artefacts often rests upon their perceived proximity (or lack thereof) to the commercial sector. He writes: 'the opposition between the "commercial" and the "non commercial" reappears everywhere. It is the generative principle of most of the judgments which, in theatre, cinema, painting or literature, claim to establish the frontier between what is and what is not art' (82). Thus, art is constructed as that which is spontaneously born out of moments of individual creative genius, while popular culture is the product of a standardized, homogenous culture industry. Such a perspective, of course, echoes the views of early critical theorists, and is informed by a problematic view of cultural distinctions and values as ahistorical and unchanging. In other words, it fails to account for the ways in which certain cultural artefacts are subject to shift within hierarchies of value. Pertinent to this discussion then, is Stuart Hall's (2006) concept of the 'cultural escalator'. According to Hall: 'Popular forms become enhanced in cultural value, go up the cultural escalator—and find themselves on the opposite side. Other things cease to have high cultural value, and are appropriated into the popular becoming transformed in the process' (483). For Hall, this process reveals that there is no inherent, fixed 'authentic' quality of a particular cultural form, which allows it to qualify as legitimate 'art'. Rather, these categories are culturally constructed by a system of institutionalized discourses. The relevance of Hall's work to this chapter is such that the trade discourses create a sense of and begin to form public opinion around fashion programming, and thus can be understood as a structuring principle in its legitimation process. In her book *Seeing Through the Eighties*, Jane Feuer (1996: 82) observes that '[s]ince television was not originally conceptualized as an art form at all, TV programs needed to be constructed as artistic artifacts. This was the function of "art discourses."' She claims '"art discourse" . . . is culturally constructed by social groups who have the power to define aesthetic value for their times' (82). Thus, later editions of the trade press play an active role in constructing fashion programming as an 'artistic artifact'.

In the 1998 issue, only one half-page article deals specifically with television, and although an increase in the column inches dedicated to television can be found within the 1999 edition, it is the 2000 issue which centralizes fashion television. The first article, 'Off the Rack and Onto the Screen' opens with the following admission: 'It's a perfect fit: fashion and cable television. Now more than ever, fashionistas are turning to broadcasting to get their designs seen by the masses, and in response the masses are tuning in and trying on what they see' (Dawn 2000a: 2). The feature article then traces the development of fashion programming within a variety of television genres, and contemplates its future. Following the 'Off the Rack and Onto the Screen' article is a full-page spread dedicated to *Sex and the City*. Notably the only full-page article dedicated to a single text within the entire catalogue of the *Hollywood Reporter: Fashion in Entertainment* special issues, 'Undressing "Sex and the City"' has secured a prime position within the trade paper—neighbouring a full-page Emporio Armani advertisement (Giorgio Armani's high-end ready-to-wear line).[4] The article performs an important cultural function in shaping attitudes towards contemporary fashion programming as it attempts to make sense of the cultural resonance the programme enjoys and to revise and challenge previous assumptions of television as a purely commercial medium.

The opening paragraph makes the often-recited claim that for a show pitched as an HBO comedy about relationships in New York City, it was the clothing which captured the interest of viewers:

> Sure, it's called 'Sex and the City'. But over the course of three HBO seasons, men have merely been second-hand goods—the clothes are what everyone's really in love with. 'The clothing is the fifth lady on the show,' explains executive producer and co-star Sarah Jessica Parker, who plays Carrie Bradshaw. 'I had no idea the clothes would be so integral!' No one did, really. (Dawn 2000b: 4)

Such a claim suggests that the success of fashion programming in general and *Sex and the City* in particular was not anticipated and therefore not the result of a carefully considered business relationship between the fashion and television industry. Thus, discourses similar to those which circulate around film are at work here: that is film is constructed as a much more *unpredictable* decentralized industry than television, and as such the success of fashion and film collaborations cannot simply be attributed to strategic business plans. Rather, it is the product of the spontaneous alignment of several intangible qualities ('chemistry' and 'luck'). As briefly discussed above, television is often viewed as the feminine and commercial 'other' to its cinematic counterpart and has resultantly been denied the legitimacy accorded to film. Yet, here the unforeseen success of *SATC* serves as evidence of its artistic 'quality' status. Significantly, concerns over the low cultural status of television are cautiously raised within the article, and quickly debunked by the show's costume designer:

> 'Sex and the City' may turn out to be one of the most influential postmillennial TV shows in terms of fashion, thanks to the collaborative spirit of [Patricia]

Field, [Rebecca] Weinberg and Parker. According to Field, she'd much rather have the small screen as her catwalk. 'Television is a great way to speak to millions of people. Anybody who pooh-poohs television is just being crotchety.' (Dawn 2000b: 4)

Field's contention is indicative of the kinds of prejudices which can be traced within earlier issues of the trade press; however, the 2000 issue marks a qualitative break with this tradition and seeks to underplay the differences between both mediums and foreground their similarities. Rather than relegating coverage of fashion and television to short fact-based pieces separate from discussion of fashion and cinema, there is a dialogue between the film and the television industry. They are presented as companion industries, for the most part, mutually supportive of fashion placement. Thus, this is part of a two-pronged approach by the trade press to legitimate fashion programming. As the above quote suggests, this first involves a process of exposing and discrediting previous assumptions regarding the aesthetic function and cultural value of television. The second approach involves a more elaborate process which has to do with disassociating fashion programming from its televisual origins and positioning it as a tangent of fashion cinema. In so doing, the emergence of fashion programming becomes associated with and is situated within a broader (and more legitimate) history of fashion and film. Consequently, the trade press perpetuates certain artistic discourses which secure cinema's position as a 'legitimate' cultural artefact precisely because the legitimacy of fashion programming is hitched to that of film.

'The Ultimate Symbiosis'?: Reimagining Fashion and Film History

This trade press construction of the film industry relies heavily on a romanticized view of cinema history, which is ardently evoked through the *Hollywood Reporter: Fashion in Entertainment* special issues and serves an important cultural function within the legitimation of fashion programming. That is to say, by tapping into a mythologized, nostalgic representation of classical Hollywood cinema, the trade press situates contemporary onscreen fashion placement within a culturally legitimate history of fashion cinema. Importantly, this particular version of cinema history deployed within the trade press runs counter to that which is constructed within academic discourse. Within Gaines and Herzog's (1990) edited collection, scholars including Charles Eckert, Charlotte Herzog, Jeanne Allen and Jane Gaines produce an account of fashion and film history as precarious, fraught and varied. Such assessments support Bruzzi's (1997: 3) claim that, '[c]outure's

3

COSTUME DESIGN, PRACTICES AND PRODUCTION CULTURES

I am a stylist, I like the commerce end of it. I love to style.
—Patricia Field in P. Wilson 2002: 6

When the trailer for David Frankel's *The Devil Wears Prada* (2006) hit cinema screens in the United Kingdom, it proudly announced that the film, brought to us by 20th Century Fox, based on the best-selling novel by Lauren Weisberger and starring Academy Award winner Meryl Streep, was costumed by Patricia Field. Indeed, the promotional process built around the film consistently foregrounded Field's involvement as costume designer in ways that had not been seen since the classical era. Field gave interviews with the quality press, fashion magazines speculated about the wardrobe and sought-after shots of the actors on set saturated the blogosphere.[1] Thus, it could easily be argued that Field's status as a costume designer rivals the likes of Gilbert Adrian and Edith Head. Her name, now synonymous with a particular visual style, is so intrinsic to the meaning of the text that she herself becomes central to the advertorial discourses.

Patricia Field, however, as a case study is in some ways exceptional. As with Adrian and Head, the visibility afforded Field is not available to all personnel within the wardrobe department; most remain unseen (and unheard). However, this is not to suggest that their roles in the meaning-making process are in any way less significant. Central to this project is the notion that the culture of production and production context inform the symbolic meaning of a text.

Traditionally, roles that have been fulfilled by women have been left out of histories of film and television production, and as such, the figure of the costume designer has rarely been examined in any level of detail. Indeed, there has been a tendency to overlook the importance of costume designers, not only in terms of their contribution to media texts, but also in regard to their involvement within the wider realm of fashion communication. In an attempt to redress this balance, this chapter has two interrelated aims.

First, it develops themes mobilized in the previous chapter regarding the cultural value of contemporary fashion programming. These themes particularly crystallize within discussions around the costume designer, a figure whose crisis of value is centralized within the trade press. Growing concerns that, following an increase in fashion placement, costume designers 'proper' are being replaced by 'creative shoppers' have sparked intense debates within industry discourse. 'Creative shopping' no longer involves designing and creating wardrobes, but rather requires the costume designer to select garments (both designer and high-street) and to 'style' characters. A change in terminology—the use of the term stylist rather than the term costume designer—reflects not only the industrial development but also an unwillingness to acknowledge contemporary costuming practices as costume design. As this chapter shall demonstrate, the economic and industrial factors which shape contemporary costume design have engendered a change in attitudes towards the figure of the television costumer. These attitudes, I argue, are predicated upon a series of assumptions to do with gender, labour and authorship that have resulted in a collective reimagining of the role within the trade press.

Within a book that promises an examination of fashion in television through the lens of identity and celebrity culture, it may seem odd to dedicate one chapter to these debates. However, this chapter is precisely concerned with the construction of professional identity and the visibility or celebrity status (or lack thereof) afforded to the costume designer. This line of argument is crucial to the chapter's second aim, which is to advance discussions within the field of production studies that examine theories of professional identity, specifically Miranda J. Banks's (2009) work on feminist production studies.

Conceptualizing Costume Design: Media Production and Gendered Labour

In her article, 'Defining Feminist Production Studies', Miranda J. Banks (2009: 87) persuasively argues that '[g]ender disparity is a critical issue in Hollywood, [and] in order to understand the nature of the professional landscape, it is crucial to look not just at the overall numbers, but to examine the gendering of individual professions within the industry.' Seeking to build on existing work in this area (D'Acci 1994; Levine 2001), Banks (2009) centres her research on the lived experience of those practitioners who are marginalized both by the industry and the academy. In so doing, she defines, 'what is truly at stake not just in the process of production but in the study of production as well' (87). Similarly,

Caldwell's (2008) monograph, *Production Culture: Industrial Reflexivity and Critical Practice in Film and Television*, also hopes to provide an understanding of the way in which the industry constructs and makes sense of itself. In his chapter 'Trade Stories and Cultural Capital,' Caldwell examines the cultural function of 'trade stories' and begins to conceptualize popular trade narratives into different genres. These genres include: 'war stories', 'against-all-odds allegories', 'Genesis myths', 'paths-not-taken parables', 'making-it sagas' and 'cautionary tales' (Caldwell 2008: 37–69). They are further categorized by context or work sectors, insofar as he suggests that the genres are specific to profession. He proposes that above-the-line workers are more likely to employ 'genesis myths' and 'paths not taken parables', whereas below-the-line staff tend to recount 'war stories' and 'against-all-odds allegories' in order to make sense of their roles.

To be sure, Caldwell acknowledges that these categories are neither exhaustive nor fixed, and thus his analysis only briefly considers the role of gender and the gendering of certain professions, an area which I seek to elaborate on within this chapter. Thus, I adopt Banks's feminist agenda and consider the role of trade stories in constructing gendered professional identities. Moreover, I also seek to consider, as Banks does, the professional identity of the costume designer. However, rather than focus on the oral history of practitioners, I assess their representation in the trade press in order to examine how the industry, as a whole, imagines the role.

In accordance with Banks, I also view the experience of below-the-line workers as an important area for scholarly attention. An examination of their treatment within the industry reveals a set of important issues regarding power, visibility and, as this chapter argues, gender. Despite their integral roles in the filmmaking process, costume designers are often considered to be below-the-line workers as opposed to writers, directors and actors, all of whom are considered above-the-line creative workers. The distinction between above- and below-the-line workers is, as Banks (2009: 89) notes, central to our understanding of production cultures. However, it also raises some troubling issues regarding the value (both economic and cultural) of certain kinds of labour which structures much of the discourse surrounding the figure of the costume designer. The line to which the terms refer is the horizontal line on a budget sheet that distinguishes creative and technical costs. Thus, the industry terms 'above the line' and 'below the line' indicate a practitioner's position on the budget sheet. The terms therefore signal a hierarchy in which creative labour is valued above technical workers, and this is consequently reflected in pay scales.

According to David Hesmondhalgh (2002), above-the-line workers contribute to the 'symbolic meaning' of a product. In other words, this kind of labour exhibits intangible qualities such as creativity, invention and artistic ability. Below-the-line workers, on the other hand, require a set of technical skills and specific subject knowledge, often learned through apprenticeships. Another significant distinction, for the purpose of this study, can be made in regard to the level of visibility practitioners receive in the public sphere. Below-the-line workers, for example, rarely achieve the celebrity status accorded to some above-the-line professionals.

While some costume designers have become public figures—and indeed this chapter shall discuss one in particular—it is important to remember that the majority remain unknown. Similarly, as David Chierichetti (1976) notes in his book *Hollywood Costume Design*, in addition to the costume designer there are 'thousands of expert seamstresses, cutters and fitters, wardrobe men and women, working long hours with little reward [who make] brilliant concepts reality' (10). This lack of public recognition has often been 'explained away' by industry professionals as a necessity for the purpose of narrative and character coherence. Indeed, one of the primary functions of costume is to contribute to an audience's sense of 'suspended disbelief'. As Sarah Street (2002: 7) argues, 'it is possible that there might be an "imagined embodiment" in process whereby the audience imagines that the character has exercised a degree of individual agency when deciding what to wear, just as they experience in their own lives.' As such, it has been argued that the costume designer must strive to deliberately remain invisible for narrative and characterization purposes. However, I would argue that this invisibility also stems from a set of gendered assumptions regarding the public and the private.

Of course, it has long been claimed that there remains a gendered division between public and private spaces; the former coded as masculine, the latter as feminine. Feminist scholars Stacy Gillis and Joanne Hollows (2009), for example, note that '[t]he private sphere was the site of the home, family life and consumption and the public sphere was identified with work, industry, commerce, politics and production' (4). This distinction has implications for the ways in which certain forms of labour are valued. That the costumer is, for the most part, obscured from public view speaks surely to the gendered nature of the role. Indeed, the technical skills required of the profession are typically associated with 'feminine' domestic labour and therefore deny the costumer the agency associated within masculine fields of work. Similarly, the element of 'styling' (i.e. sourcing and purchasing garments from fashion designers) associated with contemporary television costume design is closely tied to the activity of shopping and consumption which, as suggested above, are clearly coded as 'feminine' practices. Thus, is it important not only to note that women have traditionally dominated the profession, but also that the very nature of the work is coded as 'feminine' and therefore is bound up with the set of derogatory, and problematic, assumptions that the term inescapably brings. From this perspective it can be deduced that the lack of public recognition stems from a series of value judgements which are structured in relation to conservative (and inherently masculine) notions of production, authorship, art and commerce. Furthermore, in her examination of costuming in the classical era, Elizabeth Nielson (1990) reveals not only that a lack of respect was directed towards the costume designer, but also, significantly, that this lack of respect emerged as a direct result of the gendered nature of the role. The implicitly feminine job was 'low' in cultural and monetary value and remained distant from any artistic merit often bestowed upon fashion design (often coded as a 'masculine' profession). Seeking to clarify and expand upon some of the literature gestured towards here, this chapter examines what is at stake when these frustrations and the costume designer are made public.

The *Hollywood Reporter: Fashion in Entertainment* coverage provides a unique opportunity for costume designers to become visible (and vocal) and in so doing to stake a claim in the creative process. It includes testimonies of working costume designers as they reflect upon the precise nature of costuming in the contemporary period and provides a space in which to discuss and debate developments within the production environment. Many of these testimonies evoke characteristics of a number of the 'trade stories' associated with below-the-line staff as outlined by Caldwell (2008)—including 'war stories' and 'against-all-odds allegories'. The cultural functions of these trade stories include 'establishing craft mastery' and 'labour mystique', and showcasing a specific 'skill set': 'certitude; physique; and belief' (38). 'War stories' as the title suggests, construct production as a 'form of war' (40)—battles are won on account of individual heroism performed by below-the-line practitioners— which demonstrate 'moral character and triumph of will'. Caldwell's concept of 'war stories' are therefore profoundly masculinized. The specific examples upon which he draws even place a premium on masculine characteristics such as physical strength. Thus, the costume designer, a feminized figure, does not employ 'war stories' in quite the same way. Rather, tales of battle often involve subtly managing those 'above-the-line' individuals or external powerful forces in an attempt to protect the cultural legitimacy of the project—which thematically echoes the familiar axiom that 'behind every great man is a great woman'. The success of these wars is won on an ability to exercise 'self-sacrificing' restraint and humility (as the following will demonstrate).

'Against-all-odds allegories' operate in a similar way. As with the 'war stories', 'against-all-odds' narratives often employ myths of classic heroism designed to associate below-the-line staff with a set of specific (masculine) characteristics; 'lowly origins, physical perseverance and tenacity' (Caldwell 2008: 40). Once more, it is clear that the costume designer fails to neatly fall into the prescribed categories, not simply because of the gendered nature of the role: this also may speak to the 'liminal' position of costume designers (i.e. that they function as creative workers but are denied the status accorded to above-the-line personnel). Nevertheless, certain aspects of the 'against-all-odds allegories' are employed with regularity; specifically, the premise that 'low budgets are the mother of invention' (42). Details of difficult working conditions are central to the professional identity of the costume designer and serve to foreground the level of creativity and ingenuity the role requires. In so doing, these trade stories play an important function in 'establishing craft and mastery . . . [often] via moral character and triumph of will' (38). Establishing 'craft and mastery' is central to early issues of the trade paper, as this is the period in which the legitimacy of costume design is most in question—following the increasing use of designer fashion onscreen. Consequently, within the trade press fashions and fashion designers are posed as a 'threat' to the cultural legitimacy of costume designers. Implicitly, this speaks to a persistent hierarchy in which the work of fashion designers is valued above costumers—a hierarchy which the costume designers' trade stories seek to dismantle.

Trade Stories and Cultural Distinctions in Fashion and Costume Design

In the first of a series of *Hollywood Reporter: Fashion in Entertainment* articles, journalist Denise Abbott (1998) reports on the increasing use of onscreen designer fashion. She writes: 'As major labels begin to grab attention on-screen, costume designers are finding their relationships with fashion designers unravelling' (13). Some costume designers, such as Deborah Nadoolman Landis, are portrayed as being highly critical of the ways in which costume designers (and their contribution to the filmmaking process) are rendered invisible. Landis observes that '[o]ur frustration stems from years of being overlooked . . . Costume designers have a very low status in the industry. We are underpaid. Many earn less than hair and makeup artists. We have no ownership over our product. And there's no question fashion designers are trying to take over' (Landis in Abbott 1998: 13). Landis's comments suggest that, while abundant in (for want of a better term) 'vocational capital', the costume designer is perceived to be low in both economic and symbolic capital because they are rendered invisible. A fashion designer is able to mark their garment with a signature (and in so doing, give it value, or to use Bourdieu's (1993b) terms, 'change the social nature of the object' (137), while costume designers, on the other hand, are denied ownership over their creations, supposedly for reasons of narrative realism. In addition, as a below-the-line worker, the costume designer's creations are ultimately accountable to above-the-line creative personnel and are therefore denied creative autonomy. Similarly, if sourced clothing is used, the original fashion designer remains the 'author' of that particular product, despite any changes the costume designer may make in order for the garment to 'work' onscreen. Thus, a gendered distinction is fostered between the 'feminine' work of costume design and the 'masculine' — and thereby more 'legitimate' — field of fashion design. The remainder of the article therefore, provides a space in which costume designers seek to establish and restore their symbolic capital.

A great deal of the 'trade stories' favour an alternative discourse of value than that which privileges the craft of fashion design, and seek to make clear the ways in which costume differs from fashion. Albert Wolsky (costume designer for *You've Got Mail* (1998)), for example, contends:

> We're character driven . . . Our clothes don't have to be pretty; they can be outdated or ugly, as long as they fit the character. We tell a story with our clothes. Fashion, on the other hand, is of the moment. Its purpose is to make stars look beautiful and the audience wants to go shopping. It's not a bad purpose, but it's not my purpose. (Wolsky in Abbott 1998: 13)

For Wolsky, despite his qualification (it's not a bad purpose), it is clear that fashion is bound up with commerce. In so doing his comments serve to demystify fashion and undermine those who would seek to position it as 'art' — it is 'commercial' (and therefore not art). Costuming, on the other hand *is* a craft. Its motives are not economic; they are purely creative. These discourses of value are prevalent throughout a number of the *Hollywood Reporter: Fashion in Entertainment* special issues. For example there are several accounts in which costumers have refused items donated by fashion houses — despite the opportunity for financial gain (via tie-ins and budgetary savings) — precisely because they could not be narratively explained. Costume designer for *Felicity* (1998–2002), Linda Serijan-Fasmer recalls an occasion in which she chose not to include pieces from a Calvin Klein collection, as it did not 'fit' the character. She reveals: 'Calvin Klein wanted to fly me to New York for the clothes, but I respectfully declined because ours is the most un-Kleiny show imaginable. Felicity [Keri Russell] is an 18-year-old student, and everyone knows her character couldn't afford to dress up like that' (Serijan-Fasmer in Abbott 1999: 32). Similarly, costume designer Betsy Heinmann, when discussing the use of fashion as costume, makes the following comment. She claims that '[n]o one dresses from head to toe in one designer . . . I'm happy to use a piece here, a piece there, but it's probably not realistic to use only one designer. I'm trying to make a real person' (Heinmann in Kaufman 1999: 5). For both Serijan-Fasmer and Heinmann narrative realism is key to costuming and the primary motivation for wardrobe choices.

While the above anecdotes do not function as 'war stories' in the traditional sense, they do speak to a familiar rhetoric deployed throughout the trade press, which foregrounds the 'moral character' of the costume designer (Caldwell 2008: 38). Often the role of a costume designer involves willfully sacrificing authorship, and potential economic gain, for the 'greater good' of the project—which is in itself a heavily gendered concept. Thus, the costume designer's humility is central to several 'trade stories'. For example Debra McGuire (costume designer for *Friends* (1994–2004)), in the article 'After a Fashion', asserts:

> When you do television or movies, you're character-driven in the creation process, and you're driven by the written word, and that's the only motivation. It can't be about being seen or making a statement because what really needs to make a statement is the written word. Our job is to be a support system for the writer and help the writer realize their vision—and the job can't be any more than that. (McGuire in P. Wilson 2002: 8)

As the above passage makes clear, costume designers are encouraged to deny their own creative voice and help above-the-line personnel 'realize their vision'. Indeed, the language used to describe the role as a 'support system' echoes the way in which domestic forms of (feminine) labour are often talked about (i.e. invisible, 'behind-the-scenes' work that supports (masculine) public labour). And there is an acknowledgment and acceptance of this role. In a 1999 *Hollywood Reporter: Fashion in Entertainment* special issue, Rachael Stanley (costume designer for *Ally McBeal* (1997–2002) and *Sabrina the Teenage Witch* (1996–2003)), remarks:

> My goal is to dress my characters in the most beautiful way I can to promote the story . . . If, as a result, viewers latch onto a look, that's terrific. But that is never my motivation. I'm always shocked when I hear someone boast, 'I'm going to start a look.' Well, fine, but what if the character doesn't fit that look? Worrying about how an outfit will play in Peoria is not our job. (Stanley in Abbott 1999: 32)

For Stanley, there is a sense of disapproval towards those costumers who seek to transgress their position. Seeking to establish a public presence by initiating fashion trends threatens the integrity of the role and is viewed with at best surprise and at worst disdain. Such a view is supported by the use of 'cautionary tales', which seek to highlight the dangers of being 'seduced' by the fashion industry.

In his final category of trade stories, Caldwell (2008) suggests that 'cautionary tales' and 'making-it sagas' are typically associated with 'unregulated and nonsignatory sectors (assistants, agents, reps and clerical [workers])' (38) and perform a number of important cultural functions, including 'career salvage operations' and 'boundary and turf marking' (38). Therefore, it is somewhat unusual for costume designers to employ these genres when narrativizing their roles (not least of all because the idea of marking ones turf is coded as a 'masculine activity') and may say something of the ways in which, typically, costume designers are denied a voice or platform. Nevertheless, they are crucial in the 'Apart at the Seams' feature as costumer Marilyn Vance's anecdote makes clear. Vance recounts her experience of working with Giorgio Armani on *The Untouchables* (1987) and in so doing reveals the difficulty in reconciling the 'cross purposes' of fashion and costume design. According to Vance, despite providing Armani with well-researched, detailed storyboards and suitable fabric swatches, the designer used material from his contemporary fashion line. She claims '[s]ome of his suits were so outlandish, not even close to the right period. I spent a fortune hiring every tailor in Chicago to rework the designs' (Vance in Abbott 1998: 22), and in so doing reminds readers that fashion and costume serve alternate purposes (fashion is preoccupied with the 'new'; costume, in this case, preserves the 'old'). She goes on to detail the way in which Armani took credit for the designs and neglected to acknowledge her contribution. She maintains:

> People would call to read me these articles about how he did this and he did that. It broke my heart . . . These people are so aggressive and publicity hungry. Even Dawn Steel, who was a dear friend of mine, thought promoting his name would help the picture. I was furious with her. We costume designers serve the picture instead of publicizing ourselves or making extra money off something that sells well. I wish I had a dollar for every outfit coped from my *Pretty Woman* designs. (Vance in Abbott 1998: 22)

In so doing, Vance not only reminds readers that the costume designer's role is to suppress her own ego, but also clearly defines the concerns of the costume designer: to serve the picture.

'Career salvage operations' are central to trade press. It becomes increasingly clear that product placement is an intrinsic part of the contemporary production environment and poses a real threat to the role of costume designer. Thus, later issues make use of 'cautionary tales' and 'against-all-odds allegories' in order to make sense of the changing production conditions and legitimate contemporary costuming practices, and perhaps most importantly to demonstrate the necessity of the costume designer when the position is under threat of becoming obsolete.

Contemporary Costuming and Consumer Culture

In a 2002 issue of the *Hollywood Reporter: Fashion in Entertainment*, costume and fashion designer Bob Mackie voices concerns about the changing role of the costume designer: 'A lot of costume design now, I'm afraid is all about the shopping; most of the films are modern and sometimes (the producers) get something for free' (Mackie in P. Wilson 2002: 8). Mackie's derogatory attitude towards contemporary costume design is informed by a longstanding discourse of value in which processes of production are privileged over consumption. For Mackie, the creative processes necessary for designing and producing fashion and costume are absent from shopping or styling which, for him, lacks a certain kind of creativity. In addition, as with Wolsky, Mackie's comments also underscore the assumption that fashion is a commercial enterprise which threatens to disrupt the creative vision. Such a perspective views those contemporary costume designers or stylists who participate in the practice of 'shopping' as colluding in the economic project at the expense of the creative one. These concerns emerge from a somewhat Marxist informed view that processes of design and production are revered as inherently active and consumption practices are dismissed as inherently passive. From this perspective, meaning is inscribed on a commodity during the production process and is in turn (passively) consumed in the consumption process. In terms of fashion then, the designer participates in the 'legitimate' processes of production and is viewed as solely responsible for creating the symbolic meaning of the garment. Thus, the costume designer 'proper' (i.e. the person responsible for designing and creating costume) is thought to have encoded the garments with meaning during this process. The meaning here (as previously discussed) is supposed to in some way communicate something about the character, the narrative or both. The stylist or creative shopper is thought to have acquired clothes which are already inscribed with meaning. As such, consumption is often accepted as the 'negative other' of production (Hollows 2000: 114). Such outdated assumptions resonate within the trade press, and are at times deployed in an attempt to legitimate costume design, as the below passage, taken from a 1999 issue of the *Hollywood Reporter: Fashion in Entertainment* special issue, makes clear:

'Fashion vs. character is what I call it', says costume designer Molly Maginnis ('As Good as it Gets', 'Mighty Joe Young', 'Sister Act', 'Broadcast News'). 'Fashion designers don't think about creating a character so much as creating a look. A look is very much applied to the character as opposed to revealing it.' (Kaufman 1999: 5)

While, once again, Maginnis's claim implies that the fashion industry is driven by commercial desires—and is therefore more concerned with 'style' rather than 'substance'—it also suggests that the act of creating meaning lies with the producer; meaning is created by the fashion designer and then 'applied' to the character.

It is also important to remember, that these readings of production and consumption are gendered—passivity is equated with femininity and activity with masculinity. Indeed, even within the 'feminine' industry of fashion, Hollows (2000:

114) argues that the gendered distinction between production and consumption still applies: masculinity is associated with the production of fashion, and femininity with its consumption. Moreover, while the production of fashion is understood as a form of 'labour', consumption on the other hand is viewed 'leisure' and is consequently trivialized within patriarchal discourses. The mobilization of cultural studies as a discipline was in part created as a response to debates such as these. Indeed, the work of scholars, including Hebdige, seeks to revise the notion that meaning is only created during production. Rather, this body of work argues that consumption requires a specific set of cultural competences and is vital to the meaning-making (and remaking) process. Hebdige (1998), for example, contends that 'there can be no absolute symmetry between the "moments" of design/production and consumption/use' (80–1). As such, recent enquiries within the field seek to, as Hollows notes, consider the 'total trajectory of an object as it moves from production through exchange, distribution, mediation and consumption' (114).

The article 'Costume Drama', in the 1999 *Hollywood Reporter: Fashion in Entertainment* special issue, revisits the apparent 'turbulent' relationship between costume and fashion designers and provides important context within which to view contemporary costume design. In particular, the article focuses upon the ways in which the current production environment informs wardrobe decisions. To return to Caldwell's concept of trade stories, the article is structured as an 'against-all-odds' allegory insofar as it explicitly employs the philosophy that 'low budgets are the mother of invention', as the following passage demonstrates:

> 'Nowadays budgets are extremely low' reports Mona May [costume designer for *Clueless*] . . . 'It used to be that at least 20% to 30% of the film's overall budget went to costumes. Now, it's 10% to 12% max.'. . . Television's budgets and time constraints are even tighter, says Alexandra Welker who is currently costume designer for ABC's *Snoops*. A one-hour episodic means a new show every eight days and a voracious demand for clothes, with numerous changes for main characters, guest actors and day players. (Kaufman 1999: 5)

Thus, the article is keen to detail the precise challenges that typically preoccupy lower-level staff and speaks to their marginalization within the industry. 'Against-all-odds' narratives such as these form part of a broader agenda within this article, and subsequent coverage in the trade press serves to bolster the construction of the costume designers' 'moral character' and their ability to thrive when faced with difficult working conditions. In the contemporary production culture, costume designers rely upon their cultural competences to find new and creative ways to protect the artistic vision of above-the-line staff, and in so doing demonstrate their necessity within the creative project. This counter-discourse, employed within later issues of the *Hollywood Reporter*, rejects the traditional

Marxist assumption that meaning is created during production. This is reflected in the increasing use of the term 'creative shopping' to describe contemporary costuming practices.

The 'creative shopper' complicates the longstanding assumption that shopping is a passive process. Though this is not to suggest that the understanding is entirely rejected—indeed, the term itself relies upon the negative connotations associated with shopping in order to establish itself as different by adding the prefix 'creative'. Nevertheless, the notion of the creative shopper problematizes the understanding that meaning is encoded into a cultural product at the level of production and consumed passively. As such, the invocation of this new title serves an important 'turf-marking' and 'career-salvaging' function, insofar as it suggests a distinct attempt to revise previous attitudes towards shopping and to re-appropriate the term. Thus, creative shopping is central to the meaning-making process rather than simply absorbing existing meaning.

Television costume designers Debra McGuire's and Linda Serijan-Fasmer's anecdotes are particularly revealing of the ways in which (feminine) consumer competences are crucial to contemporary styling. For example Serijan-Fasmer believes that she possesses the aesthetic disposition which allows her to put together looks that 'the "average person" would never dream of; Birkenstock boots with a $500 Gaultier top I picked up at an outlet for $80' (Serijan-Fasmer in Abbott 1999: 30). Moreover, once again, the anecdote demonstrates her ability to work within difficult financial constraints. Similarly, McGuire makes clear that the process of 'applying' designer looks to characters also involves a specific set of cultural competences exclusive to costume designers, and attempts to challenge assumptions that 'shopping' is an inherently 'passive' practice. She claims 'I can't guarantee a designer that they're going to see what I buy from them in the state that I bought it; I might buy a dress and cut the sleeves off or reshape it, so my commitment is not to the designer at all' (McGuire in P. Wilson 2002: 8). Both accounts serve to make visible contemporary costuming practices, which too often remain hidden, while also reminding readers that, above all, the costume designer remains committed to the creative vision.

McGuire's admission that she alters designer fashion to 'fit' with character is by no means uncommon. Welker adopts a similar approach: 'There are a lot of designers out there who I identify with, but I have no qualms about changing their designs. I might buy a great coat but embellish the collar. We're always busy in the workroom' (Welker in Kaufman 1999: 6). Both McGuire's and Welker's costuming practices can be read as somewhat 'subversive'—indeed, these practices echo (masculine) subcultural practices insofar as 'intended meanings' encoded in the production process are appropriated when 'applied' to a character. As such, the 'creative shopper' challenges assumptions that 'styling' does not involve 'creative labour'. Moreover, accounts of the precise nature of contemporary costume design problematizes constructions of production and consumption as distinct and separate activities, as both are central to meaning-making processes—thus, when distinctions are made, they are often the result of essentialist gendered assumptions.

To be sure, the *Hollywood Reporter: Fashion in Entertainment* special issues perform a 'public sphere' function insofar as they offer a space for marginalized industry professionals to air grievances and make visible the kinds of labour and cultural competences of the costume designer in a 'turf-marking' exercise. In a series of ways, the trade press serves as a mediator between the disparate production sectors, allowing for 'trade stories' to jostle for position in the hope of creating some form of consensus around the professional identity of the costume designer. Thus, one final 'trade story' which is perhaps the most potent overall within the trade press is the 'success story'. Within trade discourse, Patricia Field serves as the 'success story' personified, insofar as she appears to have cultivated a successful and mutually beneficial relationship with fashion designers, while maintaining the symbolic value associated with costume design 'proper'. Thus, her frequent deployment within the *Hollywood Reporter: Fashion in Entertainment* is crucial in reimagining the role of the stylist, and restoring the cultural legitimacy of the costume designer.

Restoring Cultural Legitimacy: Patricia Field

In the opening quote of this chapter, Field makes explicit the link between 'styling' and 'commerce', something which other costume designers have been reluctant to do lest it threaten the cultural legitimacy of the 'craft'. Yet, as the remaining section of this chapter shall demonstrate, despite her acknowledgment of an economic agenda, the process of styling is reimagined as a 'legitimate' form of intellectual and creative labour.

Field's professional identity is buttressed by a 'making-it' narrative which secures her symbolic value. In the 2002 article, 'After a Fashion', Field recounts her 'accidental' break into the fashion and costuming industry:

> I started out in the retail business, and I am still in the retail business. When I was looking [to buy clothes] but it wasn't out there, I started making special things for my shop. Other shops would want to buy them, so that developed through the back door into the wholesale business. It was never really my plan to have a collection. (Field in P. Wilson 2002: 6; brackets in the original)

While Field clearly harbours a connection to the commercial sphere, equally she demonstrates her resistance to mainstream mass-produced fashion. Her success within the fashion industry (and subsequent success as a costume designer) is founded upon her ability to create 'original' one-off garments rather than sell ready-to-wear designer fashions in her boutiques. Field then represents and creates 'street style'. 'Street style' is comparable to 'folk art' insofar as it is created by 'the people'. It is created within 'urban subcultures'; according to Crane (2000) it 'suppl[ies] many of the ideas for fads and trends' (135). Therefore, the emergence of street style problematizes previous prominent sociological theories (conceptualized initially by Thorstein Veblen (1899/1994) and Georg Simmel (1904/1957)) which suggest that fashion engages in a 'trickle down' process. As discussed in the previous chapter, for Simmel this process was known as 'class differentiation', and both he and Veblen refer to the ways in which fashion trends 'trickle down' from the upper- to the lower-middle classes, stopping short of the working classes (by which time the particular trend was no longer fashionable). As such, the process maintains the symbolic boundaries between the classes. Recent work on fashion theory strongly contests the 'trickle down' concept insofar as, according to Fred Davis (1994) in his book *Fashion, Culture and Identity,* it fails to take into account 'the fashion pluralism and polycentrism that more and more characterizes contemporary dress' (112). Indeed, one of its most vocal critics, Herbert Blumer (1969), fervently argues that there is no definite direction of fashion. In his article 'Fashion: From Class Differentiation to Collective Selection', Blumer proposes a parallel theory which has subsequently been termed the 'trickle up' or 'bubble up' process. To put simply, the 'trickle up' theory is essentially a reversal of the 'trickle down' process whereby trends are initiated by 'the people' and move up through the strata before finally being incorporated into high fashion.[2] Field thus participates in this kind of 'subcultural' and 'masculine' (and by default 'legitimate') creative process which does not arise out of an intentional desire to capture the mainstream market.

Discussions of her unintentional career move into the fashion industry mirror 'rise-to-fame' narratives (see Dyer 1979/2004; Gamson 1994) which combine 'lucky breaks' with 'divine' talent, insofar as her creativity and originality are presented as solely responsible for her success; she did not seek out this career. The theme of happenstance features heavily in the construction of Field's professional identity and serves a specific cultural function. For example the following passage demonstrates that creating fashion trends is not something she anticipates when costuming; it is something that happens organically:

Field, who started out in the mid-1980s on TV series and moved on to features such as 'Miami Rhapsody' (where she first met Parker) says that to her, proper costuming is an art. 'We're like a painter who doesn't think of what the trend will be like . . . [t]rends are created from an original point of view, not thinking it's a trend.' (Dawn 2000b: 4)

In some ways her comments echo Stanley's and McGuire's contention that costume design should not be driven by the desire to ignite a 'look'. Thus, she is able to maintain the critical respect of other costumers. Indeed, she is often constructed in the same terms as other costumers featured in the trade press, and a series of familiar trade genres are employed within the *Hollywood Reporter* coverage.

In the 2000 *Hollywood Reporter: Fashion in Entertainment* special issue, an entire page spread is dedicated to *Sex and the City* and details Field's costuming practices. First, the article is keen to stress the dedication and commitment to the artistic project through trade stories associated with below-the-line staff. It reads:

> Achieving a sense of style takes long hours and lots of willingness to try and try again. Fortunately, says Field, the designers have Parker as their main model . . . Parker explains that fittings occur just about every 10 days and can last from five to seven hours at a time usually after the set has wrapped for the night. 'We can go as late as 2 or 3 in the morning.' (Dawn 2000b: 4)

The passage above employs aspects of the 'against-all-odds' narrative insofar as it details the ways in which Field must sacrifice time and energy in order to work within the tight time and budget constraints of TV production. In addition, this particular anecdote also fosters a sense of 'labour mystique' surrounding the process of styling, which Caldwell identifies as one of the central cultural functions of below-the-line trade stories. Here, a claim to the creative (and all the indefinable aspects the term conjures) is being made; Field's approach to costuming embodies those intangible qualities associated with above-the-line personnel. 'Styling' requires moments of genius that occur sporadically and inconsistently—there is no formula, and therefore many hours are needed in order to test various scenarios. One particular moment is proffered as evidence of this:

> 'Around 1 in the morning we had this brainstorm', remembers Weinberg [who co-designed early seasons with Field]. 'We thought we'd try the same shoe, but two different colours . . . So only some people will notice that, when they walk out of the hotel to go to a bar, Carrie has two shoes, different colours, but that's how we create—out of passion and fun.' (Weinberg in Dawn 2000b: 4)

The decision to put Carrie in odd shoes is presented as a moment of creative genius, born out of a brainstorming session, and as such the anecdote perpetuates a sense of mystique surrounding the process. As suggested above, traditionally, it is assumed that the designer 'proper' is thought to have encoded the garments with meaning during this process. Styling, it is often claimed, involves acquiring clothes that are already inscribed with meaning. However, as the above passage makes clear, Field's approach to costuming demonstrates how the processes of shopping for and styling a wardrobe require creativity—items are not simply 'applied' to a character, they are reworked, re-appropriated and given new meaning. The precise ways in which new meaning is created is often discussed in a necessarily vague way. For example in the same article Sarah Jessica Parker contends: 'You don't want the clothes wearing you because it looks contrived . . . People never look good when they look as if clothes were thrown on them' (Parker in Dawn 2000b: 4). Implicitly she refers to the act of styling as that which does not consist of simply 'throwing', or, to use Maginnis's term, 'applying' clothes on an actor, but rather involves a much more careful and considered process, the precise nature of which is not made clear. Nevertheless, it is clear that the stylist works as a mediator. In between the process of production and consumption, the stylist 'mediates' the meaning of the clothes in order to prevent them from appearing 'contrived'.

The 'mediation' process reconciles the differences between fashion and costume—they do not have to be antithetical in the ways that Landis suggests, and in contrast to Maginnis's claims, fashion can 'reveal' something about the character. Field, it seems, is able to embrace fashion as an asset to the creative process of costume design, as the passage below makes clear:

> For Field and Weinberg, anything goes, from vintage outfits and accessories to high-fashion designer wear. Labels aren't important per se. There are, however, favourite designers for each main character: Kim Cattrall's Samantha gets Yigal Azouel, and Chloe is favorite for Parker's Carrie, but the name is less important than how the style suits the actress. (Dawn 2000b: 4)

The use of specific labels for specific characters is supposed to reveal something about their 'identity'. In so doing, the passage suggests that the styling process requires a deep understanding of character, insofar as one should be able to 'know' the character on such a level that they might anticipate their fashion tastes. Moreover, connected to Street's observation regarding 'imagined embodiment', there is a concerted effort to put oneself in the mindset of the character when selecting garments. Consequently, the passage demonstrates a commitment to narrative realism, and thereby challenges previous assumptions that fashion poses as an innate threat to the suspension of disbelief. Thus, this conclusion has implications not only for our contemporary understanding of costume design, but also for our conceptual understanding of fashion and costume.

In the introduction to this chapter, I set out two objectives: to develop arguments proposed in the previous chapter, and to contribute to the burgeoning field of feminist production studies. Thus, I have been keen to demonstrate the precise ways in which costume designers collectively reimagine their roles during times of great industrial and economic uncertainty, in the hope of responding to these aims. In sum, the emergence of fashion programming has allowed for a re-evaluation of a series of (problematic) assumptions which structure understandings of art and value to occur. Traditionally, the 'feminine' and thus, by default, 'trivial' work that costume designers undertake is denied 'legitimate' status, unlike fashion design which has secured legitimacy through its connections to the 'masculine' sphere of art and production. However, more traditional assumptions which commend the 'labour' of production are challenged here as stylists stake a claim in the creative process. In order to do so, the role of the stylist—for which Patricia Field becomes a vanguard—is regarded as central to the creative meaning-making process, and thereby undermines longstanding assumptions that the process of meaning-making is confined to the production of garments. Rather the processes of styling—which involves the consumption, mediation and appropriation of dress—are legitimized.

Within the wider contextual apparatus, it seems that other television stylists have also enjoyed this increased level of public visibility and respect. For instance, Eric Daman, the costume designer for *Gossip Girl* and *The Carrie Diaries* (2012–) has recently been described as the 'new Patricia Field' in the *New York Post* (Lieberman 2012). The feature article discusses how Field's former assistant on *Sex and the City* is developing a visual signature which can be identified across his corpus of work. Consequently, the increased focus on stylists within the popular press encourages viewers to take note of these costuming processes. In other words, it adds importance not only to the clothes onscreen but also to how they have been put together to create meaning. In the following sections I examine these processes in detail.

PART II

TEXTUAL APPROACHES TO FASHION, COSTUME AND NARRATIVE

4

FASHION, COSTUME AND NARRATIVE TROPES IN TV DRAMA

This project envisions fashion programming as a cultural phenomenon, a product of specific economic and industrial conditions. These conditions, outlined in the previous two chapters, have implications for the content of the programmes themselves. With this in mind the following chapters identify some of the recurrent tropes across fashion television.

The trade press sought to draw favourable comparisons between contemporary fashion programming and classical 'fashion films' to ensure the continued support of fashion houses, and indeed, the texts share similar thematic terrain, such as the Cinderella narrative as discussed in Chapter 3. And as with the classical 'fashion films', the texts under discussion here vary widely in generic terms. Thus, the following discussion is concerned with the ways in which certain narrative and visual tropes are continually deployed across a seemingly disparate range of case studies.

I initiate this discussion with the programme that is thought to signal the beginning of the cycle of fashion programming, before it percolated across a range of genres: *Sex and the City*. Following *SATC*, a number of short-lived comedy dramas such as *Cashmere Mafia* (2008), *Lipstick Jungle* (2008–2009) and *Jane by Design* (2011) sought to replicate its success, as female-oriented comedy dramas served as a logical space in which to nurture the fledgling relations between the fashion and television industries. Thus, I also examine one of the most high-profile successors, *Ugly Betty* (2006–2010).

The remaining case studies are illustrative of ways in which fashion television has diversified in order to capture different markets. It is unsurprising, perhaps, that teen-oriented fashion programming shows would develop (and flourish) given the spending power of the demographic they seek to address. However, period dramas seem a more unlikely vehicle for fashion promotion, as they are concerned with the past, whereas fashion is by definition perpetually concerned with the present. And yet, *Mad Men* (2007–) and *Boardwalk Empire* (2010–)

have skilfully captured the attention of male consumers in a way that was unprecedented for the feminized medium of television. Indeed, these latter examples speak to the way in which the strategies of fashion promotion have been honed and the tropes refined to support the economic goals of the industries.

The tropes identified across Chapters 4, 5 and 6 provide a narrative explanation for the display and advertisement of fashion in television. However, this is not to say that they are devoid of cultural or ideological meaning. Conversely, these key narrative devices serve as a means by which contemporary anxieties about identity performance can be played out. This chapter isolates and examines two thematic devices employed within fashion television—specifically the use of shopping and makeover scenes. As we shall see, these tropes have long since been a staple in 'women's films', yet they have a very different import within fashion programming. Their use within the examples discussed here is not so much to provide a pleasurable moment of spectacle, but rather to make a comment on categories of femininity (idealized and failed; 'natural' and 'constructed'). In so doing, these shows express and negotiate gender performance in a so-called postmodern era.

Visual and Narrative Tropes in 'Feminine' Genres: Shopping and Makeover Scenes

The use of fashion in *Sex and the City* and *Ugly Betty* is bound up with notions of performativity and 'excess'. *Ugly Betty* relies upon an 'excessive', 'camp' aesthetic which foregrounds its own construction and in so doing adopts an ambiguous attitude towards the notion of the 'authentic' self—at times entirely rejecting it in favour of an 'image-based' identity. This image-based identity is presented as potentially subversive and resistive, challenging the assumption that the so-called postmodern self is both 'flat' and 'superficial'. *SATC* adopts a slightly different position, yet the tension between the authentic and the image-based self is still of premium importance. Within both shows, various visual and narrative strategies are invoked as a way of working through this tension—and significantly both involve, to varying degrees, transformation.

In *Hollywood Catwalk: Exploring Costume and Transformation in American Film*, Tamar Jeffers McDonald (2010) offers a nuanced account of the myriad ways in which 'transformation' is enacted and presented in cinema, identifying no less than eleven recurring thematic and visual tropes. In her discussion of the makeover scene, Jeffers McDonald observes that the most 'obvious', though not the most common, trope in American film encourages the viewer to bear witness to 'the work needed to render the "ugly duckling" into beautiful swan' (42). Various visual and aural strategies (the use of an upbeat musical track, fast editing, etc.) signal the scene as a narrative intermission, allowing viewers to take pleasure in the spectacle of fashion and beauty practices. To use Jeffers McDonald's terms, 'costume can be allowed to halt the flow of the story' (42); examples include *Clueless* (1995), *It* (1927), *Now Voyager* (1942) and *Moonstruck* (1987). In the case of *Now Voyager* and *Moonstruck* the makeover scene offers additional audience pleasures insofar as they deliver the familiar star image of the lead actors. Hitherto the transformations, the star personae of Bette Davis and Cher are obscured by thick eyebrows, greying hair and ill-fitting clothes, creating suspense as the audiences anticipate the restoration of the familiar star images. This additional pleasure of the makeover is important within *Ugly Betty* (and will be returned to in more detail shortly), as it is one that is delayed across the four seasons, and only partially achieved. The audience is continually promised certain landmark events (the removal of Betty's braces, new glasses, etc.) which are often derailed at the last moment. However, not wishing to entirely deny the audience pleasure of Betty's transformation, the show employs dream sequences which display Betty/America Ferrera in her 'glamorous' state—though importantly the audience is not permitted to view the work needed to achieve this look.

It is worth noting here that Jeffers McDonald (2010) makes a distinction between the makeover scene—in which the labour of transformation is made explicit—and those which perform alternative visual and narrative functions, such as the 'invisible transformation' (48–55) and 'the false transformation' (73–82). The 'makeover scene', she notes, holds a privileged place within lifestyle television, as the 'the television makeover show often plays up what the filmic transformation ignores: the work to achieve the transformation itself' (see for example Heller 2007; Weber 2009). Filmic representations of transformations are more likely to include the latter visual tropes. However, *Ugly Betty*, as suggested above, makes use of the 'invisible transformation'—where the audience pleasure lies in the spectacle of the 'reveal' and not in the pleasures of observing fashion and beauty practices in process—and also includes several examples of 'false transformations' (detailed below). According to Jeffers McDonald, 'false transformations' appear to include a 'radical transformation [of the central protagonist], but this is in fact not so; the change is only feigned, the new persona a masquerade' (2010: 73). *Ugly Betty* and other examples of fashion programming discussed in this volume employ the 'false transformation' in intriguing ways, and as such they call into question fashion's ability to express identity. Moreover, they also call into question broader ideas about authenticity and the existence of a natural self.[1]

Sex and the City adopts an ambiguous relationship towards fashion, femininity and identity, which is of course by no means uncommon within 'women's genres'. Building on Hilary Radner's (1995) analysis of *Pretty Woman* (1990), Charlotte Brunsdon (1997) has argued that a series of 'women's films' emerged in the 1980s and early 1990s which were preoccupied with the performance and constructedness of femininity. She refers to this collection of films as 'shopping films', precisely because of their key trope—a shopping scene. For Jeffers McDonald (2010), the shopping sequence has long since been employed as one of the most common visual tropes of transformation narratives in films such as *Why Change Your Wife?* (1920), *Gold Diggers of 1935* (1935) and *Thoroughly Modern Millie* (1967).

In many ways these films can be viewed as precursors to *Sex and the City* given their focus on fashion and femininity. That said, there are subtle textual differences between the representation and function of shopping scenes within this category of film and *SATC*. In Brunsdon's (1997) analysis of *Working Girl* (1988) and *Pretty Woman*, she demonstrates how the function of the shopping scene is informed by a 'post-feminist' logic insofar as it is representative of the 'rediscovery of the pleasures of feminine consumption' (85). These 'shopping scenes' perform a similar function to the makeover and the 'Cinderella narrative', which have long since been a staple of the 'woman's film' since the 1940s, insofar as they provide a space in which debates regarding the constructedness and performativity of femininity are enacted and worked through (see Moseley 2005a). In addition, these shopping scenes can also serve to 'educate' and inform audiences about fashion and consumption practices.

Brunsdon's (1997) analysis of *Pretty Woman*, for example, demonstrates how Vivian (Julia Roberts) is able to 'try on identities' (86); however she also notes that while Vivian is able to participate in fashion practices which allow her to construct and manipulate her identity, ultimately her 'natural' identity is privileged. While the concept of a 'natural' femininity has been rejected by more recent feminist scholars—arguing that the 'natural' self is also a construct—this body of 'women's films', as Hollows (2000: 155) has argued, seeks to 'naturalize' femininity. In other words, Vivian's transformation is less about constructing an identity for her to adopt and is more about 'revealing' her natural self. Therefore, these 'shopping films' and indeed classical 'women's films', such as *Now Voyager*, seek both to reveal the constructedness of femininity and also, somewhat contradictorily, to perpetuate the notion of a 'natural' self.

As with the 'shopping films' of the 1980s and 1990s, the performance of femininity is foregrounded in *Sex and the City*; and *SATC* also fosters this contradictory relationship to dress and the 'natural self'. The main difference between the show and its cinematic precursors that I wish to highlight here is connected to spectacle and its relationship to narrative. For example in *Pretty Woman*, Vivian's second shopping experience on Rodeo Drive (the first was a disaster) is signalled as a moment of spectacle. It is a montage sequence with little dialogue and extra-diegetic music (Roy Orbison's 'Pretty Woman') during which Vivian 'can try on identities and adopt them' (Brunsdon 1997: 86). Arguably, Vivian's function in this scene is 'to be looked at', and the lack of dialogue reinforces the fact that these moments do not exist simply to forward narrative. The shopping sequences in *SATC* are emphatically not singled out as moments of spectacle.[2] Carrie is not so much an object to be looked at as she is the holder of the gaze, with the desire to 'look' at the commodities in their own right. In so doing, *SATC* challenges early feminist criticism which views fashion as bound up with, and ultimately responsible for, the objectification of women. As Church Gibson (2000) notes, 'the "aesthetics" of fashion are not primarily sexual in nature, nor are they designed, necessarily, to attract the male gaze' (350). Rather, she writes, 'fashionable dress is a complex lexicon where the intention of sexual enticement may be absent altogether, or, if present, be unimportant in comparison to other criteria' (350). Indeed, with regard to *SATC*, fashion is either loosely, or wholly unconnected to the 'desire-to-find-Mr.-Right' narrative structure.

This is not to suggest that the shopping scenes cannot function as 'spectacle'; rather I am suggesting here that these moments are often central to the narrative focus of each specific episode. Moreover, these shopping sequences demonstrate the precise ways in which fashion as spectacle is enmeshed within the narrative. These particular scenes use fashion and consumption practices as a *metaphor* for the narrative.

Femininity, Fashion and Shopping in *Sex and the City*

Shopping scenes within *Sex and the City* are almost as frequent as the well-known 'chat-and-chew' and 'think-and-type' scenes. Consequently, this section has selected certain examples across the six seasons for further discussion. These examples have been identified on the basis that they demonstrate the varying ways in which this key narrative device can be used as a space to discuss the broader themes within a series: specifically, gender, identity and relationships.

In 'Attack of the Five Foot Ten Woman' (Season 3, Episode 3) Carrie learns that her ex-boyfriend 'Mr. Big' (Chris Noth) has married his twenty-something girlfriend, Natasha (Bridget Moynahan). When discussing the news with Charlotte (Kristin Davis), Carrie becomes upset and reveals that compared to Natasha she feels inadequate. For Carrie, Natasha embodies (if only visually) a version of domestic femininity which, as a single thirty-something in paid employment, Carrie has apparently rejected. The difference between them is central to the narrative in this episode and is played out in a shopping scene where Carrie and Natasha meet. The scene includes no fast editing and no musical interlude, and begins with a discussion between Carrie and Miranda (Cynthia Nixon) about a recent event in which Miranda's cleaning lady presented her with a rolling pin.

The pair debate whether they should feel guilty for refusing to perform the kinds of traditional domestic chores expected of them as Carrie tries on a dress in the changing room. Unbeknownst to her, Natasha is also in the changing room, and consequently when Carrie emerges from her cubical in only her underwear she is completely unprepared (and inappropriately attired) for their encounter. The costuming within this scene works to highlight the contrasting feminine identities the characters enact. Natasha's association with a 1950s version of idealized femininity is evidenced by the white-cotton shift dress she is trying on. The colour, or absence of colour, not only creates a 'bridal' look but also connotes an absence of 'personality' and 'individuality' (see Figure 1). Conversely, Carrie's mismatched underwear connotes her 'individuality' and 'quirkiness'.

In a bid to level the score, Carrie decides to attend a 'Women in the Arts' function that Natasha has organized. It becomes apparent in a 'chat-and-chew' scene with Charlotte that Carrie has purchased a new pair of shoes to wear to the event and plans to buy a dress (which she cannot afford) in an attempt to repair the damage to her self-esteem sustained during their changing-room encounter. However, Carrie's renewed self-confidence is only temporary. When she arrives at the function, Carrie is told that Natasha is unable to attend. As she enters the function room she announces, 'I charged another outfit I can't

Figure 1 Carrie meets Natasha. *Sex and the City* Season 3, Episode 3: 'Attack of the Five Foot Ten Woman', HBO, USA (2000).

afford . . . just to prove I'm amazing and I've never felt less so.' Ultimately, the episode seeks to demonstrate that Carrie's attempts to manipulate her own feminine identity through dress are fruitless and that she should celebrate her 'natural' identity—despite the fact that Carrie's 'natural' identity is shown to be constructed through dress. In other words, as with the 'shopping films' of the 1980s and 1990s, the episode demonstrates that while fashion allows Carrie the opportunity to 'try on and adopt identities', the show does in fact perpetuate the notion that Carrie somehow has an 'inner' feminine identity which is 'fixed'. Of course, it could also be argued that Natasha's conventional and domestic feminine identity represents more of a 'modernist' version of identity (thought to be shaped by more rigid 'traditional' gender roles), which Carrie resists. Thus, it is Carrie's quirkiness, individuality (and ability to complicate and negotiate the boundaries of 'gendered' identities) which are ultimately privileged and presented as part of her 'natural' self. The identity she attempts to perform as a response to her encounter with Natasha is 'inauthentic'.

The construction of identity and the performance of femininity are later challenged in Season 4. In the episode 'Change of a Dress' (Season 4, Episode 15) Carrie begins to rethink her recent engagement to her boyfriend Aidan. In an attempt to alleviate any pressure and to demystify the process of getting married, Miranda suggests that she and Carrie visit a bridal gown shop and try on the worst dresses available. In the following scene the pair emerge from their changing cubicles to reveal their dresses. Miranda, heavily pregnant at the time, wears a tight white gown with enormous puffed sleeves which she jokes, 'balances out her stomach'. Carrie, in contrast, wears an ornate high necked, beaded dress with an extremely large netted skirt. While the pair initially laugh hysterically at each other's appearance, when Carrie turns to face her reflection she suffers a panic attack. Miranda is forced to rip open the back of the dress to reveal that Carrie is covered in a red rash. Following the unsuccessful shopping trip, Carrie concludes that she is allergic to the thought of being a bride. The episode is therefore preoccupied with the performance of idealized femininity, using the wedding ceremony as shorthand for traditional domestic femininity. In her attempts to perform what she considers to be an appropriate version of femininity, Carrie is reminded that her 'authentic' identity is tied to her position as single woman. When she attempts to conform to a different model of femininity she is unsuccessful.

Carrie is reminded of this lesson in the episode 'An American Girl in Paris, Part Une' (Season 6, Episode 19). As the title suggests, the narrative revolves around Carrie's move to Paris with boyfriend Alexsandr Petrovsky; in particular, it depicts her struggles to assimilate. In an attempt to feel more at home in Paris, Carrie decides to go shopping. In a moment of screwball-inspired comedy typical of the show, Carrie enters the Dior boutique slipping on a puddle of water and slides head first into the store. The bird's eye view of Carrie spread-eagled on the floor with her belongings scattered around her demonstrates the magnitude of the fall. The camera then cuts to the faces of several sophisticated Parisian women who look on disapprovingly as Carrie attempts to recover herself from the floor. Not only does this scene demonstrate Carrie's inability to perform appropriate and sophisticated feminine behaviour, but the repercussions further serve as a reminder to Carrie that her 'authentic' identity does not belong in Paris. When she arrives back at the hotel it becomes apparent that during her fall in Dior, she misplaced her iconic 'Carrie' necklace. The necklace, as she explains to Alex, was not valuable (in the economic sense), but it was representative of who she was—thus fashion here is simply a marker of the 'natural' self.

In each of these examples, the shopping scenes provide a space for narrative concerns to be brought to the fore, serving as a metaphor for the unfolding action. As with the 'shopping film', these scenes reveal what Brunsdon (1997: 101) terms 'the labour of femininity . . . [that is] the difficulty of successfully inhabiting this contradictory position'. These shopping scenes perform the dual function of demonstrating the possibilities of 'trying on' a variety of feminine identities, but ultimately reveal the difficulty in sustaining and perpetuating those constructed identities. Indeed, these scenes serve as an ideological critique of the supposed flexibility offered by postmodern notions of identity performance, while simultaneously celebrating the supposed 'freedom' offered by consumption.

Throughout its six seasons, *Sex and the City* has often reflected on the consumption practices of women. In particular, it has raised a series of issues regarding the concept of the 'irresponsible' consumer. These debates are mobilized as early as Season 1 in 'The Power of Female Sex' (Season 1, Episode 5). In the opening scenes of the episode, the camera cuts from the outside of a Dolce and Gabbana store to the interior, panning along a selection of shoes on display before focusing on Carrie's feet trying on a pair of sandals. She makes the decision to buy the shoes only to find out that her credit card has been declined and subsequently destroyed by the shop assistant. Carrie's embarrassment is short-lived as an old female friend, Amalita (who is described in the episode as 'a professional girlfriend') buys the shoes for her. In the following scenes, Carrie becomes involved with a European architect who, after spending the night with her, leaves her $1,000. Thus, the episode centres around the moral dilemma posed in Carrie's weekly column: 'where's the line between professional girlfriend and just plain professional?' In the remainder of the episode Carrie contemplates adopting Amalita's lifestyle: dating rich men in exchange for luxury material goods. Within this episode Carrie is positioned to some extent as an 'irresponsible consumer'.

The irresponsible consumer is status-seeking, irrational, superficial, wasteful, easily manipulated and most importantly female (see Slater 1997; Miller 1995). Carrie portrays some of these traits in this episode. She allows herself to be 'manipulated' insofar as she attempts to buy a pair of shoes that she neither needs nor can afford. However, the episode does not result in Carrie changing her attitude towards fashion and consumption, and although by the end of the episode she has decided where to draw the line between professional girlfriend and professional, she keeps the $1,000 and the shoes. In other words, Carrie's 'irresponsible' consumer behaviour is questioned, but not wholly rejected.

The boundaries of acceptable consumption practices are continually challenged within *Sex and the City*. In the episode 'Ring a Ding Ding' (Season 4, Episode 16) Carrie needs to make a down payment on her apartment but is refused a loan. During a shopping scene, Miranda makes clear that the reason Carrie has no money is because she has spent over $40,000 on designer shoes. The scene begins with the pair in a non-specified shoe shop. Carrie, again, the bearer of the look, gazes longingly at the shoes on display. She then decides to 'try on' several pairs of shoes, but instructs the shop assistant not to allow her to buy them; she is trying them on for fun. This sets Carrie apart from the 'typical' irresponsible consumer, as she does not buy shoes as a means to acquire 'status' or to 'keep up with the Jones's'. Neither does she attempt to buy the shoes to attract male attention. Rather, it is implied that her desire to consume is motivated by her appreciation for beautiful objects. This is viewed as 'reasonable' consumption—thus the show refuses to condemn Carrie's behaviour.

In the show's official companion book, *Kiss and Tell*, Sarah Jessica Parker's comments on this particular episode offer some insight into why the show remains ambivalent towards Carrie's consumption practices. She claims, 'Carrie has no gal Friday. She is her own gal Friday. She doesn't have a lot of money, and she makes bad choices with her money, but she has never been anything other than completely independent' (Parker in Sohn 2004: 143). For Parker, Carrie's 'bad choices' are in some ways justified due to the fact that she is 'independent'. This speaks to the notion that postfeminist culture validates and celebrates consumer behaviour. As Tasker and Negra (2007) note, postfeminism 'elevates consumption as a strategy for healing those dissatisfactions that might alternatively be understood in terms of social ills and discontents' (2). Moreover, they demonstrate how recent postfeminist attitudes towards consumption seek to 'commodify feminism via the figure of the woman as empowered consumer' (2). Carrie moves fluidly between the positions of 'irresponsible' consumer and 'empowered consumer' throughout the six seasons of *SATC* and thereby has a complicated and, as Deborah Jermyn (2009) notes, 'questioning' (3) outlook on postfeminist notions of consumption which are continually foregrounded in the shopping sequences.

The understanding that fashion is ultimately a trivial and inherently feminine pastime is often perpetuated by the attitudes of the male characters within the show. In 'The Caste System' (Season 2, Episode 10), Miranda invites Steve (David Eigenberg) to an event hosted by her law firm. When Miranda asks Steve if he has any formal wear, he reveals that he owns a gold corduroy suit. Miranda then persuades Steve that he needs a new suit. This exchange suggests immediately that Steve lacks the cultural competences in fashion and positions him within a specific class stratum. As the title of the episode suggests, the performance of classed identities is central to the narrative and is made clear within Miranda and Steve's shopping scene. The scene begins with a shop assistant handing Miranda a glass of water, signalling that the pair are enjoying a 'luxury' shopping experience. This is further evidenced by the fact that Steve is having a suit fitted by a tailor, rather than purchasing one off the rack. In contrast to female-oriented shopping scenes, Steve is arguably positioned as the object of the gaze (both the audience and Miranda's). He appears in the centre of the frame in a designer navy-blue suit. When Miranda asks his opinion of the suit, he replies 'I think it's frightening how good I look', affirming that he is the desired object and also demonstrating the pleasure he is taking in the experience. His pleasure, however, is short lived once he realizes the price of the suit ($1,800). He registers his shock at the expense, thereby suggesting that it is irrational to spend so much on clothes. This suggests that the act of 'irrational' consumption is intrinsically 'feminine'. Yet, it doubly demonstrates his lack of cultural competences as he does not recognize the worth of the item. Miranda, in contrast, is not surprised by the price and offers to pay. Their socio-economic differences are keenly highlighted in this scene. Steve is affronted by Miranda's offer and refuses to let her pay for the suit. He claims that, had he accepted, he would start to think of her as his mother. Thus, this exchange makes clear that Steve has an understanding of conventionally 'appropriate' gender roles with regard to consumption (i.e. it is only appropriate for a female to buy him clothes if she is his mother). For Steve, it is not appropriate for Miranda, as his girlfriend, to buy him the suit he cannot afford. The shopping scene proves so distressing for Steve that he ultimately ends his relationship with Miranda, claiming that she needs to be with someone 'more on her level'. This is not the only example of a shopping scene resulting in a failed relationship.

The episode 'Lights, Camera, Relationship' (Season 6, Episode 5) opens with a shopping scene. Carrie's voice-over explains that '[i]n every relationship there comes a time when you have to take the next step . . . for some it's meeting the parents. For me, it's meeting the Prada'. Her playful monologue thereby makes clear how important fashion is to her, and suggests that it is boyfriend Berger's first time in the Prada store. As the pair enter the white, stylish and spacious boutique, Berger acknowledges its aesthetic differences to other (non-designer) outlets. He jokes, 'on my planet the clothing stores have clothes'. His witty remark not only indicates an alternative (classed) experience of shopping, but again, speaks to the notion that Carrie's world of high-end fashion is both 'ludicrous' and 'pretentious'. Shortly after they enter, the shop assistant tries to persuade Berger to buy a Prada shirt. Initially he appreciates the quality of the tailoring, claiming 'I never say fabulous, but if I did, I would. That's what a real shirt looks like.' However, as with Steve, Berger is outraged by the price and refuses to buy the shirt. In a later scene Carrie presents Berger with the shirt as a gift, as she has received an advance from her publishers. The shirt then symbolizes Carrie's financial and professional success, which Berger resents, and although he tries to overcome his feelings, their relationship ends in the following episode.

These examples of shopping scenes serve to draw attention to Carrie's and Miranda's failure to conform to idealized femininity. They signal a failed attempt to sustain a heteronormative relationship. This is not to suggest that the show takes a critical position in relation to this failure. Indeed, there is a case to be made that such scenes disturb mainstream, conservative notions of gender performance and threaten patriarchal ideology. At the very least, it reminds us that the show does not place a premium upon idealized categories of femininity, and that the show presents fashion and consumption practices as a tool in which one could (should they wish) exercise resistance.

Transformation in *Ugly Betty*

Ugly Betty adopts an equally 'questioning' and ambiguous attitude towards fashion and consumer behaviour, though these themes are explored in different ways. As previously suggested, though the promise of a makeover is an ever-looming spectre across all four seasons of *Ugly Betty*, Betty's transformation is gradual. That said, the entire series explores the possibility of transformation through fashion and beauty practices, and the makeover ultimately proves a central visual trope within the show. More specifically, *Ugly Betty* employs a version of the 'false transformation', conceptualized by Jeffers McDonald.

As Jeffers McDonald (2010) notes, the transformation narrative is precarious; it is buttressed by the notion that it must simultaneously change, but also confirm a coherent and fixed sense of self. Thus, in order to offset anxieties that fashion is inherently 'inauthentic' and responsible for obscuring the 'true' or 'natural' self, the makeover is often presented as 'make-clearer' (82). Fashion is used (as in the films discussed earlier) to reveal the 'inner' (already attractive) self of the lead protagonist. This, however, is not the case with *Ugly Betty*. The show explicitly subverts this trope and relies upon the 'false transformation' as a way of exploring the contradictions of consumer culture. Thus, *Ugly Betty* employs examples of 'makeover' and 'false transformation' scenes in order to provide a forum in which to debate the complex relationship between identity, fashion and consumption.

In the episode 'Queens for a Day' (Season 1, Episode 3), Betty, in an attempt to become more fashionable (and to gain the approval of her co-workers), seeks the advice of her sister Hilda, who suggests that Betty gets a makeover. The scene echoes the filmic representations of the makeover discussed by Jeffers McDonald (2010) insofar as it employs those strategies which encourage the scene to be read as spectacle.

Betty visits a salon in Queens, and we see a montage of shots of Betty getting her hair washed, nails manicured and make-up applied. The scene functions as 'spectacle' in Jeffers McDonald's (2010) terms, and in the final shot of the montage, the camera pans from Betty's feet to her face, revealing her new look. Betty is wearing a lime-green faux-snakeskin skirt and a one-shoulder floral Lycra top, accessorized with large gold and red hoop earrings. Her hair, permed and backcombed into an enormous 'updo', her makeup dramatic and her nails augmented by bright-red acrylic extensions—Betty's look is characterized as comical 'excess' (as can be seen in Figure 2). The reveal scene self-consciously parodies the makeover trope and provides alternative pleasures than those of the 'traditional' makeover reveal. The combination of brightly coloured, figure-hugging fabrics is presumably used with the intention of making her look 'excessive', or even 'grotesque'. It could therefore be argued that the audience is cued to pre-empt the response from Betty's co-workers and that a comedic scenario will ensue. However, while the audience is invited to laugh in anticipation, when she actually arrives at a meeting with the staff at *Mode*, Betty is publicly and cruelly humiliated by Wilhelmina (Vanessa Williams). The tone shifts immediately, through the strategic use of music and close-ups, and is no longer intended to be read as comical. Furthermore, the apparent change in mood signals that the audience is invited to share in Betty's embarrassment and perhaps to feel regret for laughing at her earlier in the episode.

The trope of the makeover recurs in the episode 'Burning Questions' (Season 2, Episode 15), in which Betty's sister Hilda also undergoes an equally complex

Figure 2 Betty's false transformation: Betty's transformation is signalled as comical 'excess'. *Ugly Betty* Season 1, Episode 3: 'Queens for a Day', Touchstone Television, USA (2006).

'false' transformation. In this particular episode, Hilda's ex-next-door neighbour and 'lifetime nemesis' Gina Gambarro (Ava Gaudet) visits Hilda's beauty salon for a manicure. Since leaving Queens, Gina has married a wealthy doctor and as such is able to indulge in conspicuous consumption. Her return is signalled by a montage which fetishizes her designer wardrobe. Close-ups of oversized gold Chanel earrings, two 'chunky' Chanel necklaces and a Gucci belt are accompanied by a hip-hop track which continually repeats the word 'ca-ching'. The camera then reveals Gina, who teams the accessories mentioned above with a leopard-skin mini skirt, bronze suit jacket and gold ruffle-necked blouse. Gina's fashion is signalled as excess through the use of sound and editing techniques.

Throughout her visit Gina divulges information about her new lifestyle, boasting a considerable clothes allowance. Upon leaving, Gina promises to return the following day for a pedicure, which prompts Hilda to visit Betty at the *Mode* offices in order to borrow designer clothes and accessories from the magazine's closet. The scene also begins with a montage of designer shoes and clothes being picked from the racks, thereby creating a comparison between this sequence and the montage before Gina's arrival. The soundtrack however, is notably different, using an upbeat Latin track to accompany the shots of various garments.

As Hilda negotiates her way around the infinite racks of the *Mode* closet, Betty follows asking why she feels the need to 'dress up' for Gina. Gesturing towards the racks, she remarks, 'Don't tell Justin I said this, but you know none of this stuff actually means anything.' To which Hilda replies, 'I know that . . . but what do I have to show for myself?' This scene therefore demonstrates that while, for the most part, Hilda appears content with her own style and takes pleasure in participating in her own individual fashion practices, she also acknowledges that these fashion practices are rooted in the popular, and that she will be judged critically by the fashion cognoscenti. Hilda is therefore aware that her own fashion practices are not considered to be 'legitimate'.

When Gina returns to the salon, the camera pans up from Hilda's feet to reveal her 'new', 'designer' look, much to Gina's displeasure. Gina then instructs Hilda that she 'can put [her] Pradas anywhere'. Hilda inspects the footwear briefly, before removing her own and concluding that Gina's shoe is in fact a 'knock off'—she claims 'this is Prada' (gesturing toward her own shoe), 'this is nada' (Gina's shoe). The scene ends with Gina storming out of the salon with her husband, who is in fact a chiropractor rather than medical doctor. Before he leaves, he turns to Hilda and retorts 'if you get your kicks out of making my wife feel lousy then your life must be pretty sad.' The camera then returns to Hilda to register her shame.

This sequence serves to reveal Hilda's ambivalent relationship with fashion. As previously argued, Hilda acknowledges in this scene that her consumer practices would be criticized by the fashion cognoscenti, in the same way that she criticizes Gina for her 'fake-ass clothes', and thus the value of high fashion is called into question. For example while Betty and Hilda are acknowledging that fashion 'doesn't mean anything', the use of close ups and frenetic camera movements glamorizes the garments, drawing attention to the spectacle of Hilda's 'shopping' experience. This contradictory attitude towards fashion and consumption is central to *Ugly Betty* and potentially threatens its position as fashion programming. Thus certain strategies are used to contain readings of fashion as ultimately 'trivial' and 'meaningless'.

To be sure, competing creative and commercial pressures affect the display of onscreen fashion and, as with other examples of fashion programming discussed here, *Ugly Betty* functions to critique but ultimately to celebrate fashion, addressing its viewers as potential consumers. Thus, the show ultimately celebrates the 'correct' use of fashion as a powerful indicator of one's 'inner personality'.

As the series progresses Betty undergoes minor changes (she grows out her fringe and changes her glasses); however, a complete and radical makeover does not take place. As previously suggested, the show denies the audience the traditional pleasure of a 'reveal', and instead deliberately derails or undermines any attempts made by Betty transform herself. In the final season, Betty is determined to have her braces removed. For such a momentous occasion, the show devotes an entire episode to the act. In 'Million Dollar Smile' (Season 4; Episode 17), Betty schedules an appointment with an orthodontist (Kathy Najimy) in time to have her 'new smile' immortalized on her new work ID card. During the appointment a series of external factors delay Betty's procedure before it is finally disrupted by a fire alarm. Wet from the sprinklers, with braces intact, Betty's ID card photo fails to capture her intended transformation. The photo shoot, which would perhaps in normal circumstances work as an effective reveal, is entirely subverted. Moreover, she then undergoes a 'digital transformation', as colleague Marc (Michael Urie) Photoshops an alternative smile and removes her glasses. Not content with the final product, Marc continues to transform the image (effectively 'whitening' her) by replacing Betty's dark hair with blonde.

Significantly, this serendipitous chain of events ultimately culminates in an unfortunate incident with the security staff at the Guggenheim museum. Convinced that Betty's ID card is counterfeit, a security guard tackles her to the ground and she is knocked unconscious. A dream sequence ensues in which Betty's orthodontist functions as a spiritual guide, able to show Betty how different her life would have been had she been born with 'perfect teeth'. During this sequence the audience is permitted to see a fully 'transformed' Betty—her glasses have been removed following laser eye surgery—yet this pleasure is tempered and undermined by the fact that they know it to be a dream sequence. Thus, it is another variation on the 'false transformation'. Moreover, the ultimate 'reveal' within the episode is that, despite her 'perfect' exterior, on the inside, Betty is now 'ugly'. Her outer transformation has resulted in an inner transformation. Thus, within this particular episode the 'inner' self is inversely connected to the 'outer' self and is, significantly, unstable (for if one is affected, so is the other). In some ways then, the scenes described above provide a critique of 'postmodern' identity performance. It provides a cautionary tale (in the most literal sense) about the superficiality of beauty and fashion practices. Thus, Betty is ultimately entitled to have her braces removed and to experience the pleasure associated with transformation, having learned how the value of her 'inner' beauty.

The use of the makeover scenes in *Ugly Betty* are visually and aurally similar to those outlined in Jeffers McDonald's (2010) work. They include a number of the same characteristics (pans of the body to 'reveal' the transformation, montage sequences accompanied by extra diegetic upbeat music, etc.). Moreover, they each permit the viewer to witness the 'labour of femininity'. In this way they can be understood as spectacle. However, this is not to suggest that they neither function solely as spectacle nor offer the same pleasures of the traditional makeover (i.e. the pleasure of the reveal). Rather, in the case of *Ugly Betty* pleasures are withheld, denied and/or parodied. Similarly, the use of shopping sequences in *Sex and the City* do not encourage a reading of pure spectacle (though this is not to suggest that such a reading is impossible); rather the scenes are not coded as spectacle in the terms previously outlined. The shopping scenes in particular function as a space where narrative concerns are foregrounded and worked through. Thus traditional understandings of spectacle and narrative are challenged and so too are spectacle and narrative's gendered connotations.

The narrative and thematic terrain of fashion programming is largely concerned with the relationship between fashion and identity, and consequently visual and narrative tropes are employed primarily to explore the ways in which identity can be made and remade in contemporary culture. In so doing, the shows tend to perform ideological critiques and explorations of postmodern models of identity. However, just as Bruzzi and Church Gibson (2004) argue with regard to *Sex and the City*, within fashion programming there is a 'residual belief in fixed character and identity [which] exists in awkward opposition to the importance it accredits fashion' (117).

These interrelated concerns of *Sex and the City* and *Ugly Betty* contribute to a broader agenda of both challenging and privileging the practice and consumption of fashion which can be found in other examples explored within this volume.

5

TEEN FASHION: YOUTH AND IDENTITY IN POPULAR TEEN DRAMAS

In 2003, the popular press identified *The O.C.* as the show which would super-sede *Sex and the City* as 'one of the greatest trendsetters' in television (Thomas 2004). Creator Josh Swartz's next project, *Gossip Girl*—named by *People* mag-azine as 'TV's most stylish series' (Triggs 2008: 119)—would also continue with greater success to foster the profitable relationship between the fashion industry and teen audiences. Taken with their contemporaries (the reboot of *90210* (2008–), the short-lived CW series *Privileged* (2008–2009) and *Revenge* (2011–)), these two shows can be viewed as representative of a broader trend within fashion programming which seeks to target the '"daughters" of the *Sex and the City* audiences' (Church Gibson 2012: 141)—a trend which appears set to continue with the recent release of the highly anticipated television adaptation of Candace Bushnell's *The Carrie Diaries* (2012–).

It is important to remember however, that this recent emergence of fashion-oriented teen drama is not exactly a new phenomenon. Market economics have long been considered a central force in shaping the content of teen TV (see Osgerby 1998; Wee 2004). Since the post-war period, the teenager has been viewed as a 'powerful economic force' (Osgerby 2004: 72) and teen TV, as a distinct category of programming, has come to be identified by its cross-promotional opportunities within multiple media platforms (Wee 2004: 88). The two shows under discussion within this chapter serve as evidence of this—both made use of online resources to promote the fashion within the show (see Kinon 2008; Lacher 2003; Stein 2009; Warner 2009). Indeed, extra-textual participation was integral to the survival of these shows; despite its initial moderate viewing figures, *Gossip Girl*'s ability to attract a fashion-conscious audience ensured that a second season was commissioned (Warner 2009).

That said, the commercial demands of teen TV are in tension with a somewhat 'public service' responsibility. In particular, teen television is thought to assist young viewers in negotiating adolescence and offer them the symbolic resources necessary to shape their 'transitional' identity. As Glyn Davis and Kay Dickinson (2004: 3) observe:

> [O]n the one hand many [teen] programmes have . . . an ethical agenda geared towards creating a certain notion of political subjecthood before the freedoms of adulthood are attained. On the other, they are also required to negotiate a further freedom that many a teen in Western society possesses in abundance: the power to buy, the power to choose some consumer items and reject others.

The narrative and visual tropes of fashion teen programming offer a space where these tensions are explored and/or managed. Thus, this chapter examines how fashion is used within *The O.C.* and *Gossip Girl* and in so doing, once again considers the conceptual relationship between fashion and costume.

The cultural knowledge and competences necessary to 'read' fashion have long since been considered an implicitly feminine skill. Fashion theorists have often remarked on the perception that men seek to distance themselves from the 'superficial' and 'trivial' world of fashion (see Craik 1994). However, what is striking about these case studies is the centrality of the male characters' fashion within extra-textual discussion. In addition, both shows have an investment in anti-fashion and typically 'masculine' practices associated with youth, subculture and style.[1] What follows is an examination of the ways in which male fashions are exhibited within the shows and as part of the narrative. As this chapter shall demonstrate, despite the investment in (masculine) subcultural practices, both shows invoke many of the key narrative tropes associated primarily with the 'woman's film' such as the makeover and Cinderella narrative, and I argue that the deployment of these tropes serves a crucial function in allowing *The O.C.* and *Gossip Girl* to fulfil the commercial and civic responsibilities expected of teen TV.

Fashion, Character and Youth Identity

Both *Gossip Girl* and *The O.C.* share similar thematic and narrative terrain. Each explores topics typically covered in teen dramas (friendship, alienation, family, sex and sexuality, drug and alcohol use, etc.) and is preoccupied with the anxieties regarding one's position within social hierarchies. These anxieties are magnified insofar as they are shored up by an exploration of class relations; both shows are 'fish-out-of-water' narratives. *The O.C.* charts main character Ryan Attwood's (Benjamin McKenzie) attempts to leave his working-class roots (and previous life of crime) behind and to begin a new life in Newport Beach; *Gossip Girl* follows the 'Brooklyn-native' Humphrey family negotiating their position within an elite private school in Manhattan. The affluent backdrops of

Manhattan and Newport Beach offer opportunities to foreground class struggles and also provide a narrative justification for spectacular luxury fashion—though this is not to suggest that fashion functions solely as spectacle and does not also serve character in the more traditional sense. Rather, onscreen fashion allows for issues of cultural identity (with a particular focus on gender and class) to be worked through. These issues are centralized within teen-oriented fashion programming and take on added importance as 'youth' is commonly perceived to be an inherently unstable and problematic identity category.

The most sustained examinations of youth and identity have been conducted by those scholars with an investment in subcultural studies. While it is not the intention of this book to provide a comprehensive review of all literature concerning youth subculture, it is perhaps worth offering a brief introduction to the key debates on youth style, which inform this examination of onscreen youth fashion. Perhaps the most influential writing on youth cultural studies has emerged from the Birmingham School's Centre for Contemporary Cultural Studies (CCCS). Stuart Hall and Tony Jefferson's (1993) collection of essays, *Resistance through Rituals: Youth Subcultures in Post-war Britain*, marks the beginning of a major intervention in the field of youth studies. Drawing on Gramscian theoretical perspectives, CCCS demonstrated a preference for textual approaches (namely semiotic/semiological analysis) to critically examine spectacular youth subcultures (punks, skinheads, mods, rockers, etc.).[2] These particular subcultures were characterized by a collective sense of (often confrontational) style which was taken to signify resistance from mainstream (bourgeois) consumer culture. Dick Hebdige's (1979) foundational *Subculture: The Meaning of Style*, details the ways in which the punk aesthetic was designed to transgress sartorial codes in a bid to expose and make strange those ideological structures which organize our sense of self and the world around us; everyday objects (safety pins, lavatory chains, bin-liners, etc.) were appropriated into ensembles to denaturalize their taken-for-granted meaning. These practices were considered 'semiotic guerrilla warfare' (Eco 1976) and spoke to the increasing (class-based) disenfranchisement within British society. Thus for Hebdige and others associated with CCCS, subculture could not be viewed in isolation from matters of class (and class conflict).

Several subsequent scholars have noted that such a perspective tends to celebrate youth subcultures. According to Hollows (2000), 'youth subcultures are valued positively because, it is supposed, they are *actively produced* by young people themselves; they are defined by their distance from *commerce*; they are therefore more "*authentic*"; they are a means by which young people express their difference; and they are *deviant, resistant* and *oppositional*' (162, emphasis in original). All these characteristics are implicitly coded as masculine. In opposition, the popular or mainstream, and the characteristics such terms inescapably bring ('passive', 'inauthentic', 'conformist') have long since been identified as feminine. The absence of girls from youth subcultures was remarked upon in McRobbie and Jenny Garber's (1993) contribution to *Resistance through Rituals*, which sought to redress this imbalance and place girls and girlhood squarely within the discussion of subcultures. McRobbie has since developed this line of enquiry to consider the practices of 'teenyboppers', bedroom culture and the 'subcultural entrepreneurs' of London's rag markets.

With the exception of McRobbie and Garber, the CCCS's approach to sub-culture has been criticized for the importance it accorded to class at the expense of other equally important factors (see Hesmondhalgh 2005). Consequently, subsequent work has moved away from a Marxist-informed approach, favouring other theoretical perspectives (such as postmodernism). The work of scholars such as Andy Bennett (1999), David Muggleton (2000), Steve Redhead (1997) and Sarah Thornton (1997) comes to represent 'post-subcultural theory', in which the view is held that the political potential of style as resistance has long been overstated. Recent work in this area challenges the notion that there is an 'intrinsic subcultural quality' (see Muggleton and Weinzierl 2003). For some 'post-subcultural' theorists, the use value of the term 'subculture' has been called into question (Bennett 1999; Shank 1994; Straw 1991). For Bennett (1999: 605), the term fails to capture 'unstable and shifting cultural affiliations which characterize late modern consumer-based identities'. Equally, Muggleton (2000) and Ted Polhemus (1997) have expressed a need to account for increasingly ephemeral groupings no longer exclusively bound by class. That being said, empirical research carried out by Steven Miles (2000) suggests that dress continues to play an important semiotic function in constructing particular groups. When examining images of young people, Miles's respondents were able to make judgements and assumptions about individuals based upon sartorial choices, suggesting that young people possess sophisticated competences in creating and *reading* (sub)cultural identities.

Thornton's (1997) work on club cultures is, in my view, the most persuasive account of contemporary subcultures and provides a useful theoretical framework within which to examine male fashion and subculture within teen TV. In a measured critique of previous literature she contends that: 'a great deal of extant research on youth subcultures has both over-politicized their leisure and at the same time ignored the subtle relations of power at play within them' (14). Influenced by Pierre Bourdieu's (1986) concept of capital, Thornton problematizes earlier constructions of the mainstream (calling for more work on the kinds of hierarchies that exist within popular culture), acknowledging that club cultures are 'taste' cultures, rife with cultural hierarchies. Coining the phrase 'subcultural capital' to describe a form of 'hipness', Thornton argues that, as with cultural capital, 'subcultural capital' can be 'objectified or embodied' (11). She writes, 'subcultural capital can be objectified in the form of fashionable haircuts and carefully assembled record collections . . . [in addition] subcultural capital is embodied in the form of being in the know' (11). Moreover, this should all appear to be 'second nature' (12). Significantly, subcultural capital differs from cultural capital insofar as it is not as class-bound. She writes, 'This is not to say that class is irrelevant simply it does not correlate in any one-to-one-way with levels of youthful subcultural capital. In fact, class is wilfully obfuscated by subcultural distinctions' (12). Another marked difference between cultural and subcultural capital, according to Thornton, is the role of the media in the circulation of the latter. While Bourdieu has been criticized for neglecting to consider the role of radio and television within the construction of cultural hierarchies, Thornton suggests that the media are a 'network crucial to the definition and distribution of cultural knowledge' (14).

Indeed, this project began with the notion that media culture, and television specifically, plays an important role in providing viewers with the symbolic resources for viewers to make, remake and enact different models of identity (see Ott 2007; Kellner 1992) and youth audiences in particular are thought to use popular culture to make sense of and to construct their own gendered identities (Nayak and Kehily 2008). The examples of teen television under discussion in this chapter, as the following section demonstrates, provide a space in which viewers are 'educated' in those competences.

Fashioning Masculinity in *The O.C.*

In her article, 'The Monsters Next Door: Media Constructions of Boys and Masculinity', Mia Consalvo (2003) notes an absence of sustained studies which examine the mediated representation of young or adolescent boys. Informed by Robert Connell's (1987, 1995, 1998) influential work on multiple masculinities, Consalvo (2003: 28) argues that these representations are especially important and revealing, as they often depict gender 'as a process being worked out— rehearsed, refined and modified'. Within *The O.C.* and *Gossip Girl*, masculinities are relational: different categories of masculinity are represented often with the aim of shoring up one dominant version. Consequently, costume articulated as fashion becomes the central way in which to construct and express difference. With regard to *The O.C.*, masculinity is presented as a process in which the final goal is the achievement of hegemonic masculinity—which, as Michael Kimmel (2000) argues, is only available to a minority. This process is played out onscreen and employs the visual strategies and narrative tropes outlined in the previous chapter.

In the opening scenes of the pilot (Season 1, Episode 1), various costuming strategies serve to establish Ryan's socio-economic class position. His jeans, hooded sweatshirt, white T-shirt and leather jacket are traditionally associated with cinematic depictions of a specific version of working-class, heterosexual masculinity. The leather jacket for example has a cinematic heritage dating from the 1950s (famous examples include Marlon Brando's character in *On the Waterfront* (1954) and James Dean in *Rebel without a Cause* (1955), which are of course bound up with anxieties surrounding youth and masculinity). From the 1990s onwards, the white T-shirt has become synonymous with the male star's 'eroticism' and positions him as an 'object of sexual desire' (Bruzzi 2005: 48). Similarly, the white vest is traditionally associated with muscular action film heroes of the 1980s (such as Bruce Willis and Sylvester Stallone) and draws attention to a corporeal masculinity. Ryan's developed physicality is showcased by the white T-shirt in this scene and also by his white vest, which becomes his sartorial trademark throughout the series. As with the garments described above, the white vest also communicates the class difference between Ryan and other characters. In using the white vest, or 'wife-beater' as it is (problematically) described in the show (and in popular vernacular), *The O.C.* not only seeks to position Ryan within a specific socio-economic category but also associates him with a specific version of masculinity. As the misogynistic term 'wife-beater' suggests, the white vest carries negative connotations regarding criminal activity and is associated with decidedly working-class masculinity. These negative connotations are widely recognized in British and American culture, and beyond.

While Ryan is arguably designed to be read in these terms in the opening scenes of the pilot, the remainder of the episode depicts his transformation, which is played out in a (typically feminine) makeover scene. During his stay with the Cohens, Ryan is forced to attend a charity fashion show event (under the assumed guise of a cousin from Boston). In the scenes leading up to the event, an over-the-shoulder shot in a mirror slowly pans upwards to reveal that Ryan is not wearing a white 'wife-beater', but actually a white-cotton dress shirt. The shot resembles a 'reveal' in a makeover programme; however, rather than surprise and joy, Ryan's facial expression reveals a feeling of unease, culminating in a moment of frustration when he fails to successfully tie his tie. Not only does the costuming reflect the class difference between Ryan and his peers, but it also suggests a lack of cultural competences in fashion practices. Moreover, Ryan becomes a point of entry for potential audiences who lack the competences required for 'reading' fashion. They are invited to learn, as Ryan does throughout the series, the competences in fashion practices and to decode their meanings.

When Ryan appears in the suit (clearly an expensive, quality item), he embodies an alternative version of masculinity to that signified by the white vest. As Church Gibson (2005) argues in her article 'Brad Pitt and George Clooney, the Rough and the Smooth: Male Costuming in Contemporary Hollywood', two types of leading men dominate the screen: the 'rough and ready' Brad Pitt type and the 'smooth' George Clooney type (to use her own examples). The Brad Pitt character demonstrates his masculinity and overt sexuality through the availability of the body on display, while George Clooney is characterized by his concealed, but still apparent, physicality. Within cultural studies of fashion, the suit is often understood as a garment which represents 'ideal' masculinity, associated with those who comply with Robert Hanke's (1998: 186) criteria: 'white, middle class, heterosexual, professional-managerial men'. Hegemonic masculine attire is, as Bruzzi (1997: 69) notes, 'traditionally characterized by consistency, functionality and durability, [and is therefore] exemplified by the suit'. The costuming in this scene therefore represents Ryan, to use Church Gibson's (2005) terms, as an archetypal 'suited hero' (68), a recurrent figure in contemporary popular cinema, whose (hetero)sexuality and physical attractiveness is enhanced by the structure of the suit (the broadening of the shoulders and chest). While symbolizing Ryan's achievement of ideal masculinity, the suit also serves as masquerade, concealing his 'authentic' class identity (which troubles and threatens his status). As such, the pilot episode invokes a 'Cinderella' narrative, which, as Moseley (2005a) notes, is 'always bound up with dress' (116), and is 'profoundly tied to the acquisition of subjectivity and a classed subjectivity at that' (118). In the pilot episode of *The O.C.* Ryan is granted temporary access to a higher social status, which is articulated through dress.

According to Moseley (2005a), within the Cinderella narrative, 'a question lingers over whether "class" can ever really be acquired, or whether it can only be performed, more or less successfully' (117). In response to this question, the narrative traditionally exposes the 'real' identity of the Cinderella, thereby stripping her of her acquired status before ultimately allowing her to transcend her lower class position. This narrative structure is played out within *The O.C.*, and by the end of the pilot episode Ryan's 'real' identity as a working-class, petty criminal is exposed, yet the return to a lower class position is short-lived (by Episode 3 Ryan is formally adopted by the Cohen family). As with other interpretations of the Cinderella narrative, the pilot episode presents Ryan as deserving of this higher social status in order to offset anxieties which may arise from his adopting an identity to which he is not (socially) entitled; his bravery, intelligence and loyalty are underlined throughout the series.

Like Ryan, the character of Seth (Adam Brody) is also an outsider in the community, and this is reflected in his costuming. While Seth has access to the same level of economic capital as his peers, he does not share their taste in leisure activities. Thus, in a series of ways Seth represents what has been termed a 'subordinate' masculinity, as opposed to 'conservative masculinity' (Hanke 1992; Consalvo 2003). Though Hanke uses the term specifically to refer to gay-male subculture, it can and has been extended to include other marginalized versions of masculinity. For example, Consalvo (2003) notes with regard to the school system that 'male "geeks" have less social standing than "jocks," even if they may later go on to positions of greater power and influence' (30). Despite Seth's position as a white, heterosexual, affluent male, his position (or lack thereof) within the school hierarchy temporarily excludes him from achieving and enacting ideal masculinity. That said, his costuming emphasizes a wish on his part to (actively) mark a departure from the versions of masculinity embodied by other male characters (those which would be considered 'ideal' masculinities).

While Ryan, for the most part, demonstrates an ambivalent attitude towards dress, Seth 'actively' participates in fashion practices and cultivates a 'resistive' identity. As briefly gestured towards in the introduction to this chapter, fashion is often considered 'trivial', and the women who devote their time to it 'dupes', yet the men who participate in fashion are perceived as worse. This is because, as Cara Buckley and Brian L. Ott (2008: 212) explain, 'it violates traditional notions of masculinity'. However, Seth escapes these pejorative connotations insofar as he engages in those subcultural fashion practices, characterized as 'active', 'masculine' and 'resistive'. Moreover, he is constructed as abundant in 'subcultural capital', demonstrated through his extensive knowledge of 'punk' and 'emo' music.

Viewed as a descendent of 'hard-core punk', 'emo' (short for emotive or emotional) is constructed as lacking in the cultural legitimacy of its predecessor, yet it can nonetheless be recognized as a youth subcultural grouping. In contrast to the punk movement, the 'emo' style is less concerned with an overtly 'political' agenda; rather than appropriating everyday items in confrontational ways, 'emo' fashion is more concerned with 'appropriating' certain forms of dress, including those traditionally associated with punk. For example, the Converse All Star shoe, initially designed to capture the basketball shoe market, was appropriated by the punk movement and has subsequently become part of the 'emo' style. Similarly, tartan fabric, also appropriated by punk, has since been adopted by 'emo'. Other garments associated with the look are striped polo shirts, dark hooded sweatshirts, Vans skate shoes, jeans and slogan T-shirts—all of which are incorporated into Seth's wardrobe. Nevertheless, as with the 'spectacular' subcultures of the 1970s, 'emo' fashion challenges certain authorized codes, particularly those associated with gender presentation. In some cases, male 'emo' fashion is characterized by long, carefully crafted hair swept over one eye and dramatic eyeliner (though it should be noted that this is not the case in *The O.C.*). Nevertheless, Seth can still be considered, in Hebdige's (1979) terms, a subcultural bricoleur insofar as his style of dress involves appropriating certain garments and 'placing them in a new symbolic ensemble which [serves] to erase or subvert their original straight meaning' (104).

In a documentary special feature of the Season 1 DVD box set, the show's costume designer, Karla Stevens, remarks on how she puts together a simple polo shirt with a pair of what she terms 'man trousers' (smart, men's-fitted trousers) and a pair of Vans or Chuck Taylor shoes. The re-appropriation of the 'man trousers', usually associated with seriousness, work and 'power', are used in Seth's wardrobe for different effect. Arguably, his desire is to 'make strange' the conservative pair of trousers, and in so doing, demonstrate his resistance to the kind of meaning they stand for. Similarly, the polo shirt, which has been appropriated within 'emo' subculture, is also associated with a mainstream 'preppy' style—which Seth seeks to distance himself from. This, again, highlights the ways in which Seth seeks, at least in part, to 'disrupt' traditional codes of fashion. Furthermore, it not only indicates that Seth is equipped with the 'subcultural capital' and cultural competences to do so, but is symptomatic of the ways in which the show addresses a potential audience with the skills in reading costume and fashion so that they can interpret this meaning. While as Wilson (1985), among others, claims subcultures have a tendency to incorporate and 'caricature' more traditional forms of dress into their styles, there is of course the possibility that an individual may be unable to recognize that the garment is being appropriated. Thus, with regard to *The O.C.*, some audience members might read Seth's character differently; he could be mistaken for one of the 'preppy' 'Newpsies' (a pejorative term used to describe residents of Newport Beach) that he wishes to distance himself from. I should note here, that the 'Newpsies' display attributes associated with 'irresponsible' consumers (outlined in the previous chapter). Moreover, they are coded as 'middlebrow', insofar as they are presented as abundant in economic capital, but lacking in (sub)cultural knowledge and competences and thus in 'legitimate' taste. To return briefly to Thornton's (1997) conceptualization of subcultural capital, it is clear that within *The O.C.* Seth's subcultural identity is not bound up with a (working) class-based distaste of middlebrow culture, for he has an abundance of economic and cultural capital. However, as Thornton acknowledges, class is still of primary importance. This is most certainly the case within both *The O.C.* and *Gossip Girl*. As previously discussed, both texts are preoccupied with the negotiation of class relations and make use of similar visual and narrative strategies (such as the Cinderella motif) in order to work through such issues.

Relational Masculinities in *Gossip Girl*

The Cinderella motif is playfully acknowledged in the pilot episode of *Gossip Girl* (Season 1, Episode 1), and arguably reflects the show's self-reflexive approach to fashion.[3] In an attempt to make himself known to his childhood crush (the 'socialite' Serena van der Woodsen (Blake Lively)), Dan Humphrey (Penn Badgley) visits the Palace Hotel, where she is currently living. While Dan (also known in the series as 'Lonely Boy') fails to introduce himself, the pair literally collide in the hotel lobby, resulting in Serena accidentally leaving behind her mobile phone— just as Cinderella does her shoe. Although the short sequence, in isolation, may not immediately remind audiences of the fairy tale, it echoes a similar moment in the Disney teen film *A Cinderella Story* (2004), starring Hilary Duff, in which the mobile phone functions as a metaphor for the shoe. In addition, in a later scene Dan explicitly makes the comparison during an exchange with a member of the hotel staff. As he attempts to return the phone, the concierge, unconvinced by Dan's account of events, begins to interrogate him, and the following exchange takes place:

Concierge: How did you know it was Miss van der Woodsen . . . and if you are not a guest at the hotel what were you doing there?

Dan: When Prince Charming found Cinderella's slipper, they didn't accuse him of having a foot fetish.

Concierge: And you're Prince Charming?

The short scene calls attention to Dan's class position, marking his difference from 'Prince Charming' in social status. In addition to the above exchange, Dan's 'ordinary' clothing appears somewhat 'out of place' against the backdrop of the Palace Hotel (see Figure 3).

Within the social hierarchy of the high school, Dan is characterized by his 'invisibility'. Referred to as 'Lonely Boy' by the anonymous writer of the fictional gossip blog, *Gossip Girl*, Dan is ostracized by his peers, in part due to his family's (somewhat ambiguous) class position. The narrative continually reminds us of their differences from Dan's affluent peers, yet the Humphreys manage to afford a spacious loft in Brooklyn and the tuition fees for a Manhattan-based private school. In addition, certain aspects of his costuming undermine and betray Dan's socio-economic status. His wardrobe, though perhaps the least 'spectacular' within the series, includes several pieces which are not narratively justified (i.e. his pair of Italian-leather, designer loafers). In a documentary special feature of

Figure 3 Dan Humphrey attempting to return Serena's phone: Dan's costuming serves to demonstrate his 'difference' in terms of social status. *Gossip Girl* Season 1, Episode 1: 'Pilot', College Hill, USA (2007).

the Season 1 DVD box set, the cast accredit Dan's sense of style to costume designer Eric Daman, and joke that without him Dan would have considerably less 'flair'. Rather, his style would be much more unflattering and explicitly reflect his 'awkwardness'.

The importance *Gossip Girl* accords fashion is made clear in the documentary feature, as Josh Schwartz—adopting the rhetoric often employed in discussions of *Sex and the City*—remarks that he wanted fashion 'to be a character'. Implicit within the claim is the assumption that the fashion is elevated from its position as mise en scène. To be sure, the press response to *Gossip Girl* would suggest that fashion is read in this way. In 2009, *Vogue* journalist Alessandra Stanley describes the costume as teetering 'between unattainable chic and self-parody' (198). Indeed, Stanley's remarks echo criticisms often levelled at *SATC* (see T. Banks 2000). Furthermore, in the same *Vogue* article, actress Blake Lively remarks, 'The fashion is just unbelievable. You can watch our show on mute and be entertained' (Lively cited in Stanley 2009: 168). Her comments are thus reminiscent of Edith Head's philosophy that costume should 'carry enough information about characters so that the audience could tell something about them if the sound went off in the theatre' (Gaines 1990: 188). However, whilst Head's comments demonstrate a preoccupation with serving narrative and characterization, Lively's speak to the pleasure offered by costume as 'spectacle'. Despite the investment in fashion as spectacle, Schwartz also acknowledges the show's commitment to representing youth and youth fashion: in the documentary feature he claims 'these [young people] definitely exist, and they definitely wear the best of the best'. While within the bounds of narrative realism, Dan supposedly cannot afford to wear the 'best of the best'; his costuming still must 'make sense' for and speak to a youth audience.

In *Gender, Youth and Culture: Young Masculinities and Femininities,* Nayak and Kehiliy (2008) contend that one of the key ways in which young men and women construct their own gender identities is 'through and against one and other and alongside imaginary notions of masculinity and femininity' (4). Indeed, the three central young-male characters in *Gossip Girl* are defined against one another, and difference is expressed through dress. Dan, as previously discussed, is marginalized by his peers; however, his dress suggests an element of deliberate resistance. According to Daman, Dan's costuming (though within the context of the show is perhaps the most unremarkable) draws inspiration from the 1960s 'French New Wave' aesthetic; his 'signature' pieces include a military coat, skinny tie, skinny jeans, button-down shirts and cardigans. Without wishing to simplify New Wave into a discrete category of films with a clear set of cohesive attributes, an argument can be made that the phenomenon tends to inspire an association with a particular (leftist) ideological position and a certain kind of masculinity, characterized by a series of (albeit contradictory) traits, including boyishness, sensitivity and rebellion. Thus, Dan's costume serves as a visual reminder of his difference from his peers (not only in terms of class but also in values) and notably sets him apart from the two other young-male characters: Nate Archibald (Chase Crawford), a descendent of the Vanderbilt clan, and the notorious 'playboy', Chuck Bass (Ed Westwick), the son of a wealthy entrepreneur. As demonstrated in Figure 4, Dan's costuming is much simpler in comparison to Chuck's flamboyant formal wear and Nate's slightly dishevelled 'corporate' attire. Indeed, the versions of masculinity enacted within *Gossip Girl* are not fully realized or given meaning when viewed in isolation—they are, as Nayak and Kehily (2008) contend, relational.

Nate performs a category of masculinity that is highly valued within the social hierarchy of the school. He is constructed, within the first season, as a counterpart to Blair (Leighton Meester). In the pilot episode the pair are constructed as the school's 'power couple', and their costuming is deeply evocative of John F. Kennedy and Jackie Kennedy; thus their wardrobe reflects their privileged position. Nate adopts a 'preppy', 'all-American' style of dress that speaks to his two defining characteristics: wealth and sporting ability.[4] Consequently, his masculine identity is contrasted with Dan's, and the pair become constructed around a series of binary oppositions: rich vs poor, athleticism vs intellect, surface vs depth.

The oppositions set up between Nate and Dan can be read as a comment upon style (and the inherent depthless-ness the term inescapably brings) and

Figure 4 Nate, Chuck and Dan: *Gossip Girl* Season 6, Episode 1: 'Gone Maybe Gone', CBS Television, USA (2012).

identity. Nate may be seen to represent 'style over substance' insofar as he performs status without actually possessing (sub)cultural capital. However, as with Dan, there are also sartorial signals of resistance; while Nate often dons designer clothing (specifically those associated with all-American style; i.e. Ralph Lauren and Abercrombie & Fitch), he also demonstrates a disinterestedness in fashion: his button-down shirts are often wrinkled and his altogether look is, for the most part, scruffy (as can be demonstrated in Figure 5). On the one hand, this speaks to confirm his conservative, 'ideal' masculinity (i.e. that he would not 'waste time' with 'trivial', 'feminine' preoccupations). On the other, it suggests an uneasiness with the societal expectations placed upon him by peers and family—a theme explored within the narrative of Season 1.

Chuck's costuming, on the other hand, demonstrates an active interest in and knowledge of high fashion. In the pilot episode, he makes no secret of the fact that he relishes the privileges afforded him as a result of his social position and participates in conspicuous consumption. He is characterized as an urban 'dandy' and a member of the 'idle rich'. Chuck's costuming is the most elaborate and flamboyant of the male characters within the show. It often includes pieces which serve to signify his association with the figure of the dandy (i.e. two-toned blazers, cravats, carnations, etc.) as can be seen in Figure 6. However, unlike the figure of the dandy (discussed at length in Chapter 8), Chuck's 'heteronormative' masculinity is never questioned. In terms of his cinematic predecessors, Chuck's wardrobe is perhaps most similar to that of the screen gangster insofar as it is

Figure 5 Nate Archibald: Though dressed in formal wear, Nate's dinner shirt is wrinkled, demonstrating his indifference when it comes to fashion. *Gossip Girl* Season 5, Episode 14: 'The Back Up Dan', CBS Television, USA (2012).

riddled with ambiguity. In her analysis of the Franco-American gangster, Bruzzi (1997) observes that the figure of the gangster is able to participate in and take pleasure from the processes of adornment (the wardrobe of the screen gangster evidences his increasing social and economic power) with no threat to his heteronormative masculine identity. She writes:

> When considering the costumes of the screen gangster the spectator is struck by this ambivalence, that here are characters who have both cultivated an aggressively masculine image and are immensely vain, and whose sartorial flamboyance, far from imitating femininity or effeminacy, is the most important sign of their masculine social and material success. (1997: 70)

The characteristics associated with the screen gangster, as outlined by Bruzzi, are encapsulated by Chuck. Indeed, the comparison also speaks to his moral ambivalence within the show. In early episodes, he is cast as a villain, and indeed throughout the series his morality is continually questioned. In the pilot episode, Chuck attempts to sexually assault both Serena and Dan's younger sister, Jenny (Taylor Momsen). His 'deviant' behaviour places him outside of 'ideal' masculine identity. However, as a white, upper-class male, ideal masculinity *is* available to him and is periodically achieved at various points across the series. Chuck is able to 'achieve' 'ideal' masculinity when he secures a (normative) romantic relationship with Blair (Leighton Meester). That said, the on–off nature of this relationship ensures that Chuck's masculine identity remains unstable throughout the series. After one break-up in particular, the instability of Chuck's masculinity is played out both within the narrative and costuming. In the final episode of Season 3, Chuck and Blair fail to repair their relationship after his one-night stand with Jenny is revealed. In the climatic final scenes, Chuck, distraught to have lost Blair, is the victim of a mugging during which he is (non-fatally) shot. Following his near-death experience, Chuck finds himself in Paris with no formal identification, under the care of Eva (Clémence Poésy)—an unassuming (working-class) Good Samaritan—and uses the opportunity to reinvent himself as 'Henry Prince'.[5] In an attempt to redeem his previous 'deviant' behaviour, Chuck makes a pledge to 'live simply, earn people's respect [and] become a person someone could love'. This involves accepting a job as a waiter at a Parisian bar and restaurant and a stark costume change. His 'workwear'—a white shirt, black waistcoat and trousers—would perhaps connote 'authentic' working-class masculinity; however, this costuming on the usually flamboyant Chuck becomes almost parodic. The 'simple' costuming is a significant departure from his usual attire and is symbolic of his weakened and impotent masculinity. This use of costuming echoes that of the gangster films discussed at length by Bruzzi (1997). She writes in regard to the screen gangster that 'his masculinity is directly measured by his narcissism: the smarter the clothes,

Figure 6 Chuck Bass as 'Urban Dandy': *Gossip Girl* Season 2, Episode 1: 'Summer Kind of Wonderful', College Hill, USA (2008).

the more dangerous the man, and the more damaged the clothes the more vulnerable the man' (93).

Chuck's performance of vulnerable masculinity is short-lived—as soon as his 'working-class' look is achieved it crumbles, serving as a reminder of the instability of his masculine identity. During an exchange with Blair he is reminded that dressing 'poorly' doesn't mean he can escape his 'real' (socio-economic) identity, and in the subsequent scene he returns to his 'spectacular' wardrobe, which involves a pinstripe suit, pale-pink shirt and matching carnation. As with the screen gangster, his masculinity is unstable and continually reworked throughout the series. As such, the viewer is frequently reminded that 'clothes only make the illusion of a man' (94).

Since Connell's path-breaking discussion of multiple masculinities, a great deal of work within the fields of fashion and cultural studies has reconsidered the relationship between masculinity and fashion. Consequently, Tim Edwards (1997) argues that the study of fashion and masculinity 'often highlights the very artificial or constructed—as opposed to the natural or essential nature of masculinity itself, for in fashion, masculinity, like clothes and accessories, is put on, swapped around and played with, like costumes in a masquerade or theatre' (4).

Within the shows discussed here, the 'work' that goes into creating and managing gendered identities is made explicit, and in so doing viewers are offered insight into consumer competences and fashion practices which construct masculinity/ies. A number of visual and narrative strategies are employed to expose and to render unstable the authorized codes designed to regulate and police the boundaries of gendered identity (the use of the Cinderella narrative, the makeover scene, etc.). Nevertheless, both shows occupy an ambiguous position when it comes to notions of selfhood in late modernity and postmodernity. While there are a number of masculinities on display which are defined in relation to one another, a dominant ('natural') category of masculinity is ultimately served. All the male characters discussed here are 'eligible' for 'ideal' masculinity; they are white, middle-class (if not initially middle-class they are permitted to transcend their class boundaries) heterosexual men. There is little racial, ethnic or sexual diversity within these shows. Thus, the function of these programmes ultimately is to showcase precisely how (through fashion practices) a specific category of young men are able to negotiate adolescence and achieve 'ideal' masculinity.

6

FASHIONING THE PAST: GENDER, NOSTALGIA AND EXCESS IN 'QUALITY' PERIOD DRAMA

We always have two reactions to every episode of *Mad Men*. There's the reaction to the story and characters, and then there's the reaction to the costuming.

—*Tom & Lorenzo* 2012

The clothing we are presenting [on *Boardwalk Empire*] seems to truly fascinate the audience.

—Donn in Laverty 2011

Since premiering on AMC in July 2007, Matthew Weiner's *Mad Men* has become one of the most widely acclaimed US prime-time dramas in recent years. Endorsed by both the quality and popular presses, *Mad Men* has been celebrated for its compelling storytelling, complex characters and historical fastidiousness as it depicts an unapologetic vision of 1960s America. Its pervasiveness in contemporary culture has been much remarked upon in the first academic anthology on the show, in which Gary R. Edgerton (2011) observes that *Mad Men*'s influence can be located in 'TV commercials and print advertisements, magazine covers and feature articles, designer fashion and department store displays, and all sorts of ancillary merchandize from cigarette lighters to hip flasks to assorted media-related tie-in such as soundtrack CDs, episode downloads and season-long DVD sets' (xxii).

Further to this, the *New York Times* comments on *Mad Men*'s impact on the televisual landscape, identifying the show as a catalyst for the recent boom in what it terms 'retro programming' (examples of which include *Boardwalk Empire* (2010–), *Pan Am* (2011–2012) and *The Playboy Club* (2011)). As the term suggests, this discursive category is characterized by the way in which it 'traffic[s] in nostalgia' (Stanley 2011), but also it is important to note, for the purpose of this book, that these shows are thought to be responsible for the revived interest in and continued popularity of retro and vintage fashion. Consequently, the 'retro boom' can be viewed within the wider schema of fashion programming. However, these shows' preoccupation with 'nostalgia' and the 'past' means that they do not function in precisely the same way as other examples discussed in this volume, particularly with regard to costume and narrative. Thus, further expansion and clarification of the debates rehearsed in the previous chapters are required.

Discussions of period costume have tended to focus on the way in which onscreen clothing serves either as historical signifier, expressing temporal specificity, or as a pleasurable, 'excessive', 'aesthetic discourse' (Gaines 1990). This chapter seeks to advance this discussion through close analysis of two of the most widely acclaimed examples of 'retro programming'—*Mad Men* and *Boardwalk Empire*—with the aim of developing a more nuanced approach to historical costume and its use in television. The following discussion moves away from whether the costuming in *Mad Men* and *Boardwalk Empire* serves as a historical signifier *or* fashion; rather it seeks to examine the multiple and varied functions of period costume. Moreover, it is important to remember that when discussing television costume in serial dramas, the shows may adopt different positions which vary from episode to episode or season to season, depending on a range of external factors. For example John Dunn and Lisa Padovani, the costume designer and associate costume designer for *Mad Men*'s pilot, were replaced by Janie Bryant (significantly, Dunn and Padovani went on to costume *Boardwalk Empire*).[1] Moreover, Bryant's background in fashion design (a trade to which she has returned following the success of *Mad Men*) may inform her approach to costuming and speak to a different set of priorities when it comes to the primary function of onscreen clothing. Thus, the following chapter is organized around a series of positions regarding the function of onscreen clothing in historical drama: that is does the costume exist to simply replicate the period, does it offer some kind of social commentary on the period or does it stylize the period? Each of these positions privileges a particular discourse of value and has implications for the way in which audiences are cued to read onscreen clothing as a semiotic language.

'Oops! You Caught That!': Approaching Historical Costume

In her foundational examination of costume and narrative, Gaines observes the importance of narrative realism as a guiding principle in classical Hollywood costuming. As discussed in the introduction, costume and all elements of mise en scène were expected to serve narrative and characterization, lest they distract the viewer from the plot. This assumption resonates with popular discourses when it comes to the discussion of period costume. As Pam Cook (1996) among others (see Bruzzi 1997; Harper 1987) has observed, 'films which pay attention to verisimilitude are usually given greater value in critical terms at least, than those which take liberties with history' (67). However, Cook also notes that 'the obsession with period authenticity reveals a contradiction at the heart of the historical film: the symbolic carriers of period detail—costume, hair, décor—are notoriously slippery and anachronistic' (67). In this regard costume is, by nature, 'threatening' and 'unruly', which can be a source of great anxiety for some and great pleasure for others.

Drawing on Cook (and Harper), Bruzzi (1997) also reminds us that period clothes 'are not always transparent and are capable of being deeply ambiguous' (42). To use one of her own examples, the corset, commonly viewed as the sartorial expression of female oppression, has been recently connected to auto-erotic pleasure and sexual assertiveness. Thus, when onscreen the corset may indeed be read as a symbol of female subjugation, equally it may reveal a counter-discourse. Consequently, I would extend Bruzzi's claim and posit that period costumes are *never* transparent and *always* ambiguous in the same way that the fashion of the time was and is. Moreover, we must remember that historical films are representations of the past, constructed for the contemporary audience. We view the past through the lens of the present, and as such are informed by certain (historically and culturally specific) taste formations. Indeed, as Anne Hollander (1993) observes, this has consequences for the way in which costume designers envisage clothing onscreen. She writes that 'costume designers for the commercial stage or screen must pay attention to what has proved successful. For historical drama they must make use of historical signals to which the public responds, as well as to the demands of current fashion, which continues to include current taste in reality' (307). Therefore, we must assume that those films valued by critics for their historical accuracy simply abide by (equally historically and culturally specific) representational codes of realism; they are in no way more or less authentic than those texts identified as in 'excess' of these visual codes. Both Cook and Harper identify the Gainsborough costumes of the 1940s as representatives of those period films which privilege an 'excessive' aesthetic discourse that centres on sex and sexuality over any attempt at historical fidelity. As Cook (1996) argues, criticisms that these films are simply 'style over substance' actually spring from anxieties around the status of history as 'truth'. These films, she writes are 'uncomfortably close to presenting history as fabrication' (68). For Harper (1987), the Gainsborough costume dramas used costume to contradict the moralistic scripts, offering an alternative and additional source of pleasure for audiences. The assumption is that these films rely upon a contradiction between the verbal and non-verbal storytelling strategies. Equally,

Bruzzi's (1997: 38) analysis of a collection of recent period films suggests that historical costume can create transgressive, erotic discourses which challenge assumptions about the bearer of the look (i.e. that this is a distinctly female gaze or pleasure). Indeed, the intention of this chapter is to develop the work which begins to dismantle traditional views of costuming as either 'expressive' of historic or 'excessive', and to consider the multiple ways in which costume operates as an 'aesthetic' discourse in television period dramas.

Following its premiere in 2007, numerous blogs emerged online dedicated to dissecting *Mad Men*'s use of costume, and perhaps unsurprisingly, the discussion quickly turned to questions of historical verisimilitude. For example popular bloggers Deborah and Roberta Lipp dedicate a category on their blog to 'anachronisms' (Lipp 2008). Equally, Tom Fitzgerald's and Lorenzo Marquez's blog, from which the opening quote is taken, present themselves as experts in 1960s fashion and regularly congratulate the show on its attention to detail (*Tom & Lorenzo* 2012). The online discussion of *Mad Men*'s period fidelity supports Jeremy Butler's (2011) claim that the show 'celebrates its historical specificity and entreats us to examine its historical accuracy' (56). In particular, what is often remarked upon as evidence of the show's commitment to accurate representation of the past is the way in which the show presented an image of the 1960s which marked a departure from the 'swinging sixties' most commonly referenced in visual culture. It may well be that this was a strategic decision to ensure that *Mad Men* developed a distinct aesthetic, signalling its difference from other screen representations of the 'sixties'. Cinematographer Phil Abraham acknowledges the difficulties of working on a show set during a time which has been heavily documented onscreen. In *American Cinematographer*, he is cited as saying 'we talked about not simply referencing the period as seen in movies of that time. We wanted to be more genuine than that' (Abraham in Feld, Oppenheimer and Stasukevich 2008: 2). In so doing, Abraham alludes to the idea that there is some 'genuine' and authentic notion of the past, but that it is not something that can be realized onscreen. Conversely, *Boardwalk Empire* does not face this challenge insofar as the show seeks to capture an image of history which has been notably underrepresented onscreen; in the *Making Boardwalk Empire* featurette (available on the Season 1 box set), creator Terry Winter claims that 'there are only a handful of film and almost no television shows that have explored the era'.[2] Nevertheless, as a period text, the popular and quality presses seemed to demand an element of 'realism' from *Boardwalk Empire*—just as they had of *Mad Men*—and the respective costume designers strove to demonstrate their commitment to this goal. Both Bryant and Dunn have revealed their (implicitly gendered) approaches to costuming and research. For Dunn, this involved assuming a role as a 'detective', scouring Hollywood costume rental companies and vintage boutiques in the hope of finding articles of clothing. As the likelihood of finding original garments in a suitable condition is slim, Dunn also reveals his reliance on tailoring books from the 1920s and his acquisition of vintage dressmaking equipment (including a faggoting machine) to create garments from scratch. Bryant, on the other hand, looks to her family for inspiration; not only did she consult her grandmother's knitting magazines from the period, but also reportedly used items of her mother's clothing (Betty is said to have worn many of Bryant's mother's cashmere sweaters, and according to *Grazia* magazine, in Season 2 Joan's roommate wears Bryant's mother's engagement party dress made by Bryant's grandmother (Mulkerrins 2012)). Both Dunn's and Bryant's approach to costuming contributes to this discourse of authenticity that the shows seek to promote. Moreover, these anecdotes, I would argue, are an equally important part of constructing and maintaining codes of realism, and thus offset concerns related to the notion of history as fabrication.

Costume designers often remark upon the need for period costume to satisfy anxieties of discerning audiences. Indeed, there are many accounts of audience backlash following onscreen historical inaccuracies in costume and production design: the director's commentary for the *Mad Men*'s pilot for example includes an anecdote about the audience's negative reaction when production designers were forced to use typewriters that were not of the period. Thus, despite Weiner's well-documented meticulous approach to the show (he supposedly approves all props, costumes, actors and hairstyles), mistakes are nevertheless made.[3] Similarly, in an interview with the blog *On Screen Fashion*, Dunn is asked if it was a deliberate decision to not have the stem of the Enoch 'Nucky' Thompson's signature red carnation going through the button hole of his lapel, to which he replied 'Oops! You caught that!' (Dunn in Rennie 2012). Thus, these unfortunate (and genuine) errors do not speak to a desire to wilfully misrepresent the past in favour of some other visual agenda.

In the same interview Dunn remarks upon the importance of authenticity not only for audience pleasure but also for aiding the actors:

> We try to be as authentic as possible; this is for several reasons. I like to help the actors to submerge themselves deeply into the period so we like to keep the clothing as 'real' as possible . . . Also, I've seen way too many period films re-interpret a period to ill-effect. I try to avoid an egotistical 'look at me' approach to period design and instead try to give the audience a visual portal into the period. (Dunn in Rennie 2012)

Implicit in his desire for verisimilitude is also the idea that, as discussed in previous chapters, costume should go unnoticed, much like an edit. (The saying goes that a good edit is the one you ignore: it simply propels the narrative forward without drawing attention to itself. It must be smooth and seamless.) However, one might encounter a problem when applying this logic to costume. That is, costume is a 'visual language'. It can only communicate meaning when it is observed, yet there remains an assumption that costume shouldn't 'knock your eyes out'.[4] This is complicated further by the fact that, at least for *Mad Men* (though the same could be said for *Boardwalk Empire*), the era it seeks to depict is known for being one of the most iconic (and frequently revisited) periods in fashion history. Thus, in spite of Dunn's attempts to avoid a 'look-at-me' approach to period design, both of the shows discussed here employ particular visual strategies that at times encourage the audience to take note of onscreen clothing.

Visual Strategies and Reading Costume

In Hollander's (1993) discussion of period costume in theatre, she argues that the 'costumes worn by extras automatically convey more than principal actors' or singers' do, since they are performing a *purely visual function . . .* The costumes are the drama, the characters are known by what they wear, and any accompanying words support the clothes not the other way around' (238, my emphasis). Both *Mad Men* and *Boardwalk Empire* rely on a series of (non-verbal) textual attributes to encourage its clothing to be read as 'the drama'—including (to pursue Hollander's argument) the extensive use of crowd scenes with little or no dialogue.

In *Making Boardwalk Empire*, production designer Bob Shaw reveals that two of the most intricate and large-scale sets—built entirely from scratch—include the boardwalk itself and Babette's Supper Club. Both sets were created to replicate real-life locations and to play important roles in creating the aesthetic identity for *Boardwalk Empire*. In the pilot episode we see both the boardwalk and Babette's Supper Club providing the backdrop for a number of visually 'spectacular' crowd scenes populated by extras in period costuming. The boardwalk scene, according to Dunn, required 150 extras to be dressed in their 'holiday best'.[5] The wide shots used to capture the set (and its extras) allow the audience to view the detail and texture of the clothing and the vibrant colour palette. Indeed, Dunn has frequently commented on the fact that most visual representations of the 1920s appear in black and white (photographs, postcards and film), and consequently there is a common misconception that fashion in the post–First World War era often employed sepia tones. Thus, Dunn's use of much richer colours for the extras on the boardwalk, he claims, was in fact representative of the time. His justification for using vibrant colours is particularly important because the fact that *Boardwalk Empire* is filmed in colour draws attention to its own construction and status as a contemporary programme. Audiences are made aware that they are not watching archival footage, filmed during the time period. Therefore, Dunn's comments may appease those viewers who take pleasure in witnessing historical verisimilitude.

Babette's Supper Club is frequently used as the backdrop for various 'spectacular' functions, such as Nucky's birthday party, Jimmy Darmody's rival party and the 'funeral' party following the prohibition of alcohol in the United States—a scene in which Dunn and Padovani were tasked with dressing 400 'swells'. These scenes undoubtedly offer audience pleasures of 'looking', though this is not to suggest that they function solely as 'spectacle'. Often, the pleasures of looking at 'spectacular' clothes are rudely interrupted with visual and verbal reminders of the sexual and racial discrimination rife in the 1920s. Take for example the prohibition party in the pilot episode. The camera follows Nucky, dressed in a tuxedo and signature red carnation, as he makes his way to the party along the crowded boardwalk towards Babette's. Lively jazz music accompanies the scene in which the audience is encouraged—via the use of a long tracking shot—to absorb and take pleasure in the striking aesthetic of period costume en masse until confronted with the jazz band, consisting of a number of musicians in blackface. Thus, the pleasures one might take from the 'excessive' visual style of *Boardwalk Empire* are suddenly halted by the presence of racist imagery.

While perhaps not on the same scale as *Boardwalk Empire*, *Mad Men* also makes use of wide shots to the same effect. The open-plan offices of Sterling Cooper (and in later seasons Sterling Cooper Draper Price) are often filmed in the wide, revealing a number of female extras dressed in vibrant period costuming. In addition, the frequent 'party' scenes in *Mad Men*, particularly in the later seasons, serve to showcase the female characters' clothing (such as Don's birthday party in Season 5, Episode 1, and the Christmas party in Season 5, Episode 10). Drawing focus to female characters is often achieved through composition of the frame—and this is not limited to the crowd scenes.

To take an arguably unremarkable scene from 'Marriage of Figaro' (Season 1, Episode 3), as an example, in which a meeting takes place between the executives of Sterling Cooper and Rachel Menken (an owner of a department store the firm represents), the composition of the frame and the use of colour draw attention to Rachel's wardrobe.[6] Rachel appears in a woollen two-piece fuchsia suit and a light-pink feathered hat, against a backdrop of well-tailored but nondescript grey polyester suits in a low-lit boardroom. There are, of course, multiple readings that could be extracted from this one scene; it could be that the choice of colour and the style of the suit serves to replicate the style of the period and is a likely choice for a person of Rachel's gender, ethnicity and class position; alternatively, it could be suggested that the decision to dress Rachel in this way reinforces Mulvey's contention that the woman onscreen is designed primarily 'to be looked at' and serve the interest of the male spectator; or finally, it could be argued that the composition functions simply as stylistic creativity and bears no narrative significance. However, the composition of the frame—that is that she appears as the *only* one in colour (and that this marks a departure from her previous wardrobe choices)—suggests that this scene cues the viewer to *read* into the costuming, to take note of it and to decode its message. When read in context with the episode's narrative it becomes clear that this scene indicates visually what is not being said verbally. First, it signals Rachel's difference, in every sense of the word. Rachel's introduction in the pilot episode is designed to provide one of *Mad Men*'s signature 'jarring' moments of unabashed sexism. Don mistakenly introduces himself to a fellow male employee of the firm whom he believes to be the client. When Don is corrected by Roger Sterling, we witness a fleeting moment of embarrassment. However, in a subsequent scene the meeting turns aggressive when Rachel disagrees with Don's proposed strategy. Don announces that he 'won't let a woman talk to [him] like that' and promptly leaves the room. As a Jewish woman Rachel is, in societal terms, Don's subordinate; however her visual representation onscreen underscores her character's agency. Her costuming ensures that she does not fade into the background literally or figuratively.

Such sequences serve to 'fetishize' clothing, allowing costume to serve as a non-verbal discourse. Another recurring trope within both shows, which also fetishizes costume, is the frequent use of dressing sequences. These sequences, though not separate from narrative and characterization, privilege costume above the spoken word. In *Boardwalk Empire*, we often witness characters being dressed by others; Nucky for example is regularly dressed by his butler. However, it is often the female characters that appear in extended dressing sequences. This is partly explained by the fact that in Season 1, Episode 3 Margaret Schroder (Kelly MacDonald) is hired and subsequently works as a dresser in a French boutique (*La Belle Femme*)—a job Nucky arranged for her. On her first day, she is told by the proprietor, Isabelle Jenuet, that her role involves dressing and modelling the clothes for clients, but most importantly she is 'to be seen and not heard'. This phrase is repeated several times during their exchange and says something of the way in which fashion onscreen traditionally functions—however, within these scenes the costume does not 'fade into the background'. In the same episode, Margaret is required to assist Lucy (Nucky's girlfriend) in trying on lingerie (see Figure 7). The dressing scene uses costume to foreground issues of power and vulnerability (characteristics typical of the gangster genre). Prior to this sequence, the audience has witnessed Margaret change from her working class, 'peasant' clothes into a teal gown supplied by her employer. Margaret dresses quickly—though we are offered a fleeting glance at her 'functional' undergarments—before taking time to assess her appearance in a full-length mirror. The 'reveal' shot functions as a traditional 'makeover' convention, demonstrating Margaret's transformation and social mobility; however, it also becomes a central point of comparison which shapes the way in which we view Lucy's dressing scene. Though visibly pleased by her appearance in the new gown, Margaret expresses a sense of unease within her new role, which is reflected in the dressing sequence by the speed at which she changes, signalling her awkwardness. Lucy, on the other hand, spends several minutes in front of the mirror posing and examining her naked body. In some ways the shot speaks to her narcissism, but also to her sexual assertiveness. In addition, the sequence reveals the power relations between the pair and becomes an important storytelling device in later episodes. For example in Episode 6, Lucy visits the boutique again and, aware that Nucky and Margaret have begun to develop a romantic relationship, requests that Margaret model 'vampy' lingerie. The scene once again is prefaced with a short exchange which reveals a great deal about the function of onscreen fashion within *Boardwalk Empire*. Isabelle is suggesting 'conservative' undergarments to Lucy, at which point she remarks, dissatisfied, 'why do women buy underwear?' Isabelle replies, 'some women want to hide, others wish to reveal'. Upon hearing the remark, Lucy's gaze turns to Margaret, and Lucy demands that Margaret try on black-lace lingerie. In the subsequent scene, Margaret removes her own, 'functional' underwear and allows Lucy to insult her figure, before retorting that Lucy's own body must not be the draw she believes it to be (as Nucky has sought Margaret's company). In this sequence, Margaret feels no need to hide her figure and demonstrates the same sexual assertiveness accorded to Lucy in the previous dressing scene.

Mad Men also includes dressing sequences. In the pilot episode, we see Don dress in his office. He opens a desk drawer to reveal (via close-up) a selection of clean white shirts; he takes one out and puts it on. This exact sequence of shots is often repeated in the early episodes of the show, and in the director's commentary Weiner discusses his desire to include the scene as it demonstrates

Figure 7 Dressing sequence: *Boardwalk Empire* Season 1, Episode 3: 'Broadway Limited', HBO, USA (2010).

the 'reality' of the show. He demands that desk drawers, suitcases and pockets be full in order to assist with the suspension of disbelief. That said, he also remarks that the dressing scene demonstrates the amount of 'business' that occurs within *Mad Men*. He clarifies that by business he is referring to acting without dialogue—thus, the act of dressing is a significant non-verbal device for both narrative and characterization.

One dressing sequence, in particular, is worthy of exploration, though it should be noted that this scene is considered atypical of the show. In Season 2, Episode 6, entitled 'Maidenform', opens with a dressing montage of Betty, Peggy and Joan. All three principal female characters appear in a state of undress, which is later contextualized, as the episode's narrative revolves around Sterling Cooper's attempts to create a Playtex campaign. The scene denies the audience the pleasure of a 'makeover' reveal and ends with the characters still in their underwear. There is no dialogue in this two-minute sequence, only an extra-diegetic soundtrack. Curiously, it is the only scene to use extra-diegetic music which is not of the period; the musical accompaniment to the sequence is a contemporary song by The Decemberists entitled 'The Infanta'. Notably, this is the only occasion in which *Mad Men* radically breaks with its commitment to historical accuracy and acknowledges the contemporary (and this was subsequently met with disdain by audiences and critics alike). Nevertheless, the scene serves a very important purpose. It reminds us that we are viewing this (re)construction of the past in the present and encourages us to read *Mad Men* in these terms (i.e. through a contemporary, critical lens). And just as this has implications for the way in which we read the overt sexism, racism and homophobia (and even excessive smoking), it also has implications for the way in which we read costume and fashion.

Redressing the Past: Melodrama and Social Commentary in *Mad Men* and *Boardwalk Empire*

While the use of contemporary music in *Mad Men* is an isolated event, there are other textual (and intertextual) strategies employed to cue the audience to read onscreen fashion as a social critique of 1960s cultural politics. To be sure, both *Mad Men* and *Boardwalk Empire* have cultivated and are often celebrated for their unique aesthetic identity; however, both also draw heavily from popular culture. As previously discussed, *Mad Men* (more so than *Boardwalk Empire*) has a rich cinematic and televisual history from which to draw inspiration— discussed at length in Edgerton's (2011) anthology. Robert Thompson's (2011) foreword for example remarks upon the influence of *The Twilight Zone*

(1959–1964), while Jeremy Butler (2011) acknowledges the visual references to 1950s and 1960s Hollywood melodramas. In particular, Butler calls attention to the similarities between the Drapers' home and Cary Scott's (Jane Wyman) in Douglas Sirk's *All that Heaven Allows* (1955). Significantly for Butler, this is not read as blank, uncritical 'pastiche', rather this is indicative of *Mad Men*'s deeply political and intellectual agenda. Indeed, it is widely agreed that Sirk's melodramas use elements of mise en scène to comment on cultural politics. For Klinger (1994), drawing on Sirk's own comments about visual style, 'objects in the mise-en-scène . . . are no longer ciphers, vivid stylistic flourishes without certain significance; they embody social critique or a self reflexive awareness of the conditions of representations' (9). Thus, the use of melodrama in both *Mad Men* and *Boardwalk Empire* plays an important role in reminding viewers of the importance of costume as social commentary.

To return once again to Gaines's (1990) work on costume and narrative, it is important to note that there was one genre which refused to abide by the codes of narrative realism, and which relished in spectacle for spectacle's sake. Drawing on Peter Brooks's (1985) theorization of the genre in *The Melodramatic Imagination*—in which he claims that melodramas are characterized by their 'rhetorical excess' (36)—Gaines (1990) argues that from the 1920s through the 1950s, melodramas allowed for onscreen wardrobes to push the boundaries of 'realism' (204). The melodrama relies upon visual language to convey meaning as much as it does verbal. She writes, 'the realist aesthetic is never sufficient to the melodrama's project, a project which requires vehicles that can express the grandiose and the profuse' (204). It is perhaps unsurprising then that attempts to delineate the genre have often remarked upon the recurring features of visual opulence and emphasized emotional register. For John Mercer and Martin Shingler (2004), the melodrama is characterized by the way in which 'action is worked up to bold climaxes . . . swinging suddenly from one emotion to its extreme opposite' (7). Moreover, they claim that a key feature of the melodrama is 'its dependence upon an established system of non-verbal signs, gesture, *mise-en-scène* (sets, props, costume and lighting) and music' (7; italics in the original).

Butler (2011) gestures towards these debates about costume and narrative, or, as he terms it, 'narrative-versus-ornamentation' (60). Following his remarks about *Mad Men*'s open-ended and 'oblique' story lines, he poses a rhetorical question: 'Could it be . . . [that] we take greater pleasure in *Mad Men*'s mise-en-scène than its narrative development or closure or in the characters' attainment of goals?' (60). A valid question, but perhaps a more crucial issue is to consider why we continue to see these two aspects as separate and often diametrically opposed, rather than deeply interconnected. For most critics, the way in which melodrama subverts traditional screen hierarchies of costume over narrative has been read as 'excessive' visual representation and has helped to secure its position as a much-maligned 'feminine' genre. However, within the work of some feminist critics who are seeking to rescue the melodrama from its lowly status, the use of 'excessive' non-verbal signs is political and worthy of serious academic attention.

The melodrama in television has most often been associated with soap operas. Consequently, emotional storylines involving familial relations and domesticity have been at the foreground. This is, of course, the case with *Mad Men* and *Boardwalk Empire*, yet what seems perhaps at odds here is the way in which both shows maintain a 'quality' status, while the melodrama and particularly the soap opera remain subject to critical debasement. Thus, this speaks to the way in which masculine cultural forms remove pejorative connotations of the mode or genre (see for example Kathleen Rowe's (1995) analysis of post-classical romantic comedies in which she demonstrates how elements of melodrama have been employed in cinema, often to tell the hero's story). It seems banal to note that the gangster film in cinema has long since been noted as a masculinized (and culturally legitimate) melodrama, however, for my purposes, it is important to remember that the gangster genre opens up an intriguing space for costume and fashion to be explored. In her discussion of the gangster film's ambiguous approach to costume, Bruzzi (1997: 70) remarks, 'here are characters who have cultivated an aggressively masculine image and are immensely vain, and whose sartorial flamboyance far from imitating femininity or effeminacy, is the most important sign of their masculine social and material success'. As previously discussed, men's participation in fashion and conspicuous consumption is often met with disdain or suspicion, with the exception of the gangster film. This particular genre renders men's pleasure in fashion and adornment safe (and undoubtedly masculine). Thus, what might be read as deviant sartorial excess in other cultural forms is normalized and celebrated. Indeed, both *Boardwalk Empire* and *Mad Men* encourage a reading of fashion as potentially 'unruly' and radical for both its male and female characters. In *Mad Men* in particular, onscreen fashion provides an alternative discourse for the female characters, who are denied expression by the social and cultural expectations of the period.

As with *Ugly Betty* (discussed in Chapter 4)—which, in terms of costume, draws inspiration from the 1960s—the women's clothes in *Mad Men* are initially coded as 'ugly' with regard to contemporary canons of taste, and possibly even for the time (with perhaps Joan Holloway as an exception). This is not to suggest that *Mad Men* lacks in visual style but rather that the wardrobe paradoxically complements the overall 'slick' aesthetic of the show. Moreover, this 'ugliness' reveals the show's position on 1960s cultural politics. In *Mad Men*, Betty's wardrobe for example reflects a resistance to changing ideas about modernity, fashion and style. Within the show's earlier seasons, Betty was often featured at home wearing full-skirted shirtdresses, invoking the 'New Look' silhouette. The 'New Look', popularized in the late 1940s and 1950s, was used frequently in these early seasons and served to signal *Mad Men*'s difference from those representations of the 'swinging sixties' most visible in popular culture, and to remind viewers that the social, cultural and political upheaval which has retrospectively characterized the decade did not occur until the late 1960s. The period represented in early seasons of *Mad Men* focuses on what Edgerton (2009) has termed the 'calm before the cultural storm'. Consequently, the ideals and values associated with the 1950s continued to exercise a strong hold on American culture in the early 1960s, and this was represented in *Mad Men*'s costuming. However, as the series progresses, Betty continually returns to the New Look. In Season 4, set in 1965, we begin to see a shift in onscreen costuming towards a 'modern' and 'European' aesthetic (personified, perhaps, in the character of Megan); however, Betty continues to wear the same cotton, full-skirted dresses.

In her article, '"It will be a magnificent obsession": Femininity, Desire, and the New Look in 1950s Hollywood Melodrama', Bruzzi (2011) complicates readings of the 'New Look' as a signifier of 'traditional femininity' (160). The New Look, she argues, became a 'sartorial touchstone' in 1950s melodrama, which communicated superficially conventional femininity, while also being worn by characters experiencing sexual frustration; 'their appearance thereby suggests a lack of erotic interest, at the same time as they themselves indicate discontent with this imposed identity' (160). In her conclusion she singles out *Mad Men* as an example of quality television that offers 'contemporary retrospectives on the . . . paradoxical nature of the New Look as it has been appropriated in mainstream American culture' (177). Betty, as the epitome of Betty Friedan's disconsolate housewife, struggles to reconcile social expectations with her own desires, and as Bruzzi notes, it is no coincidence that she appears in one of the most 'eye catching' New Look evening gowns—'a garishly spotted evening gown that is both preppish, "safe" and eye-catching underneath which nestle several springy petticoats that give it a dollish bounciness' (178)—when she confronts Don about his adultery. In the episode 'A Night to Remember' (Season 2, Episode 8), Betty hosts a dinner party for Don's co-workers. After the event Betty asks Don about his alleged affair, which he denies. The following day, still wearing the dress—and looking increasingly dishevelled—Betty searches through Don's wardrobe attempting to find evidence of his indiscretion. Unsuccessful, Betty collapses on the bed in the dress and begins to weep. The image of Betty on the bed, engulfed by the dress which the previous night had aided her performance of an idealized category of femininity, now has the very opposite meaning. The scene borrows heavily from the 'paranoid women's films' of the 1940s in its composition, and her 'eye-catching' gown now functions as a very different kind of spectacle. In other words, the costume becomes a contrapuntal discourse in this episode (see Figure 8).

Figure 8 'The Sad Clown Dress': *Mad Men* Season 2, Episode 8: 'A Night to Remember',
AMC, USA (2008).

The use of the costume as a contrapuntal discourse is frequently invoked in
Mad Men in general, and in Betty's storylines in particular. In an earlier episode,
'The Shoot' (Season 1, Episode 9), Betty—grappling with the cause of her
unhappiness—decides to return to her career as a model. She is approached
by an associate of Don's, Jim Hobart (whose agenda is primarily to poach Don
for his own company), to model for a Coca-Cola advertising campaign. During
their short exchange he continually compliments Betty, telling her that she is
a 'dead ringer for Grace Kelly' and that her 'European' look would work for
the international target market. In the following scenes, Betty, notably happier,
begins to 'relive' her modelling days—she retrieves her collection of haute
couture gowns from storage (created for her by an Italian designer for whom she
was a muse), and models them for a friend.

For her audition, Betty selects a strapless, New Look, black-, white- and pink-
striped dress (the skirt is perhaps the fullest we've seen) with a large 'pussy bow'
on the front. The dress is revealed as the camera pans across a waiting room
full of potential models, appearing in 'everyday' woollen suits. Betty glances to
the models at her side with a slightly uncomfortable look on her face, and we
begin to see here that Betty is 'out of date'. This is exacerbated by the fact that
we, the contemporary audience, read the New Look, in these terms: as a relic of
the past. Following her final photo shoot, she appears in a peach-silk New Look
dress heartbroken upon learning that the campaign is being taken in a different
direction (more Audrey Hepburn, less Grace Kelly); Betty is 'left behind'—a
theme developed in Season 4 when Don remarries a young, European brunette
(an Audrey Hepburn type), whose costuming evolves to represent the high

fashion of the late 1960s.[7] This not to suggest, of course, that Megan does not experience a similar sense of dissatisfaction with her situation as Don's second wife. In Season 5, having recently wed Don, Megan decides that she wishes to reattempt a career as an actor. In the final episode of the season she appears in a commercial, having exploited Don's business connections. As with Betty's audition scene, 'spectacular' costuming plays an important role here, as she appears in a garish red-and-yellow Heidi dirndl dress (the theme of the advertisement is Cinderella). The dress serves not only to infantilize Megan but also to maintain its status as 'costume' within the diegesis, which speaks to its position as artifice and masquerade and reminds us that Megan's success in the world of acting is also founded upon deception and nepotism, not 'genuine' talent. To return to an earlier point, the deployment of Megan's dress in this scene is also representative of the ways in which 'ugly' clothes function as commentary.

Both examples of 'retro programming' discussed here foster complex relationships with the present, and this is nowhere more explicit than in their uses of fashion. The difficulties the shows face stem from a series of assumptions regarding the function of costume in period drama, assumptions which shore up contradictory value systems. The main aim of this chapter has been to identify the problems with thinking about period costume in these terms. To view onscreen fashion in historical drama as either a signifying system of historical accuracy, or blank stylistic expression is reductive insofar as it fails to account for the myriad functions of costume and the varying ways in which audience extract pleasure from onscreen clothing. With regard to *Mad Men* and *Boardwalk Empire*, an analysis of the tropes and uses of costume reveals that fashion can be used as a historical signifier, stylistic flourish and social commentary simultaneously, or that it can move freely between the three positions.

As previously discussed, it is understood that costume designers working on period pieces are encouraged to reconcile contemporary commercial desires with the narrative needs of historical costume; to use Cook's (1996: 75) terms, 'costume has to reflect contemporary fashion as well as the suggested period'. This is not simply to create opportunities for commercial tie-ins, though for *Mad Men* there have been plenty (Janie Bryant's Mod collection for QVC, an underwear collection for Maidenform, Michael Kors's Fall 2008 collection and Banana Republic's *Mad Men* collection), but also to ensure that historical texts resonate with the contemporary audience.[8]

This chapter has identified some of the textual attributes which can be read as cues for the audience to foreground certain readings of costumes over others. However, this is not to suggest that this is how the audience makes sense of onscreen clothing, nor that the audience is only cued by the text. With regard to tie-ins, for example, Diane Waldman (1984: 48) has argued that commodity tie-ins can serve to 'foreground preferred readings of the text and to constrain oppositional ones'. Thus, one should not dismiss the possibilities of additional readings of costume encouraged through a cross-media promotion. With this in mind, the final section offers an exploration of the extra-textual material that surrounds fashion programming and its role in the sense-making of viewers and consumers.

PART III

CONCEPTUALIZING FASHION AND CELEBRITY CULTURE

7
FASHIONING CELEBRITY: CLASS, TASTEMAKING AND CULTURAL INTERMEDIARIES

Many of the examples of fashion programming discussed in this volume have engaged with the idea, articulated by Stuart and Elizabeth Ewan (1992: 186–7), that within contemporary consumer society there is no fashion, '*only fashions* . . . No rules, only choices . . . [today] everyone can be anyone' (emphasis in original). This neo-liberal discourse has divided cultural critics. For some it holds the promise of a more egalitarian society and suggests a move towards freedom and individual choice. For others, it depoliticizes the subcultural and anti-fashion practices of marginalized groups and threatens fashion's status as a marker of cultural identity. It is not the purpose of this book to evaluate the validity of these viewpoints. Rather, this book is concerned with the ways in which these conflicting philosophies inform (and in some sense are informed by) fashion programming and its wider contextual apparatus. Thus, this final section considers the symbolic meaning of onscreen fashion as it moves beyond the text into the realm of celebrity culture. In particular, it examines how the construction and circulation of the celebrity image serves the interests of the fashion system by educating audiences in fashion, taste and consumption practices during a moment of supposed instability.

A central theme running through the remaining chapters is the way in which the lead actors (who have achieved fashion-icon status) function as cultural intermediaries. While the term cultural intermediary has been deployed in myriad ways (see Hesmondhalgh 2006a; Negus 2002; Nixon 1997; Featherstone 2007), I return to and seek to expand upon Bourdieu's (1984) initial definition: that is a cultural intermediary engages in 'occupations involving presentation and representation (sales, marketing, advertising, public relations, fashion, decoration and so forth) . . . providing symbolic goods and services' (9). Indeed, Bourdieu's definition provides an appropriate framework here, as it gestures towards the importance of those individuals who enjoy some form of visibility in the mass media (his examples include TV and radio presenters and magazine journalists). With this in mind, an additional aim of Part 3 of this book is to advance the discussion of cultural intermediaries by exploring the use of 'media personalities' as fashion icons.

This chapter focuses on two examples in particular, Sarah Jessica Parker and Blake Lively. These two star images will be discussed in relation to one another as they are activated in extra-textual material in similar ways. Moreover, the popular presses have discursively constructed a relationship between the two; that is Lively has been selected as a successor to Parker, tasked with continuing her legacy as a fashion icon. Such a claim is, of course, informed by assumptions about fashionability and age, and in so doing shores up an 'ideal' type of fashion icon. Both women are eligible for the role, as they conform to a particular aesthetic (as thin, white, blonde women) but equally important are their performances of appropriate class identities. This chapter concerns itself with the way in which discourses of class are foregrounded (and class boundaries reinforced) within extra-textual material surrounding the celebrity images. Although the star images of Parker and Lively seek to promote the understanding that fashion can be 'for everyone', their construction and circulation within celebrity and fashion magazines operates within very distinct class boundaries. Both star images are informed by specific class discourses and function as arbiters of middle-class taste.

Fashion, Stardom and Class

In her article 'Bringing out the * in You', Deborah Jermyn (2006) calls for the substantial revision and re-imagining of traditional paradigms of television fame (Ellis 1992; Langer 1981). Using Sarah Jessica Parker as a case study, she demonstrates the ways in which the development of American 'quality' television complicates the longstanding assumption that 'stardom proper' is an exclusively 'cinematic phenomenon'. Deriving from Ellis's model (outlined in the introduction), it has long since been argued that celebrity inter-texts have a tendency to collapse any notion of difference between the onscreen and offscreen personae of television actors and personalities (Geraghty 2007). As such, the television actor is considered 'too familiar' and 'too ordinary' to possess 'real' star quality. However, Jermyn (2006) argues that Parker's television role as Carrie Bradshaw was vital in elevating her status. She posits that it was *Sex and the City* which granted her 'a level of visibility and public fascination which cinema did not while transforming her into a style icon, with all the connotations of distance that such status inescapably brings' (82). Thus, Parker's position as a television actor problematizes the view that fashion-icon status can only be achieved by film stars.

For Dyer (1979/2004: 35), it is film stardom which generates an interest into the 'way stars live'. As such, 'lifestyle', within which fashion is included, is often used to demonstrate the *distinctions* between stars and 'ordinary people'. Moreover, it is primarily the *display* of lifestyle within extra-textual material that contributes to the construction of the star as 'glamorous' and as an object of desire. Indeed, for Ellis, it is the supposed lack of 'glamour' associated with television personalities which prevents them from achieving 'legitimate' stardom. Underpinning both of these assumptions then, is the notion that 'conspicuous consumption' is key in the construction of the star image—in effect it is the display of lifestyle that is crucial in making stars *mean*.

The supposed shift towards consumer-based identities in the contemporary period has resulted in the display of lifestyle having added import. Indeed, it is often claimed that the display of 'lifestyle' is now the key determinant in demonstrating 'difference', replacing traditional power structures, such as class, 'race' and gender. In postmodern thought, 'lifestyle' is no longer influenced by distinct class positions. This perceived 'new' shift coincides with developments in celebrity culture, in particular the suggestion that there is an unprecedented audience fascination with the private life(style) of the celebrity.[1] Consequently, the celebrity lifestyle has an important role in conveying the 'meaning' associated with material goods, and arguably educating consumers in the practice of discrimination. In the midst of the supposed postmodern turn or 'crisis', it appears that star images serve to support the goals of the fashion system. That is they must participate in processes of meaning-making in order to maintain the cultural meaning of fashion (and, for that matter, other consumer goods) by (re)producing distinctions which have hitherto correlated with class.

The idea that social class is no longer a key determinant in identity performance throws up an opportunity and a problem for the fashion industry. On the one hand, the notion that fashion offers the promise of reinvention and transformation has perhaps more currency than it has ever had before, and can translate into an effective marketing strategy. Yet if one pursues this school of thought to its full conclusion, fashion runs the risk of becoming entirely devoid of symbolic value, exposed as fabrication and artifice. One cannot 'reinvent' oneself in the absence of a fixed point of reference. Thus, this paradox is not unlike the 'ordinary/extraordinary' concept; a delicate balance must be struck in relation to the conflicting ideologies in order for both to function.

The two star images under discussion here are vital in maintaining these interdependent positions. On the one hand, stars are thought to reinforce threatened belief systems that structure culture and society. Thus, with the decline of an extant class system, stardom serves as a substitutive experience. The star provides a moment when meanings are temporarily stabilized. They function as tastemakers, reinforcing boundaries of class identities so that meaning can be made (and remade). On the other hand, the circulation of star personae within fashion and celebrity inter-texts is often designed precisely to support the 'anyone can be anyone' philosophy and to promote the transformative nature of fashion.

Narratives of Fame: Rags to Riches and Ascribed Celebrity

Sarah Jessica Parker's 'rise-to-fame' narrative, as constructed within *People* magazine, conforms to early theoretical understandings of stardom and shores up traditional notions of the ordinary and extraordinary. In particular, Dyer's (1979/2004) concept of the 'success myth' is frequently employed in the construction of Parker's star image. The success myth draws on the concept of the 'American dream' and negotiates several (somewhat contradictory) discourses; that 'talent', 'specialness', 'hard work' and 'professionalism' will undoubtedly be rewarded, while simultaneously promoting the understanding that 'lucky breaks' can happen to anyone (48). With regard to Parker, the 'success myth' is recast as a 'Cinderella' motif. As such, Parker's image pivots on not only the understanding that hard work and talent can be converted into success, but also the notion that physical appearance and dress can be a key determinant in this process. As Moseley (2005a) observes, the Cinderella motif, with its emphasis on the 'intersection of clothes, style, power and status' (109), further reinforces the importance of fashion with regard to Parker's star image, and becomes the central explanation of her fame within *People* magazine.

Sarah Jessica Parker appears on the cover of an October 2000 issue of *People*, next to the bold headline 'Sarah Jessica Parker: Real Life Cinderella'. Below, the accompanying tagline reads: '[f]rom hardscrabble Ohio childhood to fame, a great marriage and *Sex and the City*'. As one might expect, the main article is structured around themes of poverty, struggle and hard-won success. It chronicles Parker's early 'Dickensian' childhood (*People* 2000: 118)—she recalls Christmases with no electricity and parents sacrificing their meals to feed the children—through to the height of her success as a television actor, crystallized in a moment at the 2000 Emmy Awards. The 2000 Emmy Awards ceremony represents a turning point for Parker, as it was reportedly her 'first experience of real couture' (Parker in *People* 2000: 118). *People* likened Parker to a 'giddy Cinderella' as she asked photographers to capture her pink Oscar de la Renta gown, excitedly informing them that 'each feather was hand sewn' (118). Here, fashion becomes the ultimate measure of success, for as Dyer (1979/2004: 42) argues, the star system promotes the notion that 'success is worth having in the form of conspicuous consumption'. For Parker, her impoverished roots serve to emphasize not only her worthiness, but also her appreciation for the luxurious trappings of fame.

Blake Lively's 'rise-to-fame' narrative differs somewhat from Parker's. To use Chris Rojek's (2001: 18) taxonomies, Parker represents 'achieved celebrity'; that is, Parker's success is derived from her 'perceived accomplishment . . . in open competition'. Lively, on the other hand, represents 'ascribed celebrity' insofar as her fame is concerned with 'lineage'. Her father, Ernie Lively, is a prolific film director and actor, and siblings Eric, Jason, Lori and Robyn Lively are also successful film and television actors. Consequently, Lively has been granted access to advantages and opportunities unavailable to Parker, which potentially threatens to devalue the currency of the success myth.[2] Thus, a series of strategies are implemented in order to ensure that Lively appears worthy of her fame and privilege, in order to maintain the 'ordinary/extraordinary' balance.[3]

First, there is a particular effort to construct Lively as a hardworking, professional actor. This is achieved primarily through the testimonies of other 'legitimate', 'achieved' celebrities. For example, in an interview for *Marie Claire* (2009), Rebecca Miller—Lively's director on *The Private Lives of Pippa Lee* (2009)—recounts the first day of filming, during which Lively arrived on set at 7 a.m., having only finished filming *Gossip Girl* four hours earlier. The remainder of the interview includes endorsements from co-stars Maria Bello and Julianne Moore, both of whom remarked upon her acting ability and professionalism.

Second, Lively's ability to traverse the ordinary/extraordinary paradox is also articulated through her fashion choices. Significantly around the time it was announced that Lively had become the face of Chanel's Mademoiselle handbag line, reports emerged that she was also a fan of high-street brand Topshop (Adams 2012). Indeed, these reports are buttressed by the 2011 Best Dressed special edition of *Vogue*, in which Lively appears in a Chanel sequined jacket twinned with shorts from Topshop, next to the tag line 'Plain with embellished, high with low and classic with a touch of cool' (Holgate 2011: 54). Thus, while the tagline acknowledges the disparity in symbolic value (this is a combination of high and low culture), Lively is positioned as someone with an aesthetic disposition, who is able successfully re-appropriate certain garments. Moreover, the way in which Lively is able to reconcile high and low culture, plain and embellished, classic and cool serves as a metaphor for the way in which the image also adeptly embodies 'ordinary' and 'extraordinary'.

Sarah Jessica Parker's 'rise-to-fame' narrative obviates the need for her to defend her ability or to justify her talents; thus this discourse is absent from her extra-textual circulation. Yet this is not to suggest that Parker's ordinariness is beyond dispute. Both Lively and Parker must perform ordinariness (as well as extraordinariness) in order to maintain their star image, and significantly, one strategy in particular is employed within extra-textual circulation of both star images. That is discourses of motherhood are potent within the construction of both public personae. For Parker, as a mother of three, it is perhaps unsurprising that much coverage is structured around her status as 'working mother'. Importantly, however Lively is *not* a mother. Yet even before her 2012 wedding to actor Ryan Reynolds, the spectre of motherhood (and domesticity more generally) loomed large within the extra-textual construction of her star image. Within press coverage of Lively, it becomes shorthand for an overall disinterestedness in celebrity lifestyle (i.e. 'excessive' partying, etc.) and serves to mark a departure from the pervasive media constructions of the young female celebrity as an out-of-control 'train wreck' (see Holmes and Negra 2011). An example of this can be found in the following passage taken from a 2012 interview for *Allure* magazine:

> 'I've always wanted a big family', says the actress. How many [kids does] she want? 'Oh, I'd love 30 if I could,' she says. And she shares the fact that, unlike most 25-year-olds, she enjoys practicing her parenting skills with her niece and nephews. 'I took a nine-year-old, a seven-year-old, and a four-year-old with me to New York, then did all my *Savages* press,' Lively says proudly. (Lively in Hauser 2012: 282)

The above exchange skilfully employs discourses of (pseudo)motherhood in order to position Lively as a 'grounded' young woman, one likely to succeed in the postfeminist project of managing a work-life balance. The concept of the 'working mother' is therefore a powerful device within celebrity inter-texts which seek to offer a glimpse of the private life of celebrities. As Jermyn (2008) notes, though the title 'is 'open to myriad inflections according to the class status of the woman holding it, for female stars it lends itself neatly to the ordinary/extraordinary paradigm' (165). For Sarah Jessica Parker, the 'working mother' facet of her star persona serves to demonstrate her difference from 'ultimate single girl' Carrie Bradshaw. Similarly, Lively's desire to become a 'working mother' and her investment in the 'domestic' also serves to differentiate her from the ultra-privileged Serena van der Woodsen. Moreover, Lively's and Parker's performances of 'working motherhood' (based either in reality or the imaginary) also support their position as fashion icons. Their desire for and commitment to motherhood qualifies them for 'yummy mummy' status.

Condemned by some due to its exclusive nature—it is a distinctly 'middle-class' experience (see McRobbie 2006), the 'yummy mummy' phenomenon is bound up with and born out of the 'guilt-free' consumerism offered by post-feminism. Sarah Jessica Parker, according to Jermyn (2008: 166) has become a 'figurehead' for the movement, and certainly her ability to reconcile 'fashionability' with motherhood is central to the 2011 'Age Issue' of *Vogue* (for whom, Parker is the cover 'girl'). The feature article serves as a promotional piece for her film *I Don't Know How She Does It* (2011), in which Parker plays Kate Reddy, an overworked mother attempting to successfully negotiate the work–life balance.

Within the six-page spread, Parker appears in 'spectacular' couture (including a floor-length Bottega Veneta bronze ball gown) alongside husband Matthew Broderick and their three children. The shoot adopts a 1950s aesthetic and features Parker in a domestic setting (a fictional version of the couple's home), performing 'maternal duties' (i.e. embracing one of her daughters, pointing out a mess to another, etc.). The tagline for one image in particular, though it applies to all the images, is 'Chic amongst chaos' (MacSweeney 2011). Thus while the backdrop is littered with children's toys, Parker remains immaculately dressed in Chanel suits and ball gowns, thereby demonstrating her ability to successfully perform her dual identities: mother and style icon.

In a series of ways, the shoot draws inspiration from 'star sitcoms' (Gillan 2004) of the 1950s and 1960s (such as *The Donna Reed Show* (1958–1966), *The Dick van Dyke Show* (1961–1966), etc.), not only in the use of 'retro' fashions (such as the classic Chanel suit) but also in the exaggerated gender politics. Parker appears in the domestic setting in classically 'feminine' dress (full skirts, corseted gowns, etc.), and the children also conform to gender stereotypes. The son, James Wilke, is shot in dynamic poses with swords and guitars, while the twin daughters appear more sedate, playing with stuffed animals. The overtly staged images, which adopt the kind of 'uncanny' aesthetic of the 'star sitcom' sets, are designed to resemble the 'real-life' home of the star. In so doing, they deliberately call attention to their own construction, yet simultaneously viewers are offered a glimpse of the 'authentic' celebrity persona, through the use of Parker's real-life family. The editorial affirms her position as 'real' working mother, but somewhat self-reflexively acknowledges the constructed nature of the 'celebrity' 'yummy mummy'. Thus, Parker's 'fixed' motherhood status counterbalances the playful nature of fashion and the pleasures it offers in constructing cultural identities. In addition, the photo shoot also speaks to the ways in which the concept of the celebrity working mother needs to be managed so that it most effectively serves the ordinary/extraordinary paradigm.

In a recent *Vogue* interview, Blake Lively speculates upon how she may manage her style-icon status with motherhood. She claims:

'Styling is a lot of work! I guess I would consider [getting a stylist] in the future. If I had a family and I was going on a press tour, I would not be spending my time [researching fashion]—I'd be getting my kids their Cheerios,' she told us. 'But I love it so much, it's a good outlet for my creativity. If you make a mistake [when you don't have a stylist] at least it's your own mistake.' (Lively in Niven 2012)

Not only does the comment serve to reinforce her legitimacy as a style icon (i.e. she is responsible for her own sartorial choices and takes time and effort 'researching' them), but also it reminds readers of her commitment to family values and 'ordinariness'. Thus, the ways in which the motherhood narrative is managed speaks to the very precarious position that both Lively and Parker must negotiate in order to function successfully as fashion icons and cultural intermediaries. They must simultaneously promote the conspicuous consumption associated with stardom while remaining connected to audiences through their performances of 'ordinariness'.

Due to the pejorative connotations associated with conspicuous consumption (i.e. that it is 'wasteful', 'vulgar' and 'unnecessary') both Parker and Lively must maintain a humility which allows them to traverse the boundaries between 'acceptable' and 'excessive' consumption, with no negative repercussions. Unbridled 'excess' (of any kind) threatens their positions as tastemakers. Both Parker and Lively must perform middle-class notions of 'moderation' (and respectability) if they wish to secure a middle-class mode of address. Parker must 'sanitize' her working-class roots in order achieve 'respectability'. Her background is rendered 'safe' and sanctioned within prevailing middle-class mores. For example, as previously discussed within the *People* article, there is a clear attempt to remind readers that despite her wealth and access to luxury goods (this reportedly includes a 'closet full' of Manolo Blahnik shoes and two Fendi Baguettes), her working-class background informs her relationship to fashion and consumption. One paragraph in particular, is especially revealing of this and thus is worth quoting in full:

> Yet even on Madison Avenue, memories of her 'Dickensian' childhood, as Parker once called it, are never distant. On a recent shopping trip, recalls the *Sex and the City* first assistant director Bettiann Fishman; 'she saw something she liked and she stopped and said "Oh a little pricey". I asked, "Why did that even come into your head?" And she said, "Well, you know what, let me take it and if it doesn't work I can always return it." She doesn't forget.' (*People* 2000: 118)

Two interrelated points can be drawn from this passage. First, the use of the term 'Dickensian' dispels any depreciatory associations with the working classes which can suggest a lack of cultural capital and 'respectability'. In her book *Formations of Class and Gender*, Beverley Skeggs (1997: 3) argues the working-class woman has long since been associated with 'immoral' and 'improper' sexual behaviour. Parker's 'Dickensian' childhood conjures a more wholesome image, since it is traditionally associated with Victorian Britain and therefore associates Parker with a specific set of values which pivot on sexual propriety and hard work. Second, Fishman's anecdote recalling her recent shopping trip with Parker characterizes Parker as a 'responsible consumer'. While it is clear that Parker can afford luxury goods, she carefully considers the value of the item. Thus, both the reference to her 'Dickensian' upbringing and the exchange between Parker and Fishman demonstrate Parker's ability to exercise 'restraint'. This 'restraint' is key in the construction of her star persona, insofar as it signals 'difference' between her and her onscreen persona who, as discussed in Chapter 4, is at times characterized as an 'irresponsible' consumer.

While Blake Lively bears no connection to working-class 'excess', her connection to 'middle-/upper-class' privilege also threatens to associate her with a different, though equally problematic, kind of 'excess'. That is excessive, wasteful consumption typical of the 'nouveaux riches'. Thus, the ability to exercise restraint is also a key feature of Lively's persona. Indeed, it is prominent within a 2010 *Marie Claire* interview, the tagline of which reads: 'It would be easy to cash in on her Gossip Girl fame and style-icon status but Blake Lively is seriously focused on the big picture' (Marcus 2010: 215). During the interview Lively comments upon her choice of film roles and maintains:

'I could probably make more money if I did more commercial projects. It would be nice to buy an apartment but I'm 22 and I don't need to yet . . .' When I say surely she can afford an apartment by now, she lets out a sigh and by way of explanation reminds me, 'I live in New York City. So, . . . I'm able to differentiate between what I want and need.' (Marcus 2010: 217)

Thus, despite her wealth and privilege, Lively displays self-discipline when it comes to her financial affairs. She does not display 'hedonistic excess', rather she possesses the self-control necessary to practice delayed gratification.

Within both of Parker's and Lively's public personae are foregrounded themes of self-discipline and moderation, which serve to police their class identity so that they in turn may effectively police class boundaries and taste dispositions. The final section of this chapter focuses on two particular articles which are indicative of the ways in which Parker and Lively function as tastemakers. Both articles provide a useful lens through which to examine their respective star images and to give a sense of the ways in which the competing discourses surrounding their public personae operate within specific class boundaries.

'Style Is How You Say: "This Is Who I Am Today"': Lifestyle, Class and Taste Dispositions

In July 2011, Blake Lively appeared on the cover of *Glamour* magazine, having recently been named one of *Time*'s 100 most influential people (Luhrmann 2011). This article is worthy of closer attention not simply because it coincides with *Time*'s release, but also because it marks a departure from numerous other interviews.

Firstly, the accompanying feature article is not penned by a journalist; rather it includes an informal interview conducted by musician Florence Welch (Lively's 'new celeb best friend'). Secondly, the article includes a section within which Lively's responses to interview questions are re-appropriated to function as fashion and lifestyle advice for readers. Rather than quoting the interview in full, a separate section entitled 'Outfit Advice for *You*, Straight from Blake' includes various images of Lively at certain events which have been assigned particular comments to serve as 'style advice'. For example, one image of Lively in casual wear is accompanied with the quote, 'That's a vintage medical bag I got in Paris. It's so special. I think you can take something untraditional and make it your staple. What you can't see is my DEFEND NEW ORLEANS shirt. And my tiny puppy! Three of my favourite things right there in that little shot' (Lively in Welch 2011: 102). While the comments may reveal Lively's own (decidedly middle-class) taste disposition, they are not explicitly 'style advice' for readers but are framed to appear as such. This additional feature therefore capitalizes on Lively's status as one of 2011's most influential individuals and secures her position as a cultural intermediary.

The tone of the interview is striking as it is both more informal than other material discussed here, and adopts a more 'confessional' and 'authentic' address; indeed, Lively remarks 'I'm usually shy [during interviews] but having you do it makes it easier' (Lively in Welch 2011: 102). The confessional mode of address is not uncommon within celebrity inter-texts, as it performs a crucial function in maintaining the ordinary/extraordinary paradigm. As Jo Littler (2004) argues, the confessional address is crucial in signalling a celebrity's 'authenticity', an attribute greatly valued in contemporary celebrity culture. This 'authenticity' is signalled using three key motifs. First, the star must demonstrate self-reflexivity about their celebrity status. Second, they must display 'emotional intimacy' with the audience. Finally, they must lay claim to a life before fame (13). Moreover, this discourse of authenticity is also central to the star's performance as a fashion icon. For, as Sean Redmond (2006) observes, it is

> [t]hrough the confessional text [that] the celebrity attempts to speak openly and honestly about where they have come from—their humble beginnings; . . . who they really are underneath their fame gown; and how alike they are to the everyday people who watch their films, buy their records. . . (37)

As previously discussed, Lively, unlike Parker, lacks a convincing 'rags-to-riches' narrative, thus the first two motifs outlined by Littler become the main focus of the *Glamour* interview. For example, when asked to recount her beauty regime before an event, Lively responds:

> I like it to be easy. I don't feel like I have to do so much with hair and makeup, because I'm the mannequin for these beautiful clothes, so I never want to do

anything too distracting. Most of the time, I put my hair in a ballerina bun, and I take it down and it's wavy, and then I leave. I feel shy when people are fussing on me. And my diet of choice before events is a chicken potpie from Tea and Sympathy, because they never have enough food at these things. (Lively in Welch 2011: 102)

Here, we can see both the 'presentation of emotional intimacy' and 'reflexivity about being in the position of a celebrity' at work (Littler 2004: 9). The reader is made privy to Lively's 'behind-the-scenes' fashion practices and rituals, while also being offered privileged 'access' to her emotional responses to the 'celebrity lifestyle'. Yet perhaps the most intriguing remark within this passage, given the notions of 'blankness' and absence of personality such a term conjures, is Lively's reference to herself as a 'mannequin'. This of course is at odds with academic accounts of the symbiotic relationship between fashion and celebrity culture outlined in the introduction to this book, and threatens to derail the magazine's agenda: to present Lively as a cultural intermediary, responsible for imbuing fashion with symbolic value. However, this particular claim is symptomatic of just one of the many competing discourses which circulate within the *Glamour* interview, each of which ultimately serve to confirm Lively's legitimacy as a fashion icon and cultural intermediary.

Lively's remark can be read as self-deprecating and may speak to an apparent dismissal of celebrity culture evident in other extra-textual material reviewed here. Lively denies any 'divine' 'extraordinariness' attributed to her as a star, which is of course, as discussed above, central to the maintenance of a celebrity image. Yet a contradictory discourse, which serves to simultaneously reinforce the star image's 'specialness' and 'talent', also circulates within the *Glamour* article. Consequently, both must constantly jostle for position. In addition, the article also serves to justify Lively's status as fashion icon by offering anecdotal evidence of her knowledge and consumer competences in fashion and beauty practices. Significantly, her access to social and educational capital, accorded her as a result of her class background, allowed her to develop these competences, as the following exchange makes clear:

Welch: What's amazing is that you don't have a stylist, do you?
Lively: You know, my mom modelled and made clothes, so I always had such an appreciation for design. And then *Gossip Girl* completely blew open the door to fashion for me . . . I think I became my own stylist by not knowing any better. And once I was told it was time to get one, I thought: This is one of my favourite hobbies! And I'm going to pay someone to steal my hobby from me? That's a terrible idea! (Welch 2011: 102)

Her 'appreciation' for design or aesthetic disposition thus confirms her position as a fashion icon and allows her to successfully construct her star image through fashion.

Indeed, Lively's image serves to support the postmodern philosophy that through the deployment of fashion 'everyone can be anyone': the accompanying five-page photo shoot quotes Lively as saying, 'Style is how you say: "This is who I am today"' (Lively in Welch 2011: 97). Her assertion implicitly espouses the poststructuralist notion of an unfixed identity that can be made and remade through fashion. However, this comment entirely contradicts a later remark in which Lively downplays fashion's role in the construction of identity: 'I have a strong sense of myself. That gives me a sense of security, you know? If I define myself by things that are always changing, like the public's opinion or what I'm wearing or what job I'm doing there's no stability in that' (Lively in Welch 2011: 102). Thus, these contradictions speak to the tensions which circulate around identity within the so-called postmodern era, which both Lively's and Parker's star personae must negotiate. As with the *Glamour* article, these tensions also structure the extra-textual material surrounding Sarah Jessica Parker and are particularly visible within a 2009 issue of *Harper's Bazaar.*

In the March issue, Sarah Jessica Parker appears on the cover of *Harper's* with an accompanying promotional piece for the launch of her fragrances. The main feature article foregrounds Parker as an advocate for the 'democratization' of fashion and in a very revealing anecdote, Parker promotes the myth that 'everyone can be anyone'. It reads:

> It is fascinating, the fantasy that swirls around Sarah Jessica Parker. Few can resist its pull. Exhibit A: the scene in the MTV documentary on Britney Spears in which Britney is trying on a mini sweaterdress. She and her assistant agree that said outfit is very SJP. '[But] you're Britney Spears,' the assistant says. 'You're not Sarah Jessica Parker.' 'I can be her for a day,' Britney replies. 'I heard about that,' Sarah Jessica says, clearly still computing. 'God bless her. She can be whoever she wants to be for a day. We *all* can!' (L. Brown 2009: 374; emphasis added)

Despite the apparent embracing of the postmodern identity, the anecdote is inescapably bound up with class politics and discourses of respectability. Britney Spears, characterized within contemporary media culture as 'white trash', *aspires* to 'be' Sarah Jessica Parker. Here, Parker symbolizes a notion of respectability, despite the fact that her impoverished roots are well-documented in other celebrity inter-texts. Thus, there is a distinction created between the kind of working-class femininity Spears continues to embody (despite her economic capital) and the kind of respectable, humble working-class identity characterized by Parker. It is crucial that this distinction is maintained in order for Parker to successfully function as a style icon and cultural intermediary for middle-class women, insofar as her cultural capital, and her suitability for the role, could otherwise be called into question. To be sure, it is important to note that Parker demonstrates a loyalty to her working-class roots, which is parlayed into a sense of social responsibility. For example, following directly on from the above passage, Parker comments on her relationship with 'ordinary women'; she claims 'I'm flattered by the connection with women . . . almost everything I do outside of work, I want to do it for them' (Parker in L. Brown 2009: 374). Whilst, as previously discussed, the invocation of an 'impoverished' background is common to many star/celebrity constructions, what I am suggesting here is that Sarah Jessica Parker's image also balances this with a distinctly middle-class mode of address.

In addition, the above passage clearly speaks to more traditional notions of star 'identification' practices. Sarah Jessica Parker's cultural resonance with female fans is magnified here, as the 'fan', in this case, is Britney Spears (a celebrity in her own right). However, despite Parker's claim that Spears 'can be whoever she wants to be', a counter-discourse also circulates which clearly demonstrates the *difference* between Parker and fans. For example, the opening paragraph describes Parker as 'the glamorous everywoman . . . She is someone who, if we had a bigger shoe budget, we *think* we could all be' (L. Brown 2009: 374; emphasis added). As this quote makes clear, fashion allows for a connection to be made between fans and Parker; however, Parker's abundant economic and cultural capital becomes central in maintaining this notion of difference. The accompanying photo shoot—in which Parker pays 'homage' to Diana Vreeland—is a perfect illustration of this difference.

Vreeland, an editor of *Harper's Bazaar* (1936–1962), like Sarah Jessica Parker (SJP), was famously referred to by her initials (DV). A recognized fashion icon, Vreeland fulfilled the function of cultural intermediary in the most traditional sense; she allowed readers 'access' to 'legitimate' culture (primarily haute couture) and sought to teach consumer competences through her famous 'Why Don't You . . .?' column. Within the *Harper's Bazaar*'s feature, Parker recreates famous images of Vreeland—which of course, speaks to her assertion that 'anyone can be anyone for a day'—and pens her own 'Why Don't You . . .?' column.

The sets for the accompanying editorial resemble locations associated with Vreeland; these include her famous red 'garden room', a costume exhibition and the offices of *Harper's Bazaar*.[4] Several of these images thus depict Sarah Jessica Parker undertaking 'intellectual' labour (as a museum consultant or fashion editor), which again requires a specific set of cultural competences in fashion practices and an ability to decide what is, and what is not, 'good taste'. Importantly the final image of Parker at Vreeland's desk in the *Harper*'s office accompanies Parker's 'Why Don't You . . .?' advice column, thereby dispelling any anxieties that Parker is simply *imitating* a 'legitimate' cultural intermediary, rather she is presented as a worthy *successor*; she has the competences to continue Vreeland's project.

The 'Why Don't You . . .?' column is not specifically related to fashion practices but general 'lifestyle' tips. The tagline reads: 'Sarah Jessica Parker shares her tips for a chic and *gracious* life' (L. Brown 2009: 380; emphasis added) and in so doing implicitly acknowledges Parker's appreciation for her (acquired) privilege. For the most part, Parker's advice relates to feminine practices and in some cases seeks to police femininity or femininities. Several of the tips refer to diet, exercise and activities which position the 'self as project' (see Tasker and Negra 2007). For example, she suggests that one should 'walk more', keep a bucket filled with low calorie candy to 'scratch the itch' (i.e. stave off hunger) and 'get eight hours sleep' (Parker in L. Brown 2009: 380). Similarly, she encourages readers to cook and bake from scratch, in order to boost self-confidence. The remaining tips communicate notions of appropriate, 'respectable' middle-class behaviour as it encourages readers to acquire educational and cultural capital and to perform citizenly duties. She suggests that readers give spare change to charities, regularly visit the library and read the editorial page of the local paper, which she believes 'can be terrifically provocative and perhaps a great motivational force for you to get involved in your community, regardless of your political ideology' (380). This passage speaks to Parker's loyalty to her working-class background insofar as the 'tips' above apply to *all* individuals regardless of economic status. Indeed, the 'tips' are designed to encourage self-improvement within both the lower and middle classes through the acquisition of cultural and educational capital. Moreover, this preoccupation with the 'self as project' is bound up with notions of middle-class respectability and speaks to a decidedly feminine audience. Not only then, does the article seek to demonstrate Parker's capital and affirm her status as the bearer of legitimate taste, but also makes an assumption about the readership and fan base of Parker. That is the reader is characterized as female and either middle-class or *aspiring* to achieve social mobility. Thus, it is clear that class discourses continue to pervade contemporary consumer culture and that Parker performs an important role in enforcing and policing class boundaries.

The representations of Sarah Jessica Parker and Blake Lively within extra-textual materials prove a useful lens through which to examine the social significance of their star images. If read in the context of the postmodern assumption that we are moving towards a classless society, it is possible to trace the precise ways in which both star personae are constructed in relation to, and offer a 'solution' for, the problems that this apparent shift may engender. As such, both Parker and Lively are able to reinforce boundaries of 'taste', promoting a decidedly middle-class notion of appropriate feminine identity. While, as previously discussed, the move towards a classless society promises 'individual choice', the consequential emergence of 'lifestyle' media (such as fashion magazines and lifestyle television) has resulted in what David Bell and Joanne Hollows (2005) have termed an 'over-democratization of taste'. For

Bell and Hollows, 'the over-democratization of taste . . . [inevitably leads to] a lifestyled sameness, radically devaluing the cultural capital that has been so carefully cultivated' (12). Thus, we might view Parker's and Lively's function as cultural intermediaries as a response to and corrective of this development.

Both Parker's and Lively's function as cultural intermediaries rely upon on their 'extraordinariness' and personal style to prevent 'sameness' and devaluation of fashion. However, their star images are also used to simultaneously reinforce class boundaries. While both appear committed to the 'fashion-can-be-for-everyone' philosophy, their construction within extra-textual discourses proffers a middle-class mode of address. Both of these discourses must remain in play in order for fashion to have social and cultural meaning. As such, their star personae and the celebrity inter-texts within which they are constructed are informed by complex discourses regarding fashion and social class. As a result, consumers of celebrity culture are cued to develop increasingly sophisticated consumer competences which allow them to read fashion as showcased within programming and celebrity culture. Indeed, the following chapters continue to explore the role of celebrity inter-texts in the education of potential consumers via a diverse range of case studies. In so doing, they examine the ways in which star images serve to reinforce traditional power structures in a supposedly uncertain contemporary climate.

8

CONSUMING MASCULINITY: GENDER, FASHION AND TV CELEBRITY

In her path-breaking study, *Adorned in Dreams*, Elizabeth Wilson (1985: 117) made the now oft-repeated claim that 'fashion is *obsessed* with gender' (emphasis in original). It is one of the most important markers of cultural identity and plays a significant role in the construction and maintenance of gendered difference. That said, the majority of work which explores the relationship between gender and dress has predominantly focused on women's fashion. Several explanations have been offered in an attempt to make sense of the marginalization of menswear. It has been suggested that the field of fashion studies reflects historians' preoccupation with haute couture (which until recently did not include male fashion). In addition, some attribute this lack of critical attention to the development of feminist analyses which seek to examine the 'troubling' role of fashion in the construction of feminine identity. However, recent work on masculinity and consumer culture argues that the lack of research in the area of men's fashions emerges as a result of the assumption that fashion is inherently 'feminine'. This assumption is informed by J.C. Flugel's influential work on the 'great masculine renunciation'. In *The Psychology of Clothes*, Flugel (1930) suggests that men 'renounced' the spectacular fashions of the eighteenth century in favour of a more utilitarian dress. He writes that 'modern man's clothing abounds in features of duty, of renunciation and of self-control' (113). Consequently, it is commonly understood that men are simply 'unfashionable' or 'out of fashion'.

As the previous chapter demonstrates, the examples of fashion programming under discussion in this volume have successfully created contemporary fashion icons out of their leading actresses, but this is not to suggest that male actors do not also assume that role. However, as one might expect, they operate in different ways. Building on recent work which seeks to establish men's place within the study of fashion (Edwards 1997, 2000, 2011; McNeil and Karaminas 2009; Mort 1988, 1996), this chapter considers the construction and mediation of the male fashion icon with reference to two divergent case studies: Adam Brody (*The O.C.*) and Jon Hamm (*Mad Men*). Given that the majority of male fashion icons have traditionally emerged from the more 'masculine' and thus 'legitimate' fields of music, sport or film, as television actors, Brody and Hamm prove useful yet complex case studies, due to their association with a 'feminized' and or 'feminizing' medium.

Despite their apparent differences (in terms of age and audience appeal), both operate as fashion icons in remarkably similar ways. What follows is an examination of extra-textual coverage of the male actors in order to consider the precise ways in which 'idealized' categories of masculinity are constructed and affirmed within traditionally 'feminine' cultural texts (lifestyle and celebrity magazines). Therefore, it is the contention of this chapter, with reference to the above case studies, that Brody and Hamm's connection to the 'feminine' world of fashion is positioned as a problem within their extra-textual circulation— particularly within men's magazines. Consequently, a series of strategies are implemented in order to allow the male fashion icon to negotiate a position within the 'feminine' world of fashion and simultaneously to maintain a hetero-masculine identity. In order to maintain this 'fluid' yet normative identity, the male fashion icons in question must maintain a level of 'subcultural' capital in order to protect the cultural value of their star image. This often involves the apparent rejection of 'feminine' culture.

Approaches to Fashion and Masculinity: The Dandy, the 'New Man' and the Metrosexual

The 1980s is often cited as an important period during which developments within consumer culture and the fashion industry resulted in increasing media and cultural attention to the male body (Connell 1987; Edwards 1997; Mort 1996; Nixon 1996). Often termed the 'new man', a particular incarnation of masculinity emerged which challenged the assumed truth that fashion was an exclusively feminine practice. Writing in the late 1990s, Tim Edwards (1997: 39) suggests that the 'new man arose as a primarily media-driven phenomenon in the 1980s'. Characterized by an interest in fashion and self-presentation, the 'new man' was either interpreted as, at best, 'more caring, nurturing and sensitive' than the 'old man' of the 1970s and, at worst, 'more narcissistic, passive and introspective' (39). In any case, it is thought that the 'new man's' continual appearance in popular media resulted in a greater acceptance of men as consumers of fashion. In particular, Edwards argues that the emergence of men's magazines—which he considers essential in constructing and perpetuating positive images of the 'new man'—contributed to the legitimation of consumer-based masculine identities. This is not to suggest that men were not constructed as consumers before the 1980s. Indeed, it is possible to identify specific 'boom periods' throughout history during which the male has been addressed as a consumer. As Daniel Bell (1976) among others argues, both women and men were affected by the transition to post-industrial society. The shift, Bell argues, destabilized traditional gender roles, and consequently one's sense of identity was no longer exclusively related to occupation but rather was constructed via consumption and fashion practices. That said, well-established prejudices continued to circulate regarding men's relationship to fashion, and those who created identities through the deployment of fashion risked ridicule. This is perhaps most apparent in the treatment of the dandy.

The figure of the dandy, in its various incarnations throughout history, has traditionally been viewed with suspicion. The dandy was considered a problematic individual, not only insofar as his flamboyant attire subverted sexual and gender identities, but also because he blurred class distinctions. In his article, 'The Dandy Laid Bare', Christopher Breward (2000: 237) suggests that the dandy obscures and simultaneously expresses 'tensions between notions of elite and mass taste'. Therefore, the figure of the dandy adopts a 'queer' identity, as defined by Ott and Buckley (2008: 224), in that he promotes 'a concept of the self as performance, improvisational, discontinuous and processually constructed by repetition and stylized acts'. In other words, the dandy refuses definitive categorization and instead shifts to reflect and to provide cultural commentary on masculinity and consumption within a given epoch.

It has been claimed that in the mid-1970s dandies were associated primarily with homosexuality and gay subculture. However, by the late 1970s and early 1980s it is thought that a shift occurred in which dandies became tastemakers for the general population. By the mid-1980s specific garments associated with the modern dandy became the influence for high-end designer menswear (Crane 2000). This later development coincides with a more widespread cultural acceptance of men as consumers, symptomatic of the postfeminist era.

The concept of the 'new man' in its most recent manifestation as the 'metrosexual' is vital to these contemporary attitudes towards masculinity, fashion and consumption and, as this chapter shall demonstrate, is central to the construction and circulation of the male fashion icon. For as Frank Mort (1988: 205) claims, the 'new man' movement encouraged men to take pleasure in practices previously reserved for women and to view themselves (and other men) as objects of 'consumer desire'. This development, Mort adds, opened up a space 'for some new visual codes of masculinity'.

These new visual codes of masculinity resulted in male identity becoming more fragmented and less stable. This is not to suggest that masculinity was ever 'fixed', but rather that the expression of masculine identity through dress allowed men the opportunity to make and remake their own identities to a greater degree. Indeed, there have been claims that the expansion and fragmentation of masculine identities has subverted more dominant cultural norms regarding male sexuality. Therefore, this cultural shift perhaps seeks to celebrate rather than to marginalize the fashion practices of the 'dandy'. However, as recent work on men's lifestyle magazines reveals, a counter to the 'new man' has emerged who, for some, represents a corrective to the 'feminine' masculinity he embodies. The 'new lad' is characterized by his 'ironic' misogyny which some argue ultimately proffers debasing attitudes towards feminine and feminist culture (Benwell 2003; Gill 2003; Whelehan 2000). He symbolizes a return to men's disinterestedness in feminine culture (and by extension fashion), yet paradoxically deploys fashion in order to construct this very identity.

One must not overstate the 'freedom' associated with the expansion of available masculine identities, given that these developments are ultimately determined by the needs of the market. The material surveyed as part of this chapter suggests that while it is possible to observe 'new visual codes of masculinity', these codes operate within certain parameters. Indeed, while the case studies examined here may on the surface seem wholly unconnected and representative of distinct masculine identities, similar strategies are employed to ensure that their performances as fashion icons shore up traditional hegemonic masculinity.

Adam Brody as Sophisticated Poacher

As both Edwards (1997) and Church Gibson (2005) have argued, contemporary standards of male beauty place a premium on youth. Thus, is it perhaps unsurprising that some of the most significant style icons to emerge from fashion programming play teens onscreen (e.g. Brody and his successors Chace Crawford, Ed Westwick and Penn Badgely).

Brody (following his role as Seth Cohen in the teen drama *The O.C.*) is credited with bringing 'Geek Chic' into the 'mainstream'. According to *Entertainment Weekly*'s list of '50 Pop Culture Moments That Rocked Fashion', Brody (positioned at 47) is identified as the 'poster boy for Geek Chic'. His status as a fashion icon has arguably been more consistent than his acting career (he continues to appear in fashion spreads in *GQ* and *Nylon*, despite the fact that so far his onscreen career has peaked with *The O.C.*) and thus suggests that the kind of style icon he embodies continues to fulfil an important function within contemporary fashion communication. Indeed, he has achieved fashion-icon status because he is able to bring youth 'subcultural' styles (typically coded as masculine) into the (feminine) mainstream. It is not, of course, uncommon for subcultural styles to shift into the mainstream; rather, it is almost expected. As Crane (2000) observes in her examination of men's clothing, youth subculture styles are often incorporated into mainstream consumer fashion with the help of a 'sophisticated poacher'. The 'sophisticated poacher', as Crane explains, refers to those men 'who attempt to extend the normative boundaries of acceptable male attire' (173). Brody's star image is crucial to this process of assimilation, as his style (as represented within extra-textual material) 'raids' elements of subculture and brings them into the 'mainstream'.

Significantly, 'Geek Chic' is often associated with a 'lack of style', or a re-appropriation of clothes traditionally considered unfashionable, ultimately with the aim of looking 'overly' studious, intellectual and stylish. As such, this particular style or cultural movement creates a masculine identity which draws from previous understandings of the 'new man' as feminized ('caring and sensitive') while simultaneously couched within 'masculine' youth subcultures. Brody then, occupies a position as a 'sophisticated poacher' insofar as he is able to popularize garments traditionally associated with subculture to a mainstream audience. Brody's ability to traverse the boundary of subculture and mainstream culture is, I argue, connected to his position as a 'teen' star.

Between 2003 and 2007, Brody's star image regularly appeared in teen magazines including *Teen People* (2004), *CosmoGirl* (2007), *Teen Vogue* (2004) and *Elle Girl* (2006), addressing a primarily female audience. Furthermore, in 2006, Brody was the first male ever to appear on the cover of *Elle Girl* magazine. While this particular genre occupies a low cultural status (carrying all the pejorative connotations of 'mass' culture), productive academic studies have identified 'girls'' magazines as a space within which complex cultural struggles regarding identity, femininity and consumerism are played out. In particular, McRobbie's work in the 1980s and 1990s has been especially enlightening in identifying the thematic shifts which have occurred throughout the genre's history. Pertinent to this study is McRobbie's (1991) later work, in which she acknowledges a change in address: she claims that girls' magazines in the 1970s address readers as potential wives and mothers, whereas more recent publications address readers first and foremost as consumers. As such, readers of teen magazines are offered access to a specific set of cultural competences necessary in reading fashion and cultural identities. Indeed, as McRobbie's (1991) study indicates, the teen magazine can be understood as a space in which its readers are encouraged to participate in subcultural practices with regard to style. She argues that rather than a homogenous approach towards 'mainstream' feminine fashions, they display 'a spectacular parade of retro, revivalist subcultures which coexist side by side. Fun elements and a strong emphasis on pastiche can be seen' (179). Therefore, it is clear that teen magazines are a particularly important site in which subculture and mainstream culture coexist. As such, it is precisely because the female teenage reader is constructed as adept in reading fashion practices and subcultural styles that Brody is able to negotiate a position within mainstream culture. A revealing example of this process can be found in the 2004 issue of *Teen Vogue*.[1] This example is worth singling out for particular attention insofar as it demonstrates the ways in which mainstream and subcultural styles intersect, while also making clear the strategies used to secure Brody's hetero-normative identity.

Brody shares the cover of the September 2004 issue (which promises to showcase 'over 250 looks') with former *Gilmore Girls* (2000–2007) co-star Alexis Bledel. The six-page spread includes only two short profiles on each actor; thus the focus is on the fashion shoot with Brody and Bledel modelling 'fall's most charming *date* looks' (Waterman 2004: 170; emphasis added). As such, the article foregrounds Brody's heterosexuality and thereby suggests that, while Brody's image circulates within the predominantly 'feminine' cultural spheres of both fashion and teen media, there is an investment in preserving specific assumptions about his heterosexual masculinity. This is of course nothing new, as McRobbie (1991) notes in her analysis of 1970s teen magazine, *Jackie*: notions of romance and heterosexuality have long since been crucial to the discursive address of the teen magazine. However, given the frequent moral panics which have historically been and continue to be mobilized around sexual immorality and young girls, the heterosexual mode of address must be rendered safe and 'non-threatening'. It is perhaps no coincidence, then, that the shoot employs a conservative 1950s aesthetic in both sets and costuming. The pair appears together in most photographs, in different 'traditional' (and appropriate) date locations, which include a cinema, 1950s style diner and park. Brody's wardrobe is limited to light greys and pastel-colour palettes, which again work to underline his 'feminized' and non-threatening hetero-masculinity. Moreover, pastel colours (previously associated with the figure of the dandy) are incorporated into Brody's 'mainstream' wardrobe—this particular reading of the images is complemented by the use of certain fabrics associated with sartorial extravagance, such as the pale-blue A.P.C. velour blazer. Each photograph is, of course, accompanied by details of designers and prices of the clothes worn, reminding readers that the garments (in addition to the models) are objects to be desired (and consumed). In some cases it is acknowledged that Brody is wearing his own clothes (it is revealed in the 'Cover Look' feature that throughout the shoot, Brody wears his 'trademark . . . Chuck Taylor' Converse shoes), however the designer or make of the garments is still revealed. This information arguably serves a dual purpose. First, it allows audiences a glimpse into Brody's 'real' wardrobe and thereby suggests that he has a natural interest in fashion. This, of course, is crucial insofar as it speaks to notions of authenticity which affirm his 'subcultural' capital. Second, it affirms Brody's apparent 'ownership' over his own image (and his agency), which is integral to his fashion-icon status.

While it could be argued that Brody's role in this photo shoot is no more than an 'accessory' to Bledel—given that her ensembles are often more spectacular and brightly coloured—Brody appears in one photograph alone, as its central focus. This would suggest that Brody's image, and the garments advertised, are of some importance despite the fact that the intended readership is female. Indeed, a female following is crucial to the construction of the male fashion icon. As Edward Buscombe (2000: 201) reminds us in his discussion of classical Hollywood, the male fashion icon must be 'an object of desire for women, a role model for straight men, and either or both for gay men'. Significantly, the two latter aspects are foregrounded within Brody's contemporaneous appearances in men's fashion magazines *Nylon Guys* and *GQ*.

Also in 2004, Brody appeared several times in *GQ* magazine, a publication which emerged specifically as a 'style guide' for men, positioning itself as a high-end magazine (in terms of price and content). *GQ* seeks to educate its target readership—affluent white males—in fashion and lifestyle and is often referred to as 'the magazine for men with an IQ' (cited in Edwards 1997: 80). Thus, it could be argued that *GQ* addresses the 'metrosexual' as defined by Steven Cohan. According to Cohan (2007) the metrosexual represents 'a youngish, upscale, heterosexual male who spends money on his appearance (and so much money on hairstyling, fashionable clothing and skin products) that he is readable as "gay" and too liberal to mind the mistake—but hands off please!' (181). As Cohan's comments make clear, while the metrosexual's interest in fashion and beauty practices aligns him with gay subculture, there is a concurrent discourse which affirms his heterosexuality and 'traditional' (straight) masculinity. *GQ* magazine constructs its readers in relation to these conflicting discourses insofar as it seeks to present fashion and grooming as 'acceptable' practices, while also fiercely reiterating its commitment to maintaining hetero-normative masculine values.

In the October 2004 issue, Brody serves as the focus of an editorial titled 'The Short Suit Steps Out', designed to showcase different styles of men's suits. According to Edwards (2011) the suit is often misunderstood as 'dull' and 'uniform' and too often equated with work, an assumption again buttressed by Flugel's (1930) theory of the 'Great Masculine Renunciation'. In accordance with Hollander (1993) among others, he suggests that the suit can be varied, diverse and sexually appealing. Nevertheless, Crane (2000) suggests that strict rules (imposed in the nineteenth century) continue to govern the appropriate ways in which suits are to be made and worn, compared to similar rules regarding women's hemlines, which, she observes, have disappeared. These rules include shape, collars, lapels, trouser length (and width) and colour range—often restricted to charcoal, navy and black. The fashion spread in *GQ* seeks to present the suit as a garment which has undergone subtle changes in tailoring, and the selection of Brody—as a 'sophisticated poacher'—it would seem is by no means accidental.

An unshaven Brody models Dior, Marc Jacobs, Ennio Capara and Junya Watanabe suits, signalling the difference from both his onscreen character and his 'teen-icon' image. The 'quality' aesthetic of the professional photographs coupled with the luxury items on display connects Brody to an extraordinary glamorous lifestyle associated with stardom proper. Each of these suits departs, in some way, from the more traditional rules of tailoring outlined above. For example in the first image he wears a bottle-green corduroy suit—not only, of course, is corduroy an unlikely material for a traditional 'business' suit, but also the colour deviates from the 'appropriate' muted palate. Similarly, Brody models a Junya Watanabe design which also uses non-traditional colours and material (flecked and distressed wool in crimson, charcoal and pale blue). Moreover, the Japanese fashion designer, renowned for his innovative and distinctive designs (famously displayed as a part of the 'Radical Fashion' exhibition at the Victoria & Albert Museum), abandons those precise specifications which govern proportions of trouser length and width—as the tagline suggests, 'the days of the long, drapey, soft-shouldered NBA style suits are over' (GQ 2004: 323). Thus, this particular shoot concerns itself with the re-appropriation of the suit, which as the article suggests is witnessing a revival of 1960s 'retro' styles. Brody's associations with subcultural style therefore prove useful as these 'innovative' designs are assimilated into the mainstream. His position as a 'sophisticated poacher' and cultural intermediary is exploited once more in the May 2012 issue. He 'stars' in a feature designed to encourage readers to recreate designer looks for less. Both the 2004 and 2012 fashion spreads seek to educate potential consumers in fashion practices, while his image serves to educate consumers on 'individual style'.

In June 2006, Brody appeared on the cover of Nylon Guys magazine, which by its own admission is 'not for girls'. The magazine, launched in 2006 following the success of its sister publication Nylon (launched in 2001), arguably seeks to address a younger male demographic than GQ's targeted readership. Moreover, Nylon Guys primarily focuses on 'culture and fashion' which emerges from the cultural centres New York and London, and arguably aims to present itself as slightly 'edgier' than GQ. The 'ironic' not for girls tagline would suggest that the magazine is attempting to align itself with the so-called new-lad culture, yet, Nylon Guys is clearly symptomatic of developments within the postfeminist consumer culture which encourage men to engage in fashion and grooming practices. That said, this preoccupation with fashion is framed within more 'anti-fashion' attitudes, and as such, Nylon Guys also fosters a relationship with 'subculture' and 'street style'. For example the editor's letter in the June 2006 issue promises 'tons of T-shirts, sneakers, gadgets and other stuff you never knew you wanted' (Jarrett 2006: 12). Indeed, the editor's comments are buttressed by the notion that while developments within consumer culture have resulted in an acceptance of men as consumers of fashion, there is still an underlying concern and hostility towards a society which generates irresponsible consumers (which, as previously discussed, are typically coded as 'feminine'). This speaks to the 'anti-establishment' subcultural views which structure the magazine's discourse (while of course, simultaneously engaging in and reaping the economic benefits of late capitalism).

The magazine is able to affirm its subcultural capital through its content, which according to the cover of the June 2006 issue contains '144 pages of cool sh*t!', 'The World's Top Snow-boarders Chill in Chile' and 'Hot Indie Chicks'. Again, the use of ironic language constructs the magazine as 'smart' and 'edgy', and its reader as 'sophisticated' and 'savvy'. Moreover, the inclusion of 'Hot Indie Chicks' transparently addresses a heterosexual audience. With regard to the construction of Brody's image then, an attempt has been made to contain any gay reading of his identity.

The first of a six-page spread in the magazine taps into this 'ironic' attitude towards new versions of masculinity and lad culture, arguably in an attempt to foreground a distinctly hetero-masculine identity. The tagline reads, 'Drinking? Drumming? Doing Older Women? You Bet Adam Brody is kicking his teen heart-throb image to the curb' (Long 2006: 190). Indeed, as evidenced in the *GQ* article, Brody's association with 'feminine', 'teen' and 'mainstream' culture proves problematic for a magazine which endeavours to position itself as 'alternative'. As such, the photo shoot and interview for *Nylon Guys* seems intent on drawing attention to, and subsequently distancing Brody from, his 'teen-icon' image. Furthermore, the interview and photo shoot seeks to present a more 'authentic' image of Brody than that which circulates in teen media. For example within the interview Brody discusses the *Nylon Guys* photo shoot and remarks on the constructed nature of teen media, claiming: 'I've had to do way too many teen magazines where they're like, "Giggle!" Or "Hold the bunny rabbit!"' (Brody in Long 2006: 190). Brody's disparaging comments work to create a notion of distance between his 'feminized' 'teen' magazine persona and his traditional masculine identity. Moreover, it suggests that he has evolved from his teen persona, adopting a more 'fixed' masculine identity. Indeed, a similar reading can be extracted from his 2011 shoot, which proudly announces Brody's departure from his teen 'heart-throb' past, while simultaneously reminding readers of it (the cover reads: 'Adam Brody is a long way from *The O.C.*' (*Nylon Guys* 2011)). The six-page editorial foregrounds casual designer clothing (hooded sweatshirts, button-down shirts, hand-woven cardigans and vintage T-shirts) against the backdrop of a bohemian apartment (littered with musical instruments and vinyl records). Thus, the more mature star persona constructed within *Nylon Guys* continues to pivot on a connection to 'subcultural' style that serves as the 'connective tissue' between Brody and his fans; of course, the primary function of subcultural style is to demonstrate ones allegiance to a particular group of 'likeminded' individuals. Therefore, his investment in subculture arguably seeks to strengthen the bonds between his star image and 'subcultural' fan community.

'Style Icon by Default': Jon Hamm

Though Jon Hamm has no obvious connections to youth subcultures, both his and Brody's star images (and positions as fashion icons) function in somewhat similar ways. Certain strategies employed within the print media, which contribute to the construction of Hamm's image, serve to ensure that his hetero-normative masculine identity is not in any way problematized by a connection to the 'feminine', and thereby 'trivial', sphere of 'mainstream' fashion. There are, however, obvious distinctions between Brody and Hamm which have implications for the way in which Hamm's star image operates within celebrity inter-texts. Hamm, although only eight years Brody's senior, occupies a very different space within celebrity culture. Arguably, this has to do with finding fame later in his career—in 'quality' programming no less, which ensures numerous comparisons with George Clooney. Hamm's 'claim-to-fame' narrative according to numerous print media accounts is a crucial part of his media representation and his function as a style icon.

Moving to Los Angeles in his mid-twenties, he waited on tables while taking small roles in various procedurals and network pilots (the first credit on his IMDB page is 'Gorgeous Guy in Bar' in *Ally McBeal* in 1997), before finding success ten years later (at the age of thirty-six) in AMC's *Mad Men*. Hamm attributes his initial lack of success to Hollywood's attitudes towards aging (and the way in which age is imagined). The fact that at twenty-five he looked forty (in comparison, Brody at twenty-five was playing a sixteen-year-old) proved problematic in a town which, to use his words 'not only celebrates but insists on the cult of eternal youth' (Hamm in Horkins 2012: 174). Nevertheless, as both Clooney's and Hamm's visibility within Hollywood attests, there is certainly a place for middle-aged men and the kind of masculinity they perform, within popular culture and the fashion industry.

The masculinity embodied by George Clooney and Jon Hamm is predicated upon a nostalgic longing for a mythical 'old Hollywood'. This is perhaps even more potent within Hamm's star persona, which is informed by his role in *Mad Men* (a period piece) and which is continually evoked in fashion shoots (see Figure 9). For example in a 2008 issue of *Vogue*, Hamm appears in an eight-page fashion editorial entitled 'Coastal Blend', which is keen to capitalize on his televisual persona. The prologue reads: 'On a glamorous getaway to L.A. actor Jon Hamm plays leading man opposite model Catherine McNeil, who wears a retro Hollywood worthy mix of rich, Technicolor, graphic prints, and bold bijoux' (*US Vogue* 2008: 290). The explicit references to 'retro Hollywood' provide a frame within which to view the accompanying images of Hamm. Adopting a 'Don Draper-esque "Brylcreemed"' hairstyle, Hamm models different styles of men's suits (from a formal white tuxedo to a casual sports jacket) against various locations which have a connection to classical Hollywood cinema, either in reality or in public imagination). For example part of the shoot is set at the Santa Anita race track in California, where *A Day at the Races* (1937) and *The Story of Seabiscuit* (1949) were filmed, while other backdrops tap into a mythological Hollywood—a two-page spread includes Hamm driving a red convertible 'classic' car on a clear stretch of road (incidentally, the classic car is a recurrent piece of iconography across a number of the shoots). Consequently, each locale provides a suitable backdrop for Hamm's image as 'suited hero'.

In her analysis of male costuming in contemporary Hollywood (previously discussed in Chapter 6), Church Gibson (2005) identifies George Clooney as the archetypal 'suited hero', which she reminds us 'harks back to an earlier era in the history of Hollywood' (66). The suited hero, though often fully clothed (unlike his onscreen counterpart—the 'rough-and-ready' man), functions as an object of desire, with the suit serving as a sartorial reminder of the naked body that lies underneath—and its sexual potency. This connection is made explicitly within a *Vanity Fair* (Handy 2009) shoot, in one of the rare occasions in which Hamm is bare-chested. He appears alongside onscreen wife January Jones, and while she remains fully clothed throughout, he appears at various stages of undress; in one image he is wearing an open-collared suit shirt and trousers, while in another two he appears shirtless. The naked, muscular back is on display while his grey trousers conceal his lower body, prompting the audience to make the connection between suit and sexuality. January Jones does not appear in this image—thus Hamm is presented as fetishistic spectacle—but serves to remind us of the shoot's prescribed (hetero)sexual gaze.

Figure 9 Jon Hamm as Don Draper: Hamm's onscreen performance of the 'suited hero' is established in the pilot episode and informs his extra-textual persona: *Mad Men* Season 1, Episode 1: 'Smoke Gets in Your Eyes', AMC, USA (2007).

Within the *Vogue* 2008 shoot, Jon Hamm is again partnered with an attractive female model—the considerably younger Catherine McNeil—who serves as the stereotypical 'trophy wife' of the successful 'corporate' male. The composition of the images foregrounds Hamm's (sexual) dominance—he is repeatedly positioned in front of McNeil—and in three of the five images Hamm confronts the camera's gaze while McNeil gazes longingly at him. If one were unsure how to respond to Hamm's presence within the shoot, the single-page profile included earlier in the magazine does its utmost to secure a preferred reading of his star image with sledgehammer-like subtlety. Journalist John Powers (2008) assures readers of Hamm's desirability, as he writes:

> *Mad Men* has made it obvious that this six-foot-two actor looks great in a gray vintage suit. But on the day we meet for lunch in Culver City . . . he's every bit as dashing in a Paul Smith blue pinstripe he bought off the rack. With his sturdy jaw and dark, watchful eyes, Hamm exudes an old-fashioned virility. (136)

Thus, the connection with 'old' Hollywood glamour serves as a reminder of Hamm's sexual prowess and unwavering heterosexuality. His position as a fashion icon and sex symbol is not hampered by his performance of middle age, rather it is enhanced by it. The same, as many others have noted, is not typically the case for female celebrities—only those who actively (and successfully) engage in processes to delay the physical manifestations of aging are celebrated (McCabe and Jermyn 2011). In addition, Jon Hamm's fashion-icon status is also, somewhat paradoxically, informed by an apparent disinterestedness in fashion without being 'unfashionable'. Thus, as with Adam Brody, the construction of Hamm's star image is buttressed by anti-fashion rhetoric—but importantly not subculture (in the traditional sense of the term). To clarify, it is perhaps useful at this stage to look to the work of Ted Polhemus and Lynn Procter (1978), which offers a comprehensive account of the term. For Polhemus and Procter, there is an important distinction to be made between unfashionable and anti-fashion. They write:

> With the exception of the unfashionable (those who can't keep up with fashion change but would like to), 'anti-fashion' refers to all styles of adornment which fall outside the organized systems of fashion change. The Royal Family, at least in public, wears anti-fashion . . . Hell's Angels, hippies, punks and priests wear anti-fashion . . . in no case is their dress or adornment caught up in the mechanism of fashion change, neither do they want it to be. (34–5)

Working from this definition it is clear that 'anti-fashion', as with subculture more generally, is connected to 'masculine' practices of resistance. Thus, it is possible to map a gendered distinction onto these definitions. Anti-fashion refers to those individuals who, for various (political) reasons, actively ignore seasonal trends and change. Indeed, Flugel's (1930) 'great masculine renunciation' is presented as an active decision not to participate in fashion—it is by its very nature anti-fashion, not unfashionable. The category of 'unfashionable', on the other hand, refers to those who wish to participate in fashion but are, for various reasons, excluded. It is often claimed that 'aging women' fall into this latter category (Church Gibson 2005), while Hamm's star image relies upon an association with the former, which paradoxically serves to secure his status as male fashion icon.

Jon Hamm as the suited hero is arguably the most dominant image within public consciousness (and perhaps that which has most currency in contemporary culture), yet it is not the only image of Hamm circulating. Significantly within men's magazines, there is an attempt to move away from this groomed persona towards a more 'unkempt' image. In *Esquire*, journalist Alex Bilmes refers to Hamm as the 'style icon by default' ('The square-jawed star of *Mad Men* has become a men's style icon by default and the embodiment of retro masculinity by mistake' (Bilmes 2012: 105)), meaning that there is no intention on Hamm's part to court this attention—it is effortless. The *Esquire* article then presents itself almost as a corrective—exposing a side of Hamm's public persona which is indifferent and unconcerned with the 'frivolousness' of fashion and celebrity culture, as the following passage makes clear:

> 'It's ephemeral', he says of his fame, 'and it's subject to the whims of others. There's a lot of talk about, "Oooh, you're so sexy!" If people put that mantle on you, fine but you take it with a wink and a pinch of salt. At 41 I'm like, give me a break, man, I'm not Ryan Gosling. And that's fine. I don't aspire to be that. That's not my jam.' (Hamm in Bilmes 2012: 110)

This is not to suggest that this particular facet of Jon Hamm's public persona is absent from women's magazines. Indeed, his dismissal of celebrity and consumer culture is widely observed. In a candid interview in *Elle* magazine, Hamm remarks: 'We're at a place where the idea of being "elite" is considered a negative . . . Whether it's Paris Hilton or Kim Kardashian or whoever, stupidity is certainly celebrated. Being a f***ing idiot is a valuable commodity in this culture because you're rewarded significantly' (Hamm in Horkins 2012: 176). He thereby suggests that fame, and the trappings which accompany it (i.e. luxury goods) are without value. Yet, there is, of course, a disconnect between Hamm's polemical comments and the widely circulated images in which he serves as a fashion model. Within *Esquire*, the accompanying shoot, though a departure from his 'suited hero' persona, is designed to promote a range of casual menswear. In addition, his very presence in the magazine reminds us that he is participating in those mechanisms implemented to ensure the sustaining of celebrity culture. Thus, certain strategies are employed in order to explain away this paradox.

In their comprehensive study of men's magazines, Peter Jackson, Nick Stevenson and Kate Brooks (2001: 104) argue that irony is often employed within men's (or rather 'lad's') magazines as a form of 'ideological defence against external attack'. Though they refer to the use of irony as a defence against readings of men's magazines as anti-women (those who extract such a reading are merely failing to 'get the joke'), it is applicable in this situation also. The article in *Esquire* is quick to establish a 'knowing' tone insofar as it acknowledges its role in creating the 'hoopla' surrounding Jon Hamm's onscreen persona. In the first paragraph, Bilmes (2012: 106) suggests that this hoopla is 'created and sustained, it has to be admitted, in large by magazines not unlike this one'. This first omission perhaps is designed to make the next contradiction more palatable as it admits that '[t]he image of a character created to illustrate the vacuity and amorality of consumerism is now itself used to shift product' (106). It is not only the use of irony in linguistic tropes but also the accompanying visuals. Hamm appears in casual clothing (a Ben Sherman polo shirt, Tommy Hilfiger chinos and Converse trainers) in less than glamorous locations (i.e. sprawled on a picnic bench, at a 'greasy spoon' café (in which Hamm is captured tearing into a cheeseburger and drinking hot sauce from the bottle)). In addition, he appears once again in a classic convertible, this time awkwardly lying across the passenger's seat with his feet above the steering wheel, confronting the camera with arched eyebrows. Needless to say, the shoot provides a stark contrast to the well-groomed *Vogue* images, and perhaps intentionally so. The images function, in one sense, as a commentary on the constructed nature of Hamm's 'smooth' image by deliberately including images of Hamm in disarray. Here, Hamm is far removed from his 'smooth' image and more closely resembles the 'rough-and-ready' archetype defined by Church Gibson (2005). This, I would argue, is by no means accidental. Rather, it provides a necessary counterbalance in order to protect the cultural value of Hamm's star image and the kind of heteronormative masculinity he embodies. In other words, Hamm strategically oscillates between the two categories of masculinity in order to maintain his fashion icon status and escape any connection to the 'feminine'. He functions as a desirable style icon precisely because he maintains a hegemonic masculine identity, but this identity is only available to him because he actively displays an indifference towards the 'feminine' pursuit of fashion.

Men's magazines foster a complex relationship to mainstream consumer culture. While of course they are 'mass' cultural objects, they reject the feminine connotations associated with 'mass culture', and redefine their own relationship with the world of fashion and grooming practices as masculine. As such, these texts 'raid' and re-appropriate feminine culture in order to make it 'legitimate'. It is precisely within this liminal space that the male fashion icon must negotiate a position. Adam Brody's star persona, which can be both 'masculine' and 'feminine' and 'subculture' and 'mainstream', functions as a cultural intermediary in the more traditional sense insofar as his competences in fashion are explicitly acknowledged but legitimized as they are couched within discourses of subculture. In contrast, Hamm's public persona relies upon a constructed dismissal of fashion. He simultaneously rejects and participates in fashion, in order to maintain a hegemonic masculine identity. He is not explicitly positioned as 'expert' or 'sophisticated poacher', rather it is his 'effortlessness' and 'natural' style which secure his position as a fashion icon.

The fashion and celebrity inter-texts examined here arguably seek to address a readership with cultural competences in fashion practices, who are able to read these articulations of identity. Indeed, what is particularly interesting with regard to both Adam Brody's and Jon Hamm's extra-textual representations is that they are used to not only promote the use of fashion as a marker of identity but also seek to demonstrate the artifice and performativity of fashion, and indeed their own public personas. In so doing, both serve important roles in (re)defining fashion's relationship to (hetero-normative) masculinity.

9

LOCATING THE REAL: AMERICA FERRERA, FASHION, ETHNICITY AND AUTHENTICITY

There was Rachel in *Friends*, there was Carrie in *SATC*, then there was *Ugly Betty*.

—*Marie Claire* 2007: 183

'America Ferrera, star of *Ugly Betty*, is climbing Hollywood's A-list—and she's ignoring the unwritten rule that says stars must be blond and Twizzler-thin.' So wrote *Glamour* journalist Laurie Sandell in the inaugural 'Figure-Flattery' special issue (Sandell 2007: 289). Sandell's quote typifies the discursive activity surrounding Ferrera and her celebrity body. To be sure, the female star's body has long since been subject to scrutiny within celebrity texts. Moreover, this takes place within a wider representational context in which, as Su Holmes and Sean Redmond (2006: 123) have argued, 'the celebrity self is to be prodded, probed and exposed in such a way that revels in the *processes of corporeal fabrication*, rather than the finished product itself' (emphasis in original).

While at the time of writing America Ferrera's visibility has dwindled, she nevertheless remains an important figure at the intersection of celebrity and fashion communication. Indeed, her lack of visibility is in itself important as it suggests that the ethnic female star is not permitted the 'longevity' of the white female star. Moreover, one could also make a case that Ferrera's (comparatively) short-lived fame served only to fulfil a particular function within a particular historical moment. For these reasons, her star image (and body) is treated differently from her peers.

Rather than revelling in the '*processes of corporeal fabrication*', representations of America Ferrera's star body actually 'mystify' (while seeking to appear to 'demystify') these processes. In other words, celebrity inter-texts seek to 'naturalize'—as opposed to 'denaturalize'—Ferrera's star body and in so doing wilfully neglect to acknowledge their positions as cultural constructs. This agenda awkwardly exists alongside that of the fashion industry, which seeks to promote the performative pleasures of fashion. Thus, the construction of Ferrera's star persona (and its focus on the star's corporeal self) is structured by two conflicting discourses related to fashion, identity and ethnicity. That is while Ferrera's star image is used to dramatize essentialist (albeit contradictory) ideologies regarding Latina ethnicity (as simultaneously 'authentic', 'exotic', 'dangerous' and 'excessive'), it also draws attention to the performative nature of fashion and its ability to obscure cultural identities.

'*Real* Celebrities Have Curves': Star Bodies, Ethnicity and Authenticity

In his book *Celebrity and Power: Fame in Contemporary Culture*, P. David Marshall (1997/2004: 266) argues that '[t]he intense focus on the body and its reformulation is central to the construction of the female star'. While it is often thought that the proliferation of celebrity magazines and blogs has intensified the constant scrutiny of the female star's body, the phenomenon itself is not new. Indeed, in Kathy Davis's (2006) article 'Beauty and the Female Body', it is clear that the current preoccupation with the female star body is informed by historical discourses surrounding the beautiful woman as 'muse'. Moreover, scholarship examining early and classical Hollywood stardom reveals that historically the female body has been central to the economic and symbolic value of the star. As such, initial academic inquiries into the function of star images are informed, to varying degrees, by Mulvey's (1975/1989) influential theory of the 'gaze'. This is not to suggest, however, that the female star body was relegated to function exclusively as an object of desire, for as Dyer (1986) demonstrates with regard to Marilyn Monroe, the body was also inscribed with multiple (and often disparate) meanings that worked to affirm dominant ideologies regarding gender, sexuality and 'race'. Indeed, it was precisely because the body was so important with regard to the female star that it became central to the ideological meanings that were conveyed.

Academic work with a specific focus on the ethnic female star and her representation within American media addresses this phenomenon. For example Diane Negra's (2001) *Off White Hollywood: American Culture and Ethnic Female Stardom* explores the cultural functions of ethnic female stars, in particular the way in which they 'delight and trouble the national imagination' (3). She argues that rather than functioning as a mere stereotype, the ethnic female star operates in complex and varied ways. While Negra's study focuses specifically on the ethnicity of white European American actresses, work on Latina representation in onscreen media acknowledges an equally ambivalent relationship between Hollywood and the Latina star (see Beltran 2009; Lopez 1991; Valdivia 2000).

The work cited above demonstrates the centrality of the Latina star body to its cultural and economic worth. In particular, both Valdivia (2004) and Beltran (2007) propose that the Latina star's body (as represented in Hollywood) is 'ambiguous', and as Valdivia (2004) notes, Latina stars' bodies can therefore appeal to whiteness, 'but they can also represent generalized otherness as well as more specific stereotypical Latinidad and a range of other ethnicities'. For example Beltran (2007) suggests that Jennifer Lopez's 'mainstream fame' is due to the fact that her racially 'ambiguous' and highly visible body allows her to play a range of ethnic identities in contemporary cinema. Valdivia (2004) makes a similar case for Jessica Alba: 'Since graduating from Disney, she has played the hybrid, ambiguous, and post-apocalyptic *Dark Angel* as well as African American hip hop queen in the feature length *Honey*'. This 'ambiguity', Valdivia argues, is due to the construction of the Latina identity as more mobile than other racial identities. She writes, 'Latinas as a constructed category gain meaning by virtue of their supposed location as an in between ethnicity, not white yet not black'.

Despite this ambiguity, the Latina star has been and continues to be associated with essentialist ideals of 'ethnic meaning' as characterized by Negra (2001: 138). She argues that the contemporary celebrity invokes fantasies of 'ethnic meaning' which can be divided into four categories. These are, 'Ethnicity as excess', 'Ethnicity as the sign of sincerity and/or authenticity', 'Ethnicity as a restorative response to the evacuation of contemporary culture' and finally 'Ethnicity as individual empowerment' (138). Indeed, several of these categories intersect with broader narratives of fame examined within stardom and celebrity studies. For example Gamson (1994) notes that notions of 'authenticity' are central to audience and star identification practices both historically and in the contemporary period. Thus, Negra (2001: 147) suggests that in some cases ethnicity can serve as a 'code for authenticity'. Similarly, as discussed in Chapter 7, while Dyer (1979/2004) asserts that the star image has long been used to 'reinforce values under threat', Negra (2001: 138) claims that the ethnic star functions as 'a restorative response to the evacuation of contemporary culture'. So in this regard, Negra argues that the ethnic star functions as a response to the apparent 'homogenization of American culture . . . [as a] method of claiming difference' (154). These competing discourses on ethnicity jostle for position, and can be located within the representations of America Ferrera's star image.

The intense focus on Ferrera's star body, both onscreen and offscreen, has contributed to the construction of her star persona and its symbolic value in contemporary consumer culture. Her first role in the independent 'coming-of-age' film *Real Women Have Curves* (2002), subsequent roles in *The Sisterhood of the Travelling Pants* films (2005 and 2008), *and Ugly Betty* not only foreground Ferrera's 'excessive' body within the narrative but also are key in structuring discourses surrounding the extra-textual circulation of her image. As first-generation Mexican American teenager Ana Garcia in *Real Women Have Curves*, Ferrera's 'Latina' body is positioned as a site of ideological struggle. Within the narrative, Garcia struggles to consolidate her family's wishes for her to become a seamstress and to start a family with her own desire to study at a university. This narrative is played out through a series of exchanges between Garcia and her mother which constantly refer to Ferrera's physicality—thereby binding notions of ethnicity and fantasies of assimilation directly to her 'curvy' body. In the role of Betty Suarez in *Ugly Betty* (see Chapter 4), Ferrera's ethnic body is also of narrative importance. Betty's position as 'Latina' in the fashion industry (which privileges extreme versions of Western ideals of beauty: typically white, thin bodies) exaggerates and ridicules ignorant attitudes towards racial 'otherness' in contemporary culture. As such, Ferrera's onscreen roles inform her public persona as her star body is presented as a representational tool, used to promote specific notions of ethnic femininity and assimilation in contemporary society.

'God Bless America': The American Dream and Narratives of Ethnic Stardom

As with Sarah Jessica Parker, America Ferrera's stardom is framed within a version of the success myth (see Dyer 1979/2004). However, unlike Parker, Ferrera's Latina identity is crucial to the ways in which her rise to stardom is narrativized within media discourses. For example during the promotion of *The Sisterhood of the Travelling Pants*, Ferrera and her co-stars Amber Tamblyn, Alexis Bledel and Blake Lively appeared on US talk show *The View*. Within the narrative, Ferrera's character is positioned as the antithesis of Bridget Vreeland (played by Lively)—indeed their difference is reinforced by the composition of Figure 10; however, this difference is also underlined in extra-textual discourse. During the interview Lively is asked to discuss her route into acting. In response, she recalls how her brother (actor Eric Lively) decided, on her behalf, that she would enjoy acting and 'pressured his agents' into calling her. She then reveals that she auditioned for a 'couple of months'—often cancelling auditions as she 'didn't realize what a big deal it was'—before accepting the role of Vreeland in the film.[1] As previously discussed, Lively's fame can therefore be characterized, in Rojek's (2001) terms, as 'ascribed' as opposed to 'achieved'.[2] It is through the image of the 'famous family' or 'dynasty' that Lively's fame is situated. In this televised interview she gives no indication of any difficulties she faced, rather her fame seems somewhat 'accidental'. In stark contrast, when Ferrera is asked to comment on her decision to pursue an acting career, she reveals a distinctly different experience:

> I was always a really good student and [my mother] wanted me to go to Harvard, go to Yale. She came here from Honduras mainly for us to get an education and so when I said I wanted to be an actress it was not in her plans. [S]he wasn't going to stop me but she said 'if this is something you wanna do . . . you're going to have to work for this'. So I would waitress and then get the bus to school . . . I think it was good for me. Really, really good for me.[3]

The above passage immediately demonstrates the more traditional narratives of fame and how, in America Ferrera's case, they intersect with dominant ideologies of ethnicity and class. First, it is important to note how, in contrast to Lively, Ferrera's fame can be categorized as 'achieved' (Rojek 2001). This is reflected in the question posed by Meredith Vieira, the original host of *The View*, (she stresses the word 'work') and again in Ferrera's answer, which expresses a strong work ethic (she claims not only to be an intelligent and hardworking student, but also is willing to undertake additional low-paid work in order to facilitate her dream). Ferrera is therefore characterized as the antithesis of Lively, not only in corporeal terms (as Lively is 5 ft 10 in (1.78 m), thin, white and blonde), but also in the ways in which they have achieved their celebrity status.[4] Second, it should be noted that Ferrera's 'Latina' identity is presented as central to this work ethic: she explicitly reminds viewers of her Honduran roots, which signify poverty in this context (she explains that she is one of six children, and as such her single mother was unable to drive her to auditions). Moreover, the passage above perfectly articulates a version of the American dream which is reliant on 'overcoming' ethnicity. Of course, notions of assimilation are conjured by her forename alone, but in addition Ferrera recalls how her mother moved her children to the United States as it promised a better education (and life). These narratives are not uncommon within ethnic female stardom, for as Negra (2001: 3) notes, 'As female embodiments of national fantasies, ethnic female film stars have symbolized the promise of American pluralism and proved the desirability and reliability of the American Dream (sometimes in triumphant success narratives, sometimes in negative object lessons).' As the above exchange makes clear, Ferrera demonstrates the 'desirability and reliability' of the American dream insofar as she describes how she '*really, really* wanted it' (my emphasis). Moreover, her anecdote also illustrates the 'value' of having to work for success ('I think it was good for me. Really, really good for me'). Here, Ferrera affirms her 'strong sense of self' and demonstrates how her ethnicity (and implied struggles) allowed her to achieve 'individual empowerment'.

This trope resonates in another interview with America Ferrera in fashion magazine *Marie Claire*. In the December 2007 issue, Ferrera appears on the

Figure 10 Blake Lively and America Ferrera: The composition of the shot and the use of costume serve to reinforce the difference between the characters (but also the star images): *Sisterhood of the Travelling Pants*, Ken Kwapis (Director), Debra Martin Chase (Producer), Warner, USA (2005).

cover next to the tagline: 'America Ferrera, Living the dream thanks to *Ugly Betty*'. As with *The View* interview, Ferrera's explanation of fame once again relies upon the 'success myth'—on this occasion the magazine's rhetoric explicitly references the American dream. Moreover, the article titled 'God Bless America' foregrounds Ferrera's position as a role model. Beside the title, the tagline reads: 'A Cinderella life story and a genuine antidote to Hollywood's size-zero culture, *Ugly Betty*'s America Ferrera is the reluctant role model who rewrote the rule book, both on screen and off screen' (Keeps 2007: 138). As this comment makes clear, the Cinderella motif (which as discussed in previous chapters is an incarnation of the success myth) is employed here to articulate the precise nature of Ferrera's fame. Moreover, the comment suggests that her position as a 'role model' is tied to her body. This is perhaps best evidenced by Ferrera's remarks upon the 'size-zero' culture. She claims that '[t]he tragedy about this whole image-obsessed society is that young girls get so caught up in it, they forget to realize how much more they have to offer the world' (Ferrera in Keeps 2007: 140). Inherent within Ferrera's comment is the notion that the 'image-obsessed society' is both 'trivial', and potentially 'dangerous'. This, of course, is at variance with Ferrera's fashion icon status assigned to her by the magazine. However, as I shall demonstrate, part of Ferrera's function as a fashion icon and cultural intermediary is precisely to promote a 'responsible', 'positive' understanding of fashion and its relationship to female identity (and the body).

It is important to note that this issue of *Marie Claire* is committed to promoting more 'positive' understandings of fashion—this is suggested in the publication's tagline or mission statement, titled 'Fashion with Heart'. Next to the editor's letter, which in itself boasts a commitment to 'ethical consumerism, eco trends and corporate responsibility . . . while maintaining our style cred [sic] (looking good is non-negotiable)' (O'Riordan 2007a: 15), the 'Fashion with Heart' mission statement reveals that *Marie Claire* seeks to 'publish stories that inspire our readers to make responsible consumer choices' and to '[r]aise awareness of inspirational women whose voices aren't otherwise heard' (O'Riordan 2007b: 15). Within this final agenda item, there is the implication that this includes, even if it does not explicitly refer to, women of colour. As such, America Ferrera becomes a spokesperson for 'The Fashion with Heart' campaign, and as her comments above make clear, she expresses an interest in promoting responsible consumption and fashion practices. Indeed, this is, as demonstrated in previous chapters, also central to the construction of Sarah Jessica Parker's star image and position as a fashion icon. In order to qualify Ferrera for this role, the article foregrounds her own 'individual empowerment', and sense of self. The article reads: 'Blessed with a strong sense of herself and an admirable set of boundaries, Ferrera is in no danger of becoming the next young Hollywood bad girl' (Keeps 2007: 141–3). In many ways her Latina identity 'immunizes' her against the supposed 'epidemic' of 'bad girls' which, as Su Holmes and Diane Negra (2011) suggest, are typically white and working-class. Ferrera is therefore defined against the female 'white trash' type currently pervading celebrity culture.

Ferrera's 'strong sense of self' (foregrounded in celebrity inter-texts) can be read as a response to contemporary concerns that identity is apparently becoming increasingly fragmented and unstable (as outlined in Chapter 7). Moreover, Ferrera's sense of self is 'achieved' and reliant upon the essentialist ideal of the ethnic identity as 'sincere' and 'authentic'. Within the *Marie Claire* interview, Ferrera recalls her childhood struggles, and as in the talk show appearance discussed above, she recalls the additional problems that arose precisely because of her cultural identity. For example she claims that, as a child, she realized that '[n]obody cares who I am in this world. I could just be another pregnant teen or another druggie, and it's not going to affect anyone but me, I would sit on that bus and think, "That's not going to be me. I'm going to do something with my life"' (Ferrera in Keeps 2007: 144). Here, Ferrera calls upon some of the negative stereotypes of Latinas (that they are both 'hypersexual' and 'morally ambiguous') which resonate with the white cultural imagination, and positions herself in opposition to them. Moreover, in the *Marie Claire* interview she explicitly recalls her living conditions as a child:

There was never very much to go around . . . Within a mile or two there were very, very low-income flats. Another quarter of a mile away, you had fancy lawyers' houses in gated communities. The kids I grew up with had BMWs when they were 15. It was weird moving in-between these circles of people, because I didn't really fit in anywhere. (Ferrera in Keeps 2007: 143)

If the connection between ethnicity and identity were not explicit enough, journalist David A. Keeps then affirms how this sense of exclusion is a consequence of her ethnicity as he writes: 'This was as much cultural as it was social' (143). Moreover, the article continues with Ferrera remarking on her Honduran roots. She asserts:

> I mean, sure, we ate beans and rice, but we also had pizza and burgers, so I don't know what part of my upbringing is authentically Honduran and what isn't. It's crazy—I have never even stepped foot on Honduran soil but, somehow, it is a huge part of who I am. (Ferrera in Keeps 2007: 143)

The above passage perfectly demonstrates the conflicting ideologies which inform perceptions of Latina identity. In her article, 'Ethnicities-in-Relation: Toward a Multicultural Reading of American Cinema', Ella Shohat (1991) challenges the assumption that ethnic identity is stable and unchanging. She argues that onscreen representations of ethnicities often rely upon 'textual context' in order to have meaning. For Shohat, '[e]thnicity does not constitute a fixed entity or category expressing a natural, essential difference, but rather a changing set of historically diverse experiences situated within power relations' (216). Indeed, Ferrera's comments above point to this contradiction or ambiguity regarding the Latina identity. In some ways, she perpetuates the essentialist assumption that the Latina identity has a fixed meaning, insofar as she posits that it is 'a huge part' of who she is, yet she is unable to articulate precisely what that meaning is (beyond an association with cuisine), and how it intersects with and constructs her identity. Nevertheless, she suggests that her ethnicity is somehow intrinsic, fixed and 'authentic', and seamlessly integrated into an American identity (which significantly, is also articulated through cuisine). This discourse is affirmed in a 2009 issue of *Elle* magazine. In a feature titled 'The Mentalists', which profiles twelve inspirational women, Ferrera achieved the top position 'because she made ugly the new badass' (Rosenblit 2009: 228). In the accompanying interview, Ferrera talks candidly about her ethnicity and the opportunities for Latina actresses in Hollywood. She recalls:

> When I was 17, this script I loved called for a blond girl with blue eyes. The director said, 'I think you're great, but this isn't the right thing.' So I decided, half joking and half not, to bleach my hair blonde . . . and put white powder on my face. And I put myself on tape and sent it to him. He called me, laughing, like thank you for this, but you still don't have the part. I was devastated because it was the first time I felt I wasn't given the chance to fail on my own . . . I destroyed my hair for nothing. (Ferrera in Rosenblit 2009: 229)

The above passage speaks to the pressures of the 'image-obsessed' culture discussed above and serves as a 'cautionary tale'. Here, Ferrera discourages readers from transforming their identity in order to conform to an ideal and in so doing, acknowledges the mutability of identity, while ultimately privileging a 'fixed' notion of the self.

'Ugly Betty is *HOT*!': Makeover Narratives and the 'Self as Project'

It is perhaps unsurprising that America Ferrera appears on the cover of *Glamour*'s '1st Annual Figure-Flattery' issue.[5] The image of Ferrera in a bespoke violet Versace gown is surrounded by a series of headlines related to the 'improvement' of the female body. These include: 'How any body can be a bombshell', '101 ways to dress your body better: clothes, lingerie and pro tricks to transform you' and '[t]he secret reason women gain weight and how to stop'. For the sceptical reader, these headlines might be dismissed as yet another example of the media encouraging women to conform to an (unattainable) ideal; thus we might view the use of Ferrera as the cover girl as a deliberate attempt to contain such an 'oppositional' reading. Ferrera's position as a responsible fashion icon suggests that self-surveillance and 'improvement' of the self through the fashion and beauty practices can be both pleasurable and in some way 'empowering'. Indeed, Ferrera's corporeal and ethnic difference suggests that the magazine is seeking to offer a sense of diversity. Rather than promoting a homogenous understanding of femininity, the headlines above address the readers as 'individuals' (there is an emphasis on 'how *any* body can be a bombshell', '101 ways to 'dress *your* body better' (my emphasis)). This is further reinforced by the accompanying interview in which Ferrera claims 'I know that having the perfect body doesn't make you love yourself more . . . It's all about being comfortable in your own skin' (Ferrera in Sandell 2007: 288). The article then, suggests that Ferrera embodies a Latina femininity which she is comfortable with. However, it is also important to note that, the term 'bombshell' which is repeatedly employed throughout the issue, is often used in relation to white femininity (i.e. 'blonde bombshell') (see Cook 2001). This suggests that Ferrera engages in fashion and beauty practices which allow her to police her potentially 'disruptive' and 'unruly' ethnic body. Indeed, when asked if she ever endured a 'Betty-like awkward phase', Ferrera describes her body in those terms often used to categorize the ethnic body as unruly. She professes, 'I had really frizzy hair, that extra freshman 15 from eating disgusting grilled cheese sandwiches everyday in the cafeteria and bushy eyebrows' (Ferrera in Sandell 2007: 288). This description of Ferrera pre-fame is strikingly similar to her character onscreen (whose eyebrows are constantly ridiculed by her co-workers, Marc and Amanda), yet while the copy encourages a relationship between onscreen and offscreen personae, the image of Ferrera in an Oscar De La Renta cocktail dress reminds readers that she is anything *but* 'ugly'.

Arguably, the glamorous images of America Ferrera serve as visual representations of her success, and therefore perpetuate the myth of ethnicity as 'individual empowerment', which in this case is associated with consumption. Underlying the 'success myth' and the 'fantasy of ethnicity' then, is the notion that Ferrera's potentially 'disruptive' body can be improved through participation in *Western* fashion and beauty practices. This is exemplified in another accompanying feature which positions Ferrera as 'style icon' and cultural intermediary. The feature, titled '4 Ways America Flatters Her Body' (*Glamour* 2007), details Ferrera's 'personal principles' which allow her to 'flatter' her figure (these include 'Know your body', 'Frequent your tailor', 'Have a few go-to pieces' and 'Figure out which shapes you should avoid'). Ferrera's 'personal' approach to fashion serves to reaffirm the notion that fashion and femininities are in some way 'individual' (again, there is an emphasis on *your* body). As such, Ferrera is able to assimilate through consumption and ownership of her own 'self-regulated' ethnic body. When combined, these narratives further fuel the understanding that Ferrera's ethnic star body is both 'authentic' and 'empowered'. However, the accompanying glamorous image of Ferrera in an Oscar de la Renta gown, with full makeup and hair extensions, suggests that she engages in self-regulatory behaviour beyond her personal 'tips' printed below; yet these beauty practices which allow her to achieve a 'cover-girl', 'glamorous' look remain opaque.

The headline of the *Glamour* interview reads 'Surprise! She's a Bombshell (and you can be one too)'. Not only does this suggest that the article functions as a pedagogical tool, but it also seeks to encourage a relationship between star and audience which pivots on the notion that stars are both like and unlike 'ordinary' people. Similarly, the interview invites audiences to '[r]ead on for more reasons to love her, and easy ways to dress your own body'. Arguably, the article seeks to present America Ferrera's position as the non-'ideal' body as a point of entry for readers: 'a reason to love her' (Sandell 2007: 289). As such, Ferrera's star body is associated with notions of ordinariness designed to appeal to potential audiences—audiences which, as Beltran (2007) has noted, are constructed as white.

In his article 'Makeover Morality and Consumer Culture', Guy Redden (2007) offers a detailed analysis of the function of the makeover in the contemporary moment. He suggests that a specific set of cultural and economic circumstances are in some way connected to and responsible for the ubiquity of makeover television. In so doing, he describes how the makeover speaks to, and in some ways offsets, concerns about the increasingly 'fragmented' social identities which are symptomatic of postmodern culture. He asserts that '[l]ines of social identity are not drawn uniformly in all shows. The allure of the makeover cuts across classes, ages and genders, and includes ethnic and sexual minorities'

(160). Redden therefore implies that the 'makeover' is 'inclusive' in its nature. He accounts for this 'inclusiveness' by arguing that 'the subjects of the makeovers are not made to stand for categories' (151).

It is important here not to overstate this notion of 'inclusiveness', given that the concept of the 'empowered consumer' is only available to those individuals with economic capital. Similarly, it is pertinent to acknowledge the problems inherent in the assumption that 'the subject is not made to stand for a category', as issues of social and cultural identity are *always* present within the makeover narrative. However, Redden acknowledges the importance of the individual within the makeover, which is especially useful when considering ethnicity and stardom, given that stars are said to maintain the myth of individualism (see Dyer 1979/2004). Moreover, these discourses are central to America Ferrera's construction as a fashion icon and to her appeal to audiences, as it has been argued that the makeover 'is an important source from which people draw notions of conduct for comparison and possible emulation' (Redden 2007: 160). Indeed, this function of the makeover is central to Ferrera's representation in the 'Style Watch' pages and 'Best Dressed' lists, and further demonstrates the value of fashion as the 'connective tissue' between the star and audience.

Within the style columns mentioned above, America Ferrera is constantly discussed in relation to her onscreen persona. However, the articles are committed to demonstrating her physical difference. In an August 2007 'Style Watch' feature, an image of Ferrera on the red carpet at the Imagen Awards is situated above the tagline '*Ugly* who?' (*People* 2007c: 163). Similarly, a 'Best Dressed Feature' includes Ferrera in a Badgley Mischka gown and the quote 'I have fun getting out of the Betty-wear and dressing up' (Sundel 2007: 67), and a June 2007 'Style Watch' feature, which reveals Ferrera's 'must have fashion and beauty items', asks 'What does *Ugly Betty*'s alter ego rely on to stay beautiful?' (*People* 2007b: 163). As such, the examples above seek to present Ferrera as a more glamorous version of her onscreen persona, which, of course, is reminiscent of the ways in which stars are discussed as more glamorous versions of *ourselves*.[6] This is perhaps more explicit within certain celebrity inter-texts which often use images of Ferrera in full Betty costume alongside more glamorous images of the actress, thereby functioning as a 'before and after feature'. For example *People* magazine's 'World's Most Beautiful' issue contains an article called 'Not So Ugly Betties', the tagline of which reads 'They play meek, geek and fashionably challenged on TV but off screen these sexy stars shine' (*People* 2007a: 151). This article is explicitly structured as a 'makeover' feature and uses a glamorous full-page image of Ferrera as 'the after' juxtaposed with a smaller image in the top left corner of Betty as 'the before'. The accompanying images then, offer two versions of Ferrera's image, both equally constructed (we are offered the 'glamorized' offscreen version and the comic 'un-glamorized' onscreen version). It is within features such as these that we can most clearly observe the precarious nature of stardom. In the 'Not So Ugly Betties' piece, the star could be exposed as fabrication—nothing more than a collection of fragmented images. Thus, the makeover is invoked in a particular way to prevent such a reading. To return to Jeffers McDonald's (2010: 82) work once more, the makeover, is presented as a 'make-clear'; the 'glamorous' image is presented as evidence of and reveals the 'true self'. Within all the material surveyed here, there appears to be a great investment in presenting Ferrera as 'extraordinarily' glamorous; thus it is through the makeover that she is able to skilfully negotiate the ordinary/extraordinary paradox.

While it has been claimed that contemporary celebrity texts seek to de-glamorize the celebrity image, with regards to America Ferrera there is an attempt to present the glamorous image as the 'authentic', 'real' self. Indeed it has long since been argued that the extra-textual construction of star images encourage us to 'think in terms of "really"' (Dyer 1986: 2). In other words, audiences are encouraged to search for the 'real' celebrity *behind* the image. As Gamson (1994) observes, celebrity texts have been and remain integral in both perpetuating this desire and offering audiences a site within which it may be possible to locate the celebrity's 'real' self. In the contemporary period, those 'off-guard, unkempt, unready, unsanitized' (Llewellyn-Smith 2002: 120) features committed to de-glamorizing the celebrity body are vital to this process.

America Ferrera's image rarely appears in those features designed to offer glimpses of the 'off-guard' celebrity, but rather, as previously mentioned, often appears in best-dressed lists and 'Style Watch features', which secures her position as a fashion icon. This apparent lack of desire to *deconstruct* Ferrera's star image, I propose here, is inherently connected to her ethnic meaning and its associations with 'authenticity'. As Dyer (1997) famously argues, 'whiteness' is often equated with an absence of racial identity. Similarly, Richard Alba (1990: 295) has acknowledged that '[w]hites are largely free to identify themselves as they will', and as such appear to have no fixed identity. Therefore, it is my contention that the supposed absence of racial identity of the white star is a driving force behind the contemporary preoccupation with 'prodding, probing and exposing' the *white* celebrity's 'real' identity. Moreover, in his essay, 'Thin White Women in Advertising: Deathly Corporeal', Redmond (2003: 189) argues that thin white women could be conceived as 'emptying their bodies of signs and codes of femininity'. This again points to a conclusion that the white female body lacks a coherent sense of self. Thus, the white celebrity body is often presented as in need of further deconstructing in the hope of locating the 'real' self, precisely because of its supposed fluidity or lack of identity. The non-white star image, which shores up essentialist ideologies of authenticity and ordinariness, is arguably seen to require no such deconstruction. Ferrera's authenticity is assumed, and therefore the overtly constructed images of her (as both comic un-glamorized Betty, and glamorous offscreen Ferrera) which circulate in fashion and celebrity texts are authenticated because of her associations with the essentialist Latina identity.

As such, these makeover images function to demonstrate the pleasure and benefits of constructing the 'self as project' without threatening to expose fashion as an entirely performative and disingenuous practice. Indeed, America Ferrera's makeover is presented as a successful transformation from 'beautiful-on-the-inside' Betty to legitimate glamorous star, and as such this qualifies her as both a point of entry for audiences and as a tastemaker. While narratives of transformation and self-improvement have long been central to star and celebrity culture (and indeed 'women's culture' in films and magazines), Ferrera's explicit and recurrent associations with makeover culture have required closer examination. Indeed, the makeover trope, as demonstrated above, articulates some complex and contradictory attitudes regarding the ethnic identity. Moreover, when framed within the context of celebrity culture, these discourses become in some ways magnified and have a greater social significance. As such, Ferrera's position as a cultural intermediary not only seeks to educate consumers in practices of discernment and taste but also allows readers to exercise cultural competences in reading fashion as a marker of cultural identity.

In opposition to Sarah Jessica Parker and her contemporaries, America Ferrera's role as a fashion icon aims to promote knowledge of everyday fashion and lifestyle practices rather than offering (albeit controlled) access to couture. One might take issue with this, since it reinforces boundaries which preserve couture solely for the white upper class, from which Ferrera is excluded. This is not to suggest, however, that Ferrera does not have access to couture (for as evidenced by *Marie Claire* and *Glamour* she appears in Versace and Oscar de la Renta gowns), but rather that, unlike Parker, Ferrera has not appeared on the cover of any highbrow fashion magazine—and indeed if one consults the *Vogue* cover archive, it is apparent that there is a conspicuous absence of ethnic models. That said, there is of course the possibility that Ferrera chooses to be associated with 'everyday' fashion and promote 'responsible' consumption, as evidenced by the 'Fashion with a Heart' campaign outlined above, which pivots on Ferrera's connection to ordinariness. As demonstrated with regard to the other case studies examined in this section, notions of ordinariness and authenticity are vital to the construction of the star as a fashion icon and cultural intermediary. However, as Powell and Prasad (2007) note, if celebrities become too 'ordinary' and neglect their role as 'extraordinary', 'the illusion is ruptured and the staged "ordinariness" becomes just plain ordinary' (60). Thus, the prominence of Ferrera's glamorized self is crucial to preserving her symbolic value. Ferrera's 'ordinariness' is assumed—as is her authenticity—and consequently the glamorized version of Ferrera's star image functions as 'extraordinary'. This incarnation of the ordinary/extraordinary paradox speaks to the mythology surrounding the female star body, which is perpetuated within the circulation of Ferrera's star image. Here, it is precisely Ferrera's 'ethnic meaning' which allows her to function as knowable, yet 'ambiguous', and it is therefore central to her position as a cultural intermediary and 'everyday' fashion icon.

Finally, it is important to note that (within the material surveyed throughout this final section) the claims of the increasing 'choice' and 'flexibility' of an 'image-based' identity are prominent within celebrity inter-texts. This is, of course, to be expected given that the celebrity inter-texts foreground an advertorial discourse and thus seek to encourage consumers to purchase and use material goods (which they suggest contribute to the construction and performance of self-identity). That said, it is clear that the sources also offer a counter-discourse which reinforces the importance of cultural power structures in shaping identity, and suggest that more traditional classed, gendered and racial identities remain dominant in society. In so doing, the celebrity inter-texts can offer specific competences (to specific readerships) so that readers and consumers can become adept at maintaining, or in some cases subverting and resisting, these traditional cultural identities.

10
CONCLUSION

We can all thank *Sex and the City* for really giving TV audiences a fashion education. The first episode aired in 1998 and the show was groundbreaking for fashion in popular culture . . . what we're seeing now [on television] is the evolution of that.

—Bailey in Oldenberg 2006

In the introduction to this volume, I referred to Sarah Street's call for an enquiry into the uses and functions of television costume and positioned this book as, in part, a response. For Street (2002: 103), the lack of serious attention afforded to television costume is surprising, given, as she notes, 'costumes are a key element of television dramas, soaps, sit-coms and even the news'. However, some may argue that in the contemporary moment of media convergence isolating television costume and fashion is unnecessary, as technological and economic developments increasingly destabilize the defining boundaries of media platforms. Indeed, Church Gibson (2012: 125) persuasively argues that 'images "bleed" across the media' with significant consequences for fashion and media studies. To be sure, developments within convergence culture, compounded by significant industrial changes in the late 1990s, have undoubtedly impacted aspects of fashion and television production and consumption. For as Church Gibson observes in the foreword to this volume, the online platforms which accompany shows like *Gossip Girl* invite fans to participate in an entirely immersive and interactive viewing experience. That being said, I am reluctant to ignore the specificities of television form for fear of instituting a grand narrative to explain away the relationship between fashion and media. In so doing, one may be perilously close to reproducing what Meaghan Morris (1990) refers to as the 'banality' of cultural studies. Moreover, there remains a question mark over the extent to which *all* audiences experience media convergence. Of course, there is evidence to suggest that the industry seeks to encourage these viewing and consumption practices. However, it is not yet clear whether this is fully realized at the distribution end: is this in fact an experience of the privileged few? Thus, a case can be made—at this stage—to consider the uses and function of fashion *on television*.

The fundamental aim of this book has been to examine fashion programming as a cultural phenomenon. The term phenomenon seems especially applicable because it encapsulates the feelings of 'extraordinariness' associated with fashion programming. As demonstrated in Part 1, historically specific industry conditions provided an infrastructure to support a symbiotic relationship between the fashion and screen industries. However, as the trade discourse makes clear, this relationship was engineered with film as the target screen industry. Through cinema (and its corresponding star system), it was presumed that fashion retailers could reach wider audiences. However, as explained in Chapter 2, climatic conditions meant that television was a better 'fit' for the fashion industry than cinema. Television's emerging power in fashion communication was viewed with scepticism by industry commentators. For some, television's associations with the 'ordinary' and the 'everyday' threatened the symbolic value of high fashion. Consequently, strategies were implemented to 'legitimize' fashion programming and thereby ensure the continued support of fashion retailers. Crucially, this involved significantly revising and reimagining the history of fashion and film. A romanticized view of classical Hollywood and the fashion industry runs counter to the volatile relationship presented by both film historians and industry practitioners of the time. This 'new' narrative is activated within the trade press in order to situate contemporary fashion television within a 'legitimate' history. Fashion programming was required to renounce its televisual history and operate as a successor to 'classic' fashion films. Thus, it has been my contention that this (re)presentation of fashion and film history informs and changes the meanings attached to fashion programming.

Connected to the project of rescuing fashion television from its 'lowly' status is the collective reimagining of contemporary costume designing. Substantial changes in the programming environment (i.e. the increasing reliance on fashion placement) have altered the role at a micro and macro level. The shift in terminology from 'costume designer' to 'television stylist' brought with it pejorative connotations, and consequently, the contemporary costume designer has undergone a crisis of value—something which the trade press attempts to rectify through the use of various 'trade stories' (Caldwell 2008).

The majority of costume designers mentioned in this volume have enjoyed a raised public profile. Patricia Field, Eric Daman, Janie Bryant and John Dunn have all received media attention in their own right, and several have traded on this success in order to develop their own fashion lines. Indeed, what we are seeing here is a 'celebritization' of the television stylist—a development which appears to be gaining momentum. Patricia Field's celebrity status and cultural legitimacy has since been deployed in the marketing of *Devil Wears Prada* (2006) and *Confessions of a Shopaholic* (2009). Thus, the mention of her name conjures a particular aesthetic and creates certain audience expectations. This extra-textual focus on the costume designer reminds us of the importance of fashion onscreen, but also suggests that it is not necessarily the clothes that are significant but the processes by which they are put together and made to *mean*.

The case studies under discussion in Part 2 demonstrate the ways in which fashion television accommodates fashion placement through the repeated use of narrative and visual tropes and offers a nuanced account of the ways in which fashion can function to advance the storyline and to challenge or support hegemonic norms. As described in Chapters 4, 5 and 6, the makeover, shopping and dressing scenes regularly feature and provide a space in which to debate consumption and identity performance in contemporary society. The shopping scenes in *Sex and the City* for example often function to disturb traditional notions of femininity, while *The O.C.* and *Gossip Girl* employ makeover and transformation scenes which allow for teen characters and viewers to negotiate their own 'unstable' identities. 'Quality' period dramas *Mad Men* and *Boardwalk*, perhaps the most unlikely examples of fashion programming, employ the tropes identified above to pass comment upon contemporary models of identity and fashion practices.

These shows therefore have a dual address. Viewers are of course addressed as consumers. Indeed, one cannot ignore the economic motivations for fostering this kind of programming. However, viewers are also addressed as social beings. We are encouraged to reflect upon our own consumer practices and consider fashion's place in organizing our sense of self and the world around us. Akin to the soap opera (M. Brown 1994; Hobson 1982), fashion programming enables audiences to vicariously test out ideas which bear relevance to their own moral dilemmas and to 'try on' different identities in order to better make sense of their own experiences. Moreover, these kinds of viewing practices are encouraged *outside* of the text.

As suggested in the introduction, fashion operates within a framework of discourses and exists outside of a media text. Such is the case that stars and celebrities become an important organizing principle, mediating between the audience and the fashion onscreen. Resultantly, a number of lead actors within the programmes mentioned here have achieved fashion-icon statuses, and in so doing continue the ideological and economic project of fashion programming. Those mentioned in Chapters 7, 8 and 9 function as tastemakers or cultural intermediaries, designed to (re)define or reinforce boundaries in a supposedly uncertain cultural climate.

Fashion programming fosters an uneasy relationship between fashion and identity. On the one hand, fashion serves as a key determinant in expressing the self. On the other hand, it obscures and plays with the markers of identity. Similarly, fashion icons, or indeed stardom more generally, promotes a fixed sense of self while also supporting the paradoxical notion that identity is performance. The role of fashion icons (and the function of their star images) is to ensure that these two conflicting philosophies remain in play—in order to maximize the pleasurable possibilities of fashion—in such a way that does not expose their fabrication. Each of the examples discussed in the final section of this volume adopt certain strategies which allow them to skilfully negotiate this dichotomy, though often this involves the subtle reinforcement of traditional power structures (class, 'race' and gender). These traditional markers of cultural identity are called upon in the construction of the star image so that the fashion icon may lay claim to an authentic 'fixed' self. Once this 'fixed' point has been established, the fashion icon can deviate from it and harness the 'performative' potential of fashion. Maintaining this paradox is central to both the ideological and economic goals of fashion television. Fashion is marketed through the shows and extra-textual circulation as pleasurable, playful and subversive, and audiences are encouraged to practice consumer competences which will allow them to negotiate and express their own identities. The cultural workers (in the form of costume designers and celebrities) serve important functions in securing these meanings which support the interests of fashion retailers and network executives.

The multidimensional approach used within this volume has served to reveal connections between these cultural and economic functions. It has sought to sketch a fuller picture of the ways in which changing industrial practices can impact content. For example an examination of industry discourse offers an insight into the ways in which production cultures make sense of and seek to shape others' understanding of fashion programming. Combined with close textual analysis and an examination of contexts of reception, it is possible to identify the ways in which industrial conditions have potentially informed the function of fashion onscreen, and also the ways in which other discourses contribute to meaning-making process. There are of course wider questions of reception raised throughout this work which require analysis from an audience studies perspective (which again, would require another study of this length). Indeed, it would be interesting to examine the ways in which audiences *do* respond to the star images and texts analysed here. However, I envisage this initial enquiry into television costume at the level of production, text and inter-text as a precursor to such research. As it stands, this work is relevant in myriad ways, as it can serve to illuminate developments within television culture in the contemporary period. On a theoretical and conceptual level, I hope that this book can build on work within fashion theory devoted to the consideration of the varied and complex relationship between fashion and self-identity, and advance the conceptual discussion of fashion and costume and costume and narrative. Finally, and perhaps most crucially, this book contributes to the important body of work which seeks to take both fashion and 'feminine' culture seriously.

NOTES

Chapter 1

1. When deployed in the trade press, this term includes both fiction and nonfiction programming. However, for the purposes of this book I use the term to reference fictional programming only.

2. Haute couture (French for high sewing) refers to custom-made garments made in Paris. While the term has been used to describe all made-to-order designer clothes, in order for a fashion house to use the label it must conform to formal criteria (e.g. it must have a certain number of employees and participate in specific fashion shows). A list of eligible houses is made every year by the French Ministry of Industry. In addition, most haute couture houses will produce ready-to-wear fashion (prêt-a-porter) to generate a profit. For a more detailed account see Breward (2003); Ewing (1974); Grace (1978); T. Jackson and Shaw (2005); Ley (1975).

3. I am using the term high fashion to include haute couture and designer fashion created within other cultural centres, including Japan, London and New York.

4. Consumption has become an increasingly fragmented term, and as such I employ Maggie Andrews and Mary M. Talbot's definition in *All the World and Her Husband: Women in Twentieth Century Consumer Culture* (2000: 2), in which they claim that consumption 'involves not just the purchasing and using up of items produced by the commercial world, but also bringing meanings to items, appropriating them, making them and, indeed taking them, as one's own'.

5. Doane (1987: 3) defines the 'woman's film' as that which 'deal[s] with a female protagonist and often appear[s] to allow her significant access to point of view structures . . . They treat problems defined as "female" . . . and most critically, are directed at a female audience.'

6. Though I will offer a more detailed synopsis of the precise ways in which the narrative/spectacle dichotomy is deployed within these studies in Chapter 4.

7. I am referring specifically to the emergence of 'New Hollywood Cinema' (which roughly spans from 1967 to 1976) characterized by Peter Kramer (2005: 2) as 'a period of intense formal and thematic innovation'.

8. Indeed, the numerous coffee-table books on star images and their fashion are testament to this—see Fox (1995); Eastoe and Gristwood (2008); Werle (2009).

9. It is also supposed that famous musicians and sportspersons can achieve 'star' status.

10. Indeed, it is important not to overstate the newness of this shift given that fan magazines of the classical era also sought to offer behind-the-scenes material to readers.

11. While Epstein offers a useful analysis of the importance of fashion within contemporary star-audience relationships, there is little work which examines in any detail the specific nature of the relationship between fashion and the television star. Thus, while her work and the other studies mentioned here usefully advance the discussion of fashion, stardom and identity, we cannot ignore the specificities of television fame, when theorizing the contemporary relationship between celebrity and fashion programming. Indeed, this is of particular importance given that television is thought to have been equally influenced by the so-called postmodern turn.

12. Unsurprisingly, this development is often linked to debates about 'quality TV' (see Jancovich and Lyons 2003; McCabe and Akass 2007).

13. The show continues to be a source of inspiration for contemporary fashion, as numerous fashion blogs testify. For example see: http://www.whowhatwear.com/website/full-article/currently-channeling-mary-rhoda/, accessed 21 December 2010

14. *The Hollywood Reporter* is the longest-running daily trade publication and, according to *The New York Times*, has a reported circulation of 21,619 readers (Anderson 1988)

Chapter 2

1. Hilfiger's relationship with Miramax reportedly extends beyond *The Faculty*, as, at the time of the *Hollywood Reporter*'s publication, another tie-in deal was under discussion for *Scream 3* (1999).

2. See YouTube clip at: http://www.youtube.com/watch?v=sF8Gqe9pKKE (accessed January 2012).

3. In her 1990 article, 'How Dress Tells the Woman's Story', Jane Gaines reveals that filmmakers were told not to use fashionable designs as it could date the film given the extended period between production and release.

4. Emporio Armani is the only diffusion line reportedly designed by Giorgio Armani and takes part in Milan Fashion Week.

Chapter 3

1. Moreover, a nationwide competition was launched in which potential audiences could win a brown, leather, La Rue–studded bag designed exclusively for the film.

2. A contemporary example of this 'trickle up' process would be Jean Paul Gaultier, whose collections are often influenced by street subcultural styles

Chapter 4

1. Jeffers McDonald (2010) expands on some of these themes in her discussion of the 'true self' (82–95).

2. Interestingly, *Sex and the City: The Movie* (2008) does include scenes which are signalled as spectacle: the *Vogue* scene and the packing-up-the-wardrobe scene.

Chapter 5

1.   The term *anti-fashion* is used to describe resistance from 'mainstream' fashion. This is not to suggest that the show takes an 'anti-fashion' perspective, but rather that the male fashion practices exhibited demonstrate an 'active' engagement with 'subcultural' styles.

2.   There are of course exceptions to this—see, for example, Paul Willis's *Learning to Labour* (1977).

3.   The Cinderella narrative is also referenced in Episode 2, Season 4, as Blair gives a stiletto to a Prince.

4.   In the original novels upon which the series is based, the character of Nate is fond of yachting. Daman reportedly was keen to reference this through the use of navy-blue, nautical-style dress.

5.   The particular choice of surname serves as a reference to the Cinderella motif which preoccupies the episode.

Chapter 6

1.   This is not to put forth an 'authorial' vision of costume design whereby only the principle costume designer is accredited for all wardrobe decisions, but rather this is one example of how changes in personnel, budget, et cetera may affect the visual style of a programme over time.

2.   See YouTube clip at: http://www.youtube.com/watch?v=gcs94eMxcGU (accessed 12 January 2013)

3.   *The New York Times* curiously describes him as both the 'ultimate authority and divine messenger, some peculiar hybrid of God and Edith Head' (Witchel 2008).

4.   Of course editing is a language in its own right, but I am suggesting that costume works in a slightly different way, insofar as it is traditionally a more varied semiotic system and thus has many possible readings.

5.   See YouTube clip at: http://www.youtube.com/watch?v=gcs94eMxcGU (accessed 12 January 2013)

6.   This shot is unremarkable in the sense that the technique is often employed when female employees (typically Joan and Peggy) of Sterling Cooper are in frame.

7.   Indeed Pechman's (2012) post on www.theawl.com reports on the similarities between Megan's costuming and high fashion garments in 1966 issues of *Vogue*, where Pechman painstakingly compiles a number of screen shots of Megan's outfits with the editorials.

Chapter 7

1.   Again, it should be reiterated that audiences have long expressed interest in the personal lives of celebrities, and that early fan magazines provided images of the celebrity 'at home', etc.

2.   While it may be argued that the success myth has less currency due to the increasing visibility of other explanations of fame, as the work of Gamson (1994),

among others, makes clear, the success myth still must remain in play (alongside these alternative explanations) within contemporary celebrity culture.

3. This is of particular importance given that Lively's onscreen counterpart is also a member of the 'socially elite'.

4. Later in her career, Vreeland became a consultant for the Costume Institute of the Metropolitan Museum of Art in New York in 1971.

Chapter 8

1. The magazine, created as a teen version of its sister magazine, the so-called style bible *Vogue,* adopts a somewhat didactic approach to fashion: *Teen Vogue* is designed to train young women as fashion consumers (according to the magazine's mission statement: 'Influence Starts Here' (*Condé Nast* n.d.)).

Chapter 9

1. Lively on *The View* (ABC, aired on 26 May 2005).

2. See Chapter 7 for a more detailed overview of Rojek's work.

3. Ferrera on *The View* (ABC, aired on 26 May 2005).

4. Interestingly, rumours circulated within the popular press that the pair did not get on—often this was articulated as if Ferrera was in some way 'jealous' of Lively; see *The Soup* (aired 11 August 2008).

5. Significantly, the figure-flattery issue did not continue.

6. See Chapter 1 for a more detailed discussion of the ordinary/extraordinary paradox.

BIBLIOGRAPHY

Abbott, Denise (1998), 'Apart at the Seams', *The Hollywood Reporter: Fashion in Entertainment Special Issue* (20–6 October).

Abbott, Denise (1999), 'TV Teen Threads', *The Hollywood Reporter: Fashion in Entertainment Special Issue* (19–25 October).

Adams, Rebecca (2012), 'Blake Lively "Savages" Costumes Make Her Uncomfortable', *Huffington Post* (7 June), http://www.huffingtonpost.com/2012/07/06/blake-lively-savages-costumes_n_1654141.html, accessed 11 January 2013.

Alba, Richard (1990), *Ethnic Identity: The Transformation of White America*, New Haven: Yale University Press.

Allen, Jeanne (1990), '*Fig Leaves* in Hollywood: Female Representation and Consumer Culture', in Jane Gaines and Charlotte Herzog (eds), *Fabrications: Costume and the Female Body*, London and New York: Routledge.

Allen, Robert C., and Gomery, Douglas (1985), *Film History: Theory and Practice*, New York: Random House.

Anderson, A. Donald (1988), 'Hollywood's Version of Trade Wars', *New York Times* (7 August), http://www.nytimes.com/1988/08/07/business/hollywood-s-version-of-trade-wars.html, accessed 19 January 2012.

Andrews, Maggie, and Talbot, Mary (eds) (2000), *All the World and Her Husband: Women in Twentieth Century Consumer Culture*, London and New York: Cassell.

Arthurs, Jane (2003), '*Sex and the City* and Consumer Culture: Remediating Postfeminist Drama', *Feminist Media Studies*, 3/1: 83–98.

Baker, Nancy (1984), *The Beauty Trap*, New York: Franklin Watts.

Banks, Miranda J. (2009), 'Defining Production Studies', in Vicky Mayer, Miranda J. Banks and John T. Caldwell (eds), *Production Studies: Cultural Studies of Media Industries*, New York: Routledge.

Banks, Tim (2000), 'Putting the Sex into the City', *Telegraph Magazine* (2 December).

Bauman, Zygmunt (1992), *Intimations of Postmodernity*, London: Routledge.

Bell, Daniel (1976), *The Cultural Contradictions of Capitalism*, New York: Basic Books.

Bell, David, and Hollows, Joanne (2005), 'Making Sense of Ordinary Lifestyles', in David Bell and Joanne Hollows (eds), *Ordinary Lifestyles: Popular Media, Consumption and Taste*, Maidenhead: Open University Press.

Beltran, Mary (2007), 'The Hollywood Latina Body as Site of Social Struggle: Media Constructions of Stardom and Jennifer Lopez's "Cross-over Butt"', in Sean Redmond and Su Holmes (eds), *Stardom and Celebrity: A Reader*, London: Sage.

Beltran, Mary (2009), *Latina/o Stars in U.S. Eyes: The Making and Meaning of TV Stardom*, Urbana and Chicago: University of Illinois Press.

Bennett, Andy (1999), 'Subcultures or Neo-tribes? Rethinking the Relationship between Youth, Style and Musical Taste', *Sociology,* 33/3: 599–617.

Benwell, Bethan (2003), *Masculinity and Men's Lifestyle Magazines*, Oxford: Blackwell.

Berry, Sarah (2000), *Screen Style: Fashion and Femininity in 1930s Hollywood*, Minneapolis and London: University of Minnesota.

Bilmes, Alex (2012), 'Jon Hamm Is Not the Man You Think He Is', *Esquire* (March).

Bloomer, Dexter C. (1895/1975), *Life and Writings of Amelia Bloomer*, New York: Schocken Books.

Blumer, Herbert (1969), 'Fashion: From Class Differentiation to Collective Selection', *The Sociological Quarterly*, 10/3: 275–97.

Bourdieu, Pierre (1984), *Distinction: A Social Critique of the Judgment of Taste*, Richard Nice (trans.), London: Routledge.

Bourdieu, Pierre (1986), 'The Forms of Capital', in John G. Richardson (ed.), *Handbook of Theory and Research for the Sociology of Education*, New York: Greenwood.

Bourdieu, Pierre (1993a), *The Field of Cultural Production*, London: Polity.

Bourdieu, Pierre (1993b), *Sociology in Question*, Richard Nice (trans.), London: Sage.

Breward, Christopher (2000), 'The Dandy Laid Bare', in Pamela Church Gibson and Stella Bruzzi (eds), *Fashion Culture: Theories, Explorations and Analysis*, London: Routledge.

Breward, Christopher (2003), *Fashion (Oxford History of Art)*, Oxford: Oxford University Press.

Brooks, Peter (1985), *The Melodramatic Imagination: Balzac, Henry James, Melodrama and the Mode of Excess*, New York: Columbia University Press.

Brown, Laura (2009), 'Why Don't You . . . ?', *Harper's Bazaar* (March).

Brown, Mary E. (1994), *Soap Opera and Women's Talk*, London: Sage.

Brownmiller, Susan (1984), *Femininity*, New York: Linden Press.

Brunsdon, Charlotte (1991), 'Text and Audience', in Ellen Seiter (ed.), *Remote Control: Television Audiences and Cultural Power*, London: Routledge.

Brunsdon, Charlotte (1997), *Screen Tastes: Soap Opera to Satellite Dishes*, London and New York: Routledge.

Bruzzi, Stella (1997), *Undressing Cinema: Clothing and Identity in the Movies*, London and New York: Routledge.

Bruzzi, Stella (2005), 'Gregory Peck: Anti-Fashion Icon', in Rachel Moseley (ed.), *Fashioning Film Stars: Dress, Culture and Identity*, London: BFI Publishing.

Bruzzi, Stella (2011), ' "It will be a magnificent obsession": Femininity, Desire, and the New Look in 1950s Hollywood Melodrama', in Adrienne Munich (ed.), *Fashion in Film*, Bloomington: Indiana University Press.

Bruzzi, Stella, and Church Gibson, Pamela (2000), 'Introduction', in Stella Bruzzi and Pamela Church Gibson (eds), *Fashion Cultures: Theories, Exploration and Analysis*, London: Routledge.

Bruzzi, Stella, and Church Gibson, Pamela (2004), ' "Fashion is the Fifth Character": Fashion, Costume and Character in *Sex and the City*', in Kim Akass and Janet McCabe (eds), *Reading Sex and the City*, London: I.B Tauris.

Buckley, Cara Louise, and Ott, Brian L. (2008), 'Fashion(able/ing) Selves', in Marc Leverette, Brian L. Ott and Cara Louse Buckley (eds), *It's Not TV: Watching HBO in the Post-Television Era*, London and New York: Routledge.

Buscombe, Edward (2000), 'Cary Grant', in Stella Bruzzi and Pamela Church Gibson (eds), *Fashion Cultures: Theories, Exploration and Analysis*, London: Routledge.

Butler, Jeremy G. (2011), 'Smoke Gets in Your Eyes: Historicizing Visual Style in *Mad Men*', in Gary Edgerton (ed.), *Mad Men*, London: I.B Tauris.

Caldwell, John T. (2008), *Production Culture: Industrial Reflexivity and Critical Practice in Film and Television*, Durham: Duke University Press.

Cardwell, Sarah (2006), 'Television Aesthetics', *Critical Studies in Television*, 1/1: 72–80.

Cashmore, Ellis (2006), *Celebrity Culture*, London: Routledge.

Chambers, Iain (1986), *Popular Culture: The Metropolitan Experience*, London: Routledge.

Chierichetti, David (1976), *Hollywood Costume Design*, New York: Harmony Books.

Christy, George (1998), 'Designing Minds', *The Hollywood Reporter: Fashion in Entertainment Special Issue* (20–6 October).

Christy, George (2000), 'The Hollywood Mystique', *The Hollywood Reporter: Fashion in Entertainment Special Issue* (31 October–6 November).

Church Gibson, Pamela (2000), 'Redressing the Balance: Patriarchy, Postmodernism and Feminism', in Stella Bruzzi and Pamela Church Gibson (eds), *Fashion Cultures: Theories, Explorations and Analysis*, London and New York: Routledge.

Church Gibson, Pamela (2005), 'Brad Pitt and George Clooney, the Rough and the Smooth: Male Costuming in Contemporary Hollywood', in Rachel Moseley (ed.), *Fashioning Film Stars: Dress, Culture and Identity*, London: BFI Publishing.

Church Gibson, Pamela (2012), *Fashion and Celebrity Culture*, London: Bloomsbury.

Cohan, Steven (2007), 'Queer Eye for the Straight Guise: Camp, Postfeminism and the Fab Five's Makeovers of Masculinity', in Yvonne Tasker and Diana Negra (eds), *Interrogating Postfeminism*, Durham and London: Duke University Press.

Condé Nast (n.d.), 'Product Licensing: Teen Vogue', http://www.condenast.com/content/teen-vogue-product-licensing, accessed 19 January 2012.

Connell, Robert W. (1987), *Gender and Power: Society, the Person and Sexual Politics*, Cambridge: Polity.

Connell, Robert W. (1995), *Masculinities*, Cambridge: Polity.

Connell, Robert W. (1998), 'Teaching the Boys: New Research on Masculinity, and Gender Strategies for Schools', in Barbara Balliet and Patricia McDaniel (eds), *Women, Culture and Society: A Reader*, Dubuque, IA: Kendall/Hunt Publishing.

Consalvo, Mia (2003), 'The Monsters Next Door: Media Constructions of Boys and Masculinity', *Feminist Media Studies*, 3/1: 27–45.

Cook, Pam (1996), *Fashioning the Nation: Costume and Identity in British Cinema*, London: BFI Publishing.

Cook, Pam (2001), 'The Trouble with Sex: Diana Dors and the Blonde Bombshell Phenomenoni', in Bruce Babington (ed.), *British Stars and Stardom: From Alma Taylor to Sean Connery*, Manchester: Manchester University Press.

Corner, John (2003), 'Finding Data, Reading Patterns, Telling Stories: Issues in the Historiography of Television', *Media, Culture and Society*, 25: 273–80.

CosmoGirl (July 2007).

Coward, Rosalind (1984), *Female Desire: Women's Sexuality Today*, London: Paladin.

Craik, Jennifer (1994), *The Face of Fashion: Cultural Studies in Fashion*, London and New York: Routledge.

Crane, Diana (2000), *Fashion and Its Social Agenda: Class, Gender, and Identity in Clothing*, Chicago: University of Chicago Press.

Creeber, Glen (2006), 'The Joy of Text: Television and Textual Analysis', *Critical Studies in Television*, 1/1: 81–8.

D'Acci, Julie (1994), *Defining Women: Television and the Case of Cagney and Lacey*, Chapel Hill: University of North Carolina Press.

Davis, Fred (1994), *Fashion Culture and Identity*, Chicago: Chicago University Press.

Davis, Glynn, and Dickinson, Kay (eds) (2004), *Teen TV: Genre, Consumption, Identity*, London: BFI Publishing.

Davis, Kathy (2006), 'Beauty and the Female Body', in P. David Marshall (ed.), *The Celebrity Culture Reader*, London and New York: Routledge.

Dawn, Randee (2000a), 'Off the Rack & Onto the Screen', *The Hollywood Reporter: Fashion in Entertainment Special Issue* (31 October–6 November).

Dawn, Randee (2000b), 'Undressing "Sex and the City"', *The Hollywood Reporter: Fashion in Entertainment Special Issue* (31 October–6 November).

Doane, Mary Ann (1987), *The Desire to Desire: The Woman's Film of the 1940s*, Indiana: Bloomington Press.

du Gay, Paul (ed.) (1997), *Production of Culture/Cultures of Production*, London: Sage.

Dunn, Robert (1998), *Identity Crises: A Social Critique of Postmodernity*, Minneapolis: University of Minnesota Press.

Dyer, Richard (1979/2004), *Stars*, London: BFI Publishing.

Dyer, Richard (1986), *Heavenly Bodies: Film Stars and Society*, London: Palgrave Macmillan.

Dyer, Richard (1997), *White*, London: Routledge.

Eastoe, Jane, and Gristwood, Sarah (2008), *Fabulous Frocks*, Oxford: Pavilion.

Eckert, Charles (1990), 'The Carole Lombard in Macy's Window', in Jane Gaines and Charlotte Herzog (eds), *Fabrications: Costume and the Female Body*, London and New York: Routledge.

Eco, Umberto (1976), *Theory of Semiotics*, Bloomington: Indiana University Press.

Edgerton, Gary R. (2009), 'JFK, Don Draper and the New Sentimentality', *Critical Studies in Television*, http://cstonline.tv/jfk-don-draper, accessed 2 December 2010.

Edgerton, Gary R. (ed.) (2011), 'Introduction', *Mad Men*, London: I.B Tauris.

Edwards, Tim (1997), *Men in the Mirror: Men's Fashion, Masculinity and Consumer Society*, London: Cassell.

Edwards, Tim (2000), *Contradictions of Consumption: Concepts, Practices, and Politics in Consumer Society*, Berkshire: Open University Press.

Edwards, Tim (2011), *Fashion in Focus: Concepts, Practices and Politics*, London: Routledge.

Elle Girl (June/July 2006).

Ellis, John (1992), *Visible Fictions: Cinema, Television, Video*, 2nd edition, London: Routledge.

Entwistle, Joanne (2000), *The Fashioned Body: Fashion, Dress and Modern Social Theory*, Cambridge: Polity Press.

Epstein, Rebecca (2007), 'Sharon Stone in a Gap Turtleneck', in Sean Redmond and Su Holmes (eds), *Stardom and Celebrity: A Reader*, London: Sage.

Evans, Jessica, and Hesmondhalgh, David (eds) (2005), *Understanding Media: Inside Celebrity,* Berkshire: Open University Press.

Ewan, Stuart, and Ewan, Elizabeth (1992), *Channels of Desire: Mass Images and the Shaping of American Consciousness*, Minneapolis: University of Minnesota.

Ewing, Elizabeth (1974), *History of Twentieth Century Fashion*, London: Batsford.

Featherstone, Mike (2007), *Consumer Culture and Postmodernism*, 2nd edition, London: Sage.

Feld, Rob, Oppenheimer, Jean, and Stasukevich, Ian (2008), 'Tantalizing Television', *American Cinematographer* (March), http://www.theasc.com/ac_magazine/March2008/Television/page1.php, accessed 10 January 2013.

Feuer, Jane (1996), *Seeing Through the Eighties: Television and Reganism*, London: BFI Publishing.

Fischer, Rachel (2000), 'Cruz Wear', *The Hollywood Reporter: Fashion in Entertainment Special Issue* (31 October–6 November).

Flugel, John C. (1930), *The Psychology of Clothes*, London: Hogarth.

Fox, Patty (1995), *Star Style: Hollywood Legends as Fashion Icons*, Santa Monica: Angel City Press.

Gaines, Jane (1990), 'Costume and Narrative: How Dress Tells the Woman's Story', in Jane Gaines and Charlotte Herzog (eds), *Fabrications: Costume and the Female Body*, London and New York: Routledge.

Gaines, Jane, and Herzog, Charlotte (eds) (1990), *Fabrications: Costume and the Female Body*, London and New York: Routledge.

Gamson, Joshua (1994), *Claims to Fame: Celebrity in Contemporary America*, London and California: University of California Press.

Garnham, Nicholas (1995), 'Political Economy and Cultural Studies: Reconciliation or Divorce?', *Critical Studies in Mass Communication*, 12/1: 60–71.

Geraghty, Christine (2007), 'Re-examining Stardom: Questions of Texts, Bodies and Performance', in Sean Redmond and Su Holmes (eds), *Stardom and Celebrity: A Reader,* London: Sage.

Giddens, Anthony (1992), *The Transformation of Intimacy,* Cambridge: Polity Press.

Gill, Rosalind (2003), 'Power and the Production of Subjects: A Genealogy of the New Man and the New Lad', in Bethan Benwell (ed.), *Masculinity and Men's Lifestyle Magazines*, Oxford: Blackwell.

Gillan, Jennifer (2004), 'From Ozzie Nelson to Ozzy Osbourne: the Genesis and Development of the Reality (Star) Sitcom', in Su Holmes and Deborah Jermyn (eds), *Understanding Reality Television*, London: Routledge.

Gillis, Stacey, and Hollows, Joanne (2009), *Feminism, Domesticity and Popular Culture*, New York: Routledge.

Ginsberg, Merle (2000), 'TV Ups the Fashion Quotient', *Women's Wear Daily* (28 July), www.wwd.com, accessed 28 March 2008.

Gitlin, Todd (1987), *Watching Television*, New York: Pantheon.

Glamour (2007), '4 Ways America Flatters Her Body' (October).

Glamour (July 2011).

Goffman, Erving (1959/1990), *The Presentation of the Self in Everyday Life,* Harmondsworth: Penguin.

GQ (2004), 'The Short Suit Steps Out' (October).

Grace, Evelyn (1978), *Introduction to Fashion*, New York: Prentice Hill.

Gripsrud, Jostein (1995), *The Dynasty Years: Hollywood Television and Critical Media Studies*, London: Routledge.

Grossberg, Lawrence (1987), 'The In-Difference of Television', *Screen*, 28/2: 28–46.

Hall, Stuart (2006), 'Notes on Deconstructing the Popular', in John Storey (ed.), *Cultural Theory and Popular Culture*, 3rd edition, Edinburgh: Pearson.

Hall, Stuart, and Jefferson, Tony (eds) (1993), *Resistance through Rituals: Youth Subcultures in Post-war Britain*, London: Routledge.

Handy, Bruce (2009), 'Don and Betty's Paradise Lost', *Vanity Fair* (September), http://www.vanityfair.com/culture/features/2009/09/mad-men200909, accessed 1 January 2013.

Hanke, Robert (1992), 'Redesigning Men: Hegemonic Masculinity in Television', in Steve Craig (ed.), *Men, Masculinity and the Media*, Thousand Oaks, CA: Sage.

Hanke, Robert (1998), 'Theorizing Masculinity with/in the Media', *Communication Theory*, 8/2: 183–203.

Harper, Sue (1987), 'Historical Pleasures: Gainsborough Costume Melodrama', in Christine Gledhill (ed.), *Home Is Where the Heart Is: Studies in Melodrama and the Woman's Film*, London: BFI Publishing.

Haskell, Molly (1974/1987), *From Reverence to Rape: The Treatment of Women in the Movies*, London and Chicago: Chicago University Press.

Hauser, Brooke (2012), 'Golden Girl', *Allure* (October).

Hebdige, Dick (1979), *Subculture: The Meaning of Style*, London: Methuen.

Hebdige, Dick (1998), *Hiding the Light: On Images and Things,* London and New York: Routledge.

Hebdige, Dick (2006), 'Postmodernism and "The Other Side" ', in John Storey (ed.), *Cultural Theory and Popular Culture*, Edinburgh: Peason.

Heller, Dana (2007), *Makeover Television: Realities Remodelled*, London: I.B. Tauris.

Herzog, Charlotte (1990), ' "Powder Puff" Promotion: The Fashion Show-in-the-Film', in Jane Gaines and Charlotte Herzog (eds), *Fabrications: Costume and the Female Body*, London and New York: Routledge.

Herzog, Charlotte, and Gaines, Jane (1991), 'Puffed Sleeves before Tea-Time: Joan Crawford, Adrian and Women Audiences', in Christine Gledhill (ed.), *Stardom: Industry of Desire,* London: Routledge.

Hesmondhalgh, David (2002), *The Culture Industries*, London: Sage.

Hesmondhalgh, David (2005), 'Subcultures, Scenes or Tribes? None of the Above Youth Tribes', *Journal of Youth Studies*, 8/1: 21–40.

Hesmondhalgh, David (2006a), 'Bourdieu, the Media and Cultural Production', *Media Culture and Society*, 28/2: 211–31.

Hesmondhalgh, David (ed.) (2006b), *Media Production*, Berkshire: Open University Press.

Hesmondhalgh, David, and Baker, Sarah (2013), *Creative Labour: Media Work in Three Cultural Industries*, London: Routledge.

Hobson, Dorothy (1982) *Crossroads: The Drama of a Soap Opera*, London: Methuen.

Holgate, Mark (2011), 'Blake Lively', *Vogue Best Dressed Special Issue* (November).

Hollander, Anne (1993), *Seeing Through Clothes*, Berkeley: University of California Press.

Hollows, Joanne (2000), *Feminism, Femininity and Popular Culture*, Manchester and New York: Manchester University Press.

Holmes, Su, and Negra, Diane (2011), *In the Limelight and Under the Microscope: Forms and Functions of Female Celebrity*, New York: Continuum.

Holmes, Su, and Redmond, Sean (eds) (2006), *Framing Celebrity: New Directions in Celebrity Culture*, London and New York: Routledge.

Horkins, Tony (2012), 'Mad About the Man', *Elle* (April).

Huyssen, Andreas (1986), *The Great Divide: Modernity, Mass Culture and Postmodernism*, London: Macmillan.

Jackson, Peter, Stevenson, Nick, and Brooks, Kate (2001), *Making Sense of Men's Magazines*, London: Wiley.

Jackson, Tim, and Shaw, David (2005), *The Fashion Handbook*, London: Routledge.

Jacobs, Jason (2001), 'Issues of Judgement and Value in Television Studies', *International Journal of Cultural Studies*, 4/4: 427–47.

Jameson, Fredric (1985), 'Postmodernism and Consumer Culture', in Hal Foster (ed.), *Postmodern Culture*, London: Pluto.

Jancovich, Mark, and Lyons, James (eds) (2003), *Quality TV: Cult TV, the Industry and Fans*, London: BFI Publishing.

Jarrett, Marvin Scott (2006), 'Letter From the Editor', *Nylon Guys* (June).

Jeffers McDonald, Tamar (2010), *Hollywood Catwalk: Costume and Transformation in American Film*, London: I.B Tauris.

Jermyn, Deborah (2004), 'In Love with Sarah Jessica Parker: Celebrating Female Fandom and Friendship in *Sex and the City*', in Kim Akass and Janet McCabe (eds), *Reading Sex and the City*, London: I.B Tauris.

Jermyn, Deborah (2006), ' "Bringing out the * in You": SJP, Carrie Bradshaw and the Evolution of Television Stardom', in Su Holmes and Sean Redmond (eds), *Framing Celebrity: New Directions in Celebrity Culture*, London: Routledge.

Jermyn, Deborah (2008), 'Still Something Else Besides A Mother?: Negotiating Motherhood in Sarah Jessica Parker's Star Story', *Social Semiotics*, 18/2: 201–19.

Jermyn, Deborah (2009), *Sex and the City*, Detroit, Michigan: Wayne State University Press.

Kaufman, Debra (1999), 'Costume Drama', *The Hollywood Reporter: Fashion in Entertainment Special Issue* (9–15 October).

Kawamura, Yuniya (2005), *Fashion-ology: An Introduction to Fashion Studies*, Oxford and New York: Berg.

Keeps, David A. (2007), 'God Bless America', *Marie Claire* (December).

Kellner, Douglas (1992), 'Popular Culture and the Construction of Postmodern Identities', in S. Lash and J. Friedman (eds), *Modernity and Identity*, Oxford: Blackwell.

Kellner, Douglas (1995), *Media Culture: Cultural Studies, Identity and Politics Between the Modern and the Postmodern*, London and New York: Routledge.

Kimmel, Michael (2000), *The Gendered Society*, Oxford: Oxford University Press.

King, Barry (2003), 'Embodying an Elastic Self: The Parametrics of Contemporary Stardom', in Thomas Austin and Martin Barker (eds), *Contemporary Hollywood Stardom*, London: Arnold.

Kinon, Cristina (2008), ' "Gossip" Fans are Dishing about the "Girl's" Clothes', *New York Daily News* (23 April), http://www.nydailynews.com/entertainment/tv-movies/gossip-fans-dishing-girl-clothes-article-1.283441, accessed 16 May 2009.

Klinger, Barbara (1991), 'Digressions at the Cinema: Commodification and Reception in Mass Culture', in James Naremore and Patrick Brantlinger (eds), *Modernity and Mass Culture,* Bloomington: Indiana University Press.

Klinger, Barbara (1994), *Melodrama and Meaning: History, Culture and the Films of Douglas Sirk*, Bloomington: Indiana University Press.

Kramer, Peter (2004), 'The Rise and Fall of Sandra Bullock: Notes on Starmaking and Female Stardom in Contemporary Hollywood', in Andy Willis (ed.), *Film Stars: Hollywood and Beyond*, Manchester and New York: Manchester University Press.

Kramer, Peter (2005), *The New Hollywood: From Bonnie and Clyde to Star Wars*, London: Wallflower.

Lacher, Irene (2003), 'Frock Stars', *The Hollywood Reporter: Fashion in Entertainment Special Issue* (28 October–3 November).

Landis, Deborah (2003), *Screencraft: Costume Design*, Boston: Focal Press.

Langer, John (1981), 'Television's Personality System', *Media Culture and Society*, 3/4: 351–65.

LaPlace, Maria (1987), 'Producing and Consuming the Woman's Film: Discursive Struggle in *Now Voyager*', in Christine Gledhill (ed.), *Home is Where the Heart Is: Studies in Melodrama and the Woman's Film*, London: BFI Publishing.

Laverty, Chris (2011), 'Boardwalk Empire Costume Q&A: John Dunn & Lisa Padovani', *Clothes on Film* (21 September), http://clothesonfilm.com/boardwalk-empire-costume-qa-john-dunn-lisa-padovani/22114/, accessed 15 January 2013.

Leopold, Ellen (1992), 'The Manufacture of the Fashion System', in Juliet Ash and Elizabeth Wilson (eds), *Chic Thrills: A Fashion Reader*, London: Pandora.

Levine, E. (2001), 'Toward a Paradigm for Media Production Research: Behind the Scenes at *General Hospital*', *Critical Studies in Media Communication*, 18/1 (March): 66–82.

Ley, Sandra (1975), *Fashion for Everyone: The Story of Ready-to-Wear (1870s–1970s)*, New York: Scribners.

Lieberman, Sara (2012), 'Eric Daman is the New Patricia Field' *New York Post* (6 December), http://www.saralieberman.com/wp-content/uploads/2013/03/P6M-Eric-Daman-is-the-new-Patricia-Field-December-2012.pdf, accessed 24 June 2013.

Lipp, Deborah (2008), 'Anachronisms Aren't Anachronisms', *Basket of Kisses* (19 June), http://madmenmad.wordpress.com/category/anachronisms/, accessed 21 November 2012.

Littler, Jo (2004), 'Making Fame Ordinary: Intimacy, Reflexivity and "Keeping It Real" ', *Mediactive*, 1/2: 8–25.

Llewellyn-Smith, Caspar (2002), *Poplife: A Journey by Sofa*, London: Sceptre.

Long, April (2006), 'Growing Up Brody', *Nylon Guys* (June).

Lopez, Ana (1991), 'Are All Latins from Manhattan?: Hollywood, Ethnography, and Cultural Colonialism', in Lester D. Friedman (ed.), *Unspeakable Images: Ethnicity and the American Cinema,* Urbana and Chicago: University of Illinois Press.

Lotz, Amanda D. (2007), *The Television Will Be Revolutionized*, New York: New York University Press.

Luhrmann, Baz (2011), 'The 2011 Time 100: Blake Lively', *Time* (21 April), http://www.time.com/time/specials/packages/article/0,28804,2066367_2066369_2066409,00.html, accessed 1 January 2012.

MacSweeney, Eve (2011), 'Sarah Jessica Parker: Show and Tell', *Vogue* (August), http://www.vogue.com/magazine/article/sarah-jessica-parker-show-and-tell/#, accessed 1 January 2012.

Marcus, Harvey (2010), 'Blake Lively', *Marie Claire* (October).

Marie Claire (2007), 'The 100 People We Love Right Now' (December).

Marshall, P. David (1997/2004), *Celebrity and Power: Fame in Contemporary Culture*, Minneapolis: University of Minnesota.

Mascia-Lees, Frances E., and Sharpe, Patricia (1992), *Tattoo, Torture, Mutilations and Adornment: The De-Naturalisation of the Body in Culture and Text*, Albany: Statue University of New York Press.

Mayer, Vicky, Banks, Miranda J., and Caldwell, John T. (eds) (2009), *Production Studies: Cultural Studies of Media Industries*, New York: Routledge.

McCabe, Janet, and Akass, Kim (eds) (2007), *Quality Television: Contemporary American Television and Beyond*, London: I.B. Tauris.

McCabe, Janet, and Jermyn, Deborah (2011), 'Ageing Is Not Something to Be Defied', *Guardian* (8 December), http://www.guardian.co.uk/commentisfree/2011/dec/08/ageing-not-to-be-defied, accessed 15 January 2013.

McNeil, Peter, and Karaminas, Vicki (eds) (2009), *The Men's Fashion Reader*, Oxford: Berg.

McRobbie, Angela (1991), *Feminism and Youth Culture: From 'Jackie' to 'Just Seventeen'*, London: Macmillan.

McRobbie, Angela (1994), *Postmodernism and Popular Culture*, London: Routledge.

McRobbie, Angela (2006), 'Yummy Mummies Leave a Bad Taste for Young Women', *Guardian* (2 March), www.guardian.co.uk/comment/story/0,,1721450,00.html, accessed 1 January 2013.

McRobbie, Angela, and Garber, Jenny (1993), 'Girls and Subcultures', in Stuart Hall and Tony Jefferson (eds), *Resistance through Rituals: Youth Subcultures in Post-war Britain*, London: Routledge.

Mercer, John, and Shingler, Martin (2004), *Melodrama: Genre, Style, Sensibility*, London: Wallflower.

Miles, Steven (2000), *Youth Lifestyles in a Changing World*, Buckingham: Open University Press.

Miller, Daniel (1995), 'Consumption as the Vanguard of History: A Polemic by Way of an Introduction' in David Miller (ed.), *Acknowledging Consumption: A Review of New Studies*, London: Routledge.

Miller, Rebecca (2009), 'Blake Lively Grows Up', *Marie Claire* (4 November), http://www.marieclaire.com/celebrity-lifestyle/celebrities/blake-lively-interview, accessed 1 December 2012.

Mittell, Jason (2001), 'A Cultural Approach to Television Genre Theory', *Cinema Journal*, 40/3: 3–24.

Mizejewski, Linda (1999), *Ziegfeld Girl: Image and Icon in Culture and Cinema*, Durham: Duke University Press.

Morris, Meaghan (1990), 'Banality in Cultural Studies', in Patricia Mellencamp (ed.), *Logics of Television: Essay in Cultural Criticism*, Bloomington: Indiana University Press.

Mort, Frank (1988), ' "Boys Own?" Masculinity, Style and Popular Culture', in Rowena Chapman and Jonathon Rutherford (eds), *Male Order: Unwrapping Masculinity*, London: Lawrence and Wishart.

Mort, Frank (1996), *Cultures of Consumption: Commerce, Masculinities and Social Space*, London: Routledge.

Moseley, Rachel (2002), *Growing Up with Audrey Hepburn: Text, Audience, Resonance*, Manchester: Manchester University Press.

Moseley, Rachel (2005a), 'Dress, Class and Audrey Hepburn: The Significance of the Cinderella Story', in Rachel Moseley (ed.), *Fashioning Film Stars: Dress Culture and Identity*, London: BFI Publishing.

Moseley, Rachel (2005b), 'Introduction', in Rachel Moseley (ed.), *Fashioning Film Stars: Dress Culture and Identity*, London: BFI Publishing.

Muggleton, David (2000), *Inside Subculture: The Postmodern Meaning of Style*, Oxford: Berg.

Muggleton, David, and Weinzierl, Rupert (2003), *The Post-Subcultures Reader*, Oxford: Berg.

Mulkerrins, Jane (2012), 'Janie Bryant Dishes on *Mad Men*'s Fabulous Costumes: "Betty Has Worn Many of My Mother's Sweaters!" ', *Grazia Daily* (15 May), http://www.graziadaily.co.uk/fashion/archive/2012/05/15/interview--jane-bryant-mad-men.htm, accessed 27 January 2013.

Mulvey, Laura (1975/1989), 'Visual Pleasure and Narrative Cinema', in Laura Mulvey (ed.), *Visual and Other Pleasures*, Basingstoke: Macmillan.

Nayak, Anoop, and Kehily, Mary Jane (2008), *Gender, Youth and Culture: Young Masculinities and Femininities*, New York: Palgrave Macmillan.

Negra, Diane (2001), *Off White Hollywood: American Culture and Ethnic Female Stardom*, London and New York: Routledge.

Negra, Diane (2004), 'Quality Postfeminism: Sex and the Single Girl on HBO', *Genders Online*, 39, http://www.genders.org/g39/g39_negra.html, accessed 1 November 2010.

Negrin, Llewellyn (1999), 'The Self as Image: A Critical Appraisal of Postmodern Theories of Fashion', *Theory, Culture & Society*, 16/3: 99–118.

Negus, Keith (1992), *Producing Pop: Culture and Conflict in the Popular Music Industry*, London: Edward Arnold.

Negus, Keith (1997), 'The Production of Culture', in Paul du Gay (ed.), *Production of Culture/Cultures of Production*, London: Sage.

Negus, Keith (2002), 'The Work of Cultural Intermediaries and the Enduring Distance between Production and Consumption', *Cultural Studies*, 16/4: 501–515.

Nielson, Elizabeth (1990), 'Handmaidens of the Glamour Culture: Costumers in the Hollywood Studio System', in Jane Gaines and Charlotte Herzog (eds), *Fabrications: Costume and the Female Body*, London and New York: Routledge.

Niven, Lisa (2012), 'Blake Lively Exclusive Interview', *Vogue* (6 September), http://www.vogue.co.uk/news/2012/09/06/blake-lively-interview---gucci-premiere-fragrance-fashion-and-children, accessed 1 January 2013.

Nixon, Sean (1996), *Hard Looks: Masculinities, Spectatorship and Contemporary Consumption*, New York: Palgrave Macmillan.

Nixon, Sean (1997), 'Circulating Culture', in Paul du Gay (ed.), *Production of Culture/ Cultures of Production*, London Sage.

Nylon Guys (2011), 'Here Comes the Sun' (April).

Oakley, Ann (1981), *Subject Women*, New York: Pantheon.

Oldenberg, Ann (2006), 'TV Brings High Fashion Down to the Everyday', *USA Today* (12 July), http://www.usatoday.com/life/television/news/2006-07-11-fashion-tv_x.htm, accessed 26 June 2008.

O'Riordan, Marie (2007a), 'Editor's Letter', *Marie Claire* (December).

O'Riordan, Marie (2007b), 'Fashion with Heart', *Marie Claire* (December).

Osgerby, Bill (1998), *Youth in Britain since 1945*, London: Wiley.

Osgerby, Bill (2004), ' "So Who's Got Time for Adults!": Femininity, Consumption, and the Development of Teen TV—from *Gidget* to *Buffy*', in Glynn Davis and Kay Dickinson (eds), *Teen TV: Genre, Consumption, Identity*, London: BFI Publishing.

Ott, Brian L. (2007), *The Small Screen: How Television Equips Us to Live in the Information Age*, Oxford: Blackwell.

Partington, Angela (1992), 'Popular Fashion and Working-Class Affluence', in Juliet Ash and Elizabeth Wilson (eds), *Chic Thrills: A Fashion Reader*, London: Pandora.

Pearson, Roberta E., and Messenger-Davies, Maire (2003), 'You're Not Going to See That on TV: *Star Trek—The Next Generation* in Film and Television', in Mark Jancovich and James Lyons (eds), *Quality Popular Television: Cult TV, the Industry and Fans,* London: BFI Publishing.

Pechman, Ali (2012), 'Mad Men's Megan Draper Reads (And Wears) 1966 "Vogue" ', *The Awl* (18 May), http://www.theawl.com/2012/05/mad-men-megan-draper-and-vogue, accessed 1 December 2012.

Penn, Jean (1998), 'Clothing the Deal', *The Hollywood Reporter: Fashion in Entertainment Special Issue* (20–6 October).

People (2000), 'Naughty but Nice' (2 October).

People (2007a), 'Not So Ugly Betties' (7 May).

People (2007b), 'Style Watch' (11 June).

People (2007c), 'Style Watch' (13 August).

Petro, Patrice (1986), 'Mass Culture and the Feminine: The "Place" of Television in Film Studies', *Cinema Journal*, 25/3 (Spring): 5–21.

Polhemus, Ted (1997), 'In the Supermarket of Style', in Steve Redhead, Derek Wynne and Justin O'Connor (eds), *The Clubcultures Reader: Readings in Popular Cultural Studies*, Oxford: Blackwell.

Polhemus, Ted, and Procter, Lynn (1978), *Fashion and Anti-Fashion: An Anthropology of Clothing and Adornment*, London: Thames & Hudson.

Powell, Helen, and Prasad, Sylvie (2007), 'Life Swap: Celebrity Expert as Lifestyle Adviser', in Dana Heller (ed.), *Makeover Television: Realities Remodelled*, London: I.B. Tauris.

Powers, John (2008), 'Contributors Man of the Hour', *Vogue* (December).

Radner, Hilary (1995), *Shopping Around: Feminine Culture and the Pursuit of Pleasure*, London and New York: Routledge.

Redden, Guy (2007), 'Makeover Morality and Consumer Culture', in Dana Heller (ed.), *Makeover Television: Realities Remodelled*, London and New York: I.B Tauris.

Redhead, Steve (1997), *Subculture to Clubculture: An Introduction to Popular Cultural Studies*, London: Wiley.

Redmond, Sean (2003), 'Thin White Women in Advertising: Deathly Corporeal', *Journal of Consumer Culture*, 3/2: 170–90.

Redmond, Sean (2006), 'Intimate Fame Everywhere', in Su Holmes and Sean Redmond (eds), *Framing Celebrity: New Directions in Celebrity Culture*, London: Routledge.

Rennie, Kara (2012), 'An Interview with Boardwalk Empire Costume Designer John Dunn', *On Screen Fashion* (January), http://onscreenfashion.com/2012/01/27/an-interview-with-boardwalk-empire-costume-designer-john-dunn/, accessed 6 August 2012.

Rojek, Chris (2001), *Celebrity*, London: Reaktion Books.

Romao, Tico (2004), 'Guns and Gas: Investigating the 1970s Car Chase Film', in Yvonne Tasker (ed.), *Action and Adventure Cinema*, London: Routledge.

Rosenblit, Rachel (2009), 'The Mentalists', *Elle* (April).

Rowe, Kathleen (1995), *The Unruly Woman: Gender and the Genres of Laughter*, Austin: University of Texas Press.

Sandell, Laurie (2007), 'Surprise! She's a Bombshell (and You Can Be One Too)', *Glamour* (October).

Shank, Barry (1994), *Dissonant Identities: The Rock 'n' Roll Scene in Austin Texas*, Hanover: Wesleyan University Press.

Sheridan, Jayne (2010), *Fashion Media Promotion: The New Black Magic*, Oxford: Wiley-Blackwell.

Shohat, Ella (1991), 'Ethnicities-in-Relation: Toward a Multicultural Reading of American Cinema', in Lester D. Friedman (ed.), *Unspeakable Images: Ethnicity and the American Cinema*, Urbana and Chicago: University of Illinois.

Simmel, Georg (1904/1957), 'Fashion', *The American Journal of Sociology*, 62/6: 541–58.

Skeggs, Beverley (1997), *Formations of Class and Gender*, London, Thousand Oaks and New Delhi: Sage.

Slater, Don (1997), *Consumer Culture and Modernity*, Cambridge: Polity Press.

Sohn, Amy (2004), *Sex and the City: Kiss and Tell*, London: Pan Macmillan.

Stacey, Jackie (1994), *Stargazing: Hollywood Cinema and Female Spectatorship*, London: Routledge.

Stanley, Alessandra (2009), 'East Side Story', *US Vogue* (February).

Stanley, Alessandra (2011), 'Retrofitting the Feminine Mystique', *New York Times* (16 September), http://www.nytimes.com/2011/09/18/arts/television/pan-am-playboy-club-and-whitney-new-on-tv.html?pagewanted=all&_r=0, accessed 12 January 2013.

Star, Darren (1996), *Sex and the City* 'Pilot', revised final script (4 February).

Steele, Valerie (1998), *Paris Fashion: A Cultural History*, Oxford and New York: Oxford University Press.

Stein, Louisa (2009), 'Playing Dress-Up: Digital Fashion and Gamic Extensions of Televisual Experience in *Gossip Girl*'s Second Life', *Cinema Journal*, 48/3: 11–122.

Storey, John (ed.) (2006), *Cultural Theory and Popular Culture*, 3rd edition, Edinburgh: Pearson.

Straw, Will (1991), 'Systems of Articulation, Logics of Change: Communities and Scenes in Popular Music', *Cultural Studies*, 5/3: 368–88.

Street, Sarah (2002), *Costume and Cinema: Dress Codes in Popular Film*, London: Wallflower.

Studlar, Gaylyn (2000), ' "Chi-Chi Cinderella": Audrey Hepburn as Couture Countermodel', in David Desser and Garth S. Jowett (eds), *Hollywood Goes Shopping*, Minneapolis: University of Minnesota Press.

Sundel, Jenny (2007), 'Best Dressed', *People* (12 February).

Tasker, Yvonne, and Negra, Diane (2007), 'Introduction', in Yvonne Tasker and Diane Negra (eds), *Interrogating Postfeminism*, Durham and London: Duke University Press.

Teen People (December 2004).

Teen Vogue (September 2004).

Thomas, Karen (2004), 'Is There Fashion After "Sex" ', *USA Today* (27 February), http://usatoday30.usatoday.com/life/television/news/2004-02-26-tv-fashion_x.htm, accessed 13 February 2009.

Thompson, Robert (2011), 'Foreword: From Rod Serling to Roger Sterling', in Gary Edgerton (ed.), *Mad Men*, London: I.B Tauris.

Thornton, Sarah (1997), 'The Social Logic of Subcultural Capital', in Ken Gelder (ed.), *The Subcultures Reader*, London and New York: Routledge.

Tom & Lorenzo (2012), 'Mad Style: Tom & Lorenzo' (6 June), http://www.tomandlorenzo.com/tag/mad-style, accessed 23 January 2013.

Trebay, Guy (2006), 'Roll Up Your Sleeves and Indulge in a Miami Vice', *New York Times* (20 July), http://www.nytimes.com/2006/07/20/fashion/20MIAMI.html?_r=1&pagewanted=1&n=Top/Reference/Times%20Topics/People/T/Trebay,%20Guy, accessed 21 December 2010.

Triggs, Charlotte (2008), 'Behind the Seams at *Gossip Girl*', *People* (29 September).

Turner, Graeme (2004), *Understanding Celebrity*, London: Sage.

Turner, Graeme, Bonner, Frances, and Marshall, P. David (eds) (2000), *Fame Games: The Production of Celebrity in Australia,* Cambridge: Cambridge University Press.

US Vogue (2008), 'Coastal Blend' (December).

Valdivia, Angharad (2000), *A Latina in the Land of Hollywood and Other Essays on Media Culture*, Arizona: University of Arizona.

Valdivia, Angharad (2004), 'Latinas as Radical Hybrid: Transnationally Gendered Traces in Mainstream Media', *Global Media Journal*, 3/4 (Spring), http://lass.purduecal.edu/cca/gmj/sp04/gmj-sp04-valdivia.htm, accessed 26 March 2010.

Veblen, Thorstein (1899/1994), *A Theory of the Leisure Class*, London: Allen & Unwin.

Waldman, Diane (1984), 'From Midnight Shows to Marriage Vows', *Wide Angle,* 6/2: 33–48.

Walsh, Margaret (1979), 'The Democratization of Fashion: The Emergence of the Women's Dress Pattern Industry', *Journal of American History*, 6/2: 299–313.

Warner, Helen (2009), 'Style over Substance?: Fashion, Spectacle and Narrative in Contemporary US Television', *Journal of Popular Narrative Media*, 2/2: 181–93.

Warner, Helen (2010), 'New Trends?: Industrial Strategies in Fashion, Television and Celebrity Culture', *SCAN: Journal of Media Arts Culture*, 7/2, http://scan.net.au/scan/journal/display.php?journal_id=154, accessed 1 January 2012.

Waterman, Lauren (2004), 'Mixed Doubles', *Teen Vogue* (September).

Weber, Brenda (2009), *Makeover TV: Selfhood, Citizenship, and Celebrity*, Durham and London: Duke University Press.

Wee, Valerie (2004), 'Selling Teen Culture: How American Multimedia Conglomeration Reshaped Teen Television in the 1990s', in Glyn Davis and Kay Dickinson (eds), *Teen TV: Genre, Consumption, Identity*, London: BFI Publishing.

Welch, Florence (2011), 'Ooh La La Blake!', *US Glamour* (July).

Werle, Simone (2009), *Fashionistas: A Century of Style Icons*, London: Prestel.

Whelehan, Imelda (2000), *Overloaded: Popular Culture and the Future of Feminism*, London: Women's Press.

Willens, Malerie (1998), 'Perfect Fit', *The Hollywood Reporter: Fashion in Entertainment Special Issue* (20–6 October).

Williams, Raymond (1975/2003), *Television: Technology and Cultural Form*, London: Routledge.

Willis, Paul (1977), *Learning to Labour,* London: Ashgate.

Wilson, Elizabeth (1985), *Adorned in Dreams: Fashion and Modernity*, London: Virago Press.

Wilson, Elizabeth (1992), 'Fashion and the Postmodern Body', in Juliet Ash and Elizabeth Wilson (eds), *Chic Thrills: A Fashion Reader*, London: Pandora.

Wilson, Julie (2010), 'Star Testing: The Emerging Politics of Celebrity Gossip', *The Velvet Light Trap: A Critical Journal of Film and Television,* 65: 25–39

Wilson, Polly (2002), 'After a Fashion', *The Hollywood Reporter: Fashion in Entertainment Special Issue* (22–8 October).

Witchel, Alex (2008), ' "Mad Men" Has its Moment', *New York Times* (22 June), http://www.nytimes.com/2008/06/22/magazine/22madmen-t.html?pagewanted=all, accessed 17 January 2013.

Wollen, Peter (1995), 'Strike a Pose', *Sight and Sound*, 5/3: 13–15.

Filmography and Broadcast Media

90210 (2008–), Created by Gabe Sachs, Jeff Judah, Darren Star and Rob Thomas, USA: CW Television Network.

A Cinderella Story (2004), Directed by Mark Rosman [Film], USA: Warner Bros.

A Day at the Races (1937), Directed by Sam Wood [Film], USA: MGM.

All That Heaven Allows (1955), Directed by Douglas Sirk [Film], USA: Universal International.

Ally McBeal (1997–2002), Created by David E. Kelley, USA: 20th Century Fox Television.

American Gigolo (1980), Directed by Paul Schrader [Film], USA: Paramount Pictures.

As Good as It Gets (1997), Directed by James L. Brooks [Film], USA: Sony Pictures Entertainment.

Back to the Future (1985), Directed by Robert Zemeckis [Film], USA: Universal Pictures.

Being John Malkovich (1999), Directed by Spike Jonze [Film], USA: USA Films.

Boardwalk Empire (2010–), Created by Terence Winter, USA: Home Box Office.

Breakfast at Tiffany's (1961), Directed by Blake Edwards [Film], USA: Paramount Pictures.

Broadcast News (1987), Directed by James L. Brooks [Film], USA: Twentieth Century Fox Film Corporation.

Carrie Diaries, The (2012–), Created by Miguel Arteta, USA: CW Television Network.

Cashmere Mafia (2008), Created by Kevin Wade, USA: American Broadcasting Company.

Charade (1963), Directed by Stanley Donen [Film], USA: University Pictures.

Confessions of a Shopaholic (2009), Directed by P.J. Hogan [Film], USA: Walt Disney Studio Motion Pictures.

Clueless (1995), Directed by Amy Heckerling [Film], USA: Paramount Pictures.

Dallas (1978–1991), Created by David Jacobs, USA: Warner Bros. Domestic Television Distribution.

Dark Angel (2000–2002), Created by James Cameron and Charles H. Eglee, USA: 20th Century Fox.

Designing Woman (1957), Directed by Vincente Minnelli [Film], USA: MGM.

Devil Wears Prada, The (2006), Directed by David Frankel [Film], USA: Twentieth Century Fox Film Corporation.

Dick van Dyke Show, The (1961–1966), Created by Carl Reiner, USA: Columbia Broadcasting System.

Donna Reed Show, The (1958–1966), Created by William Roberts, USA: American Broadcasting Company.

Dynasty (1981–1989), Created by Esther Shapiro and Richard Alan Shapiro, USA: American Broadcasting Company.

Faculty, The (1998), Directed by Robert Rodriguez [Film], USA: Dimension Films.

Fashions of 1934 (1934), Directed by William Dieterle [Film], USA: Warner Bros.

Felicity (1998–2002), Created by J. J. Abrams and Matt Reeves, USA: The WB Network Television.

First Contact (1996), Directed by Jonathan Frakes [Film], USA: Paramount Pictures.

Friends (1994–2004), Created by David Crane and Marta Kauffman, USA: Warner Bros.

Funny Face (1957), Directed by Stanley Donen [Film], USA: Paramount Pictures.

Gilmore Girls (2000–2007), Created by Amy Sherman-Palladino, USA: The WB Network Television.

Gold Diggers of 1935 (1935), Directed by Busby Berkeley [Film], USA: Warner Bros.

Golden Girls, The (1985–1992), Created by Susan Harris, USA: National Broadcasting Company.

Gossip Girl (2007–2012), Created by Josh Schwarz and Stephanie Savage, USA: CW Television Network.

Honey (2003), Directed by Billie Woodruff [Film], USA: Universal Pictures.

I Don't Know How She Does It (2011), Directed by Douglas McGrath [Film], USA: The Weinstein Company.

I Love Lucy (1951–1957), Created by Jess Oppenheimer [Film], USA: Columbia Broadcasting System.

It (1927), Directed by Clarence G. Badger [Film], USA: Paramount Pictures.

Jane By Design (2011), Created by April Blair, USA: ABC Family.

Letty Lynton (1932), Directed by Clarence Brown [Film], USA: MGM.

Lipstick Jungle (2008–2009), Created by Timothy Busfield, USA: National Broadcasting Company.

Mad Men (2007–), Created by Matthew Weiner, USA: American Movies Classic.

Mannequin (1937), Directed by Frank Borzage [Film], USA: Twentieth Century Fox Film Corporation.

Mary Tyler Moore Show, The (1970–1977), Created by James L. Brooks and Allan Burns, USA: Columbia Broadcasting System.

Matrix, The (1999), Directed by Andy Wachowski and Lana Wachowski [Film], USA: Warner Bros.

Men in Black (1997), Directed by Barry Sonnenfeld [Film], USA: Columbia Pictures.

Miami Rhapsody (1995), Directed by David Frankel [Film], USA: Buena Vista Pictures.

Miami Vice (1984–1990), Created by Anthony Yerkovich, USA: National Broadcasting Company.

Mighty Joe Young (1998), Directed by Ron Underwood [Film], USA: Buena Vista Pictures.

Moonstruck (1987), Directed by Norman Jewison [Film], USA: MGM.

Now Voyager (1942), Directed by Irving Rapper [Film], USA: Warner Bros.

O.C., The (2003–2007), Created by Josh Schwartz, USA: Warner Bros Television.

On the Waterfront (1954), Directed by Elia Kazan [Film], USA: Columbia Pictures.

Pan Am (2011–2012), Created by Jack Orman, USA: American Broadcasting Company.

Playboy Club, The (2011), Created by Chad Hodge, USA: National Broadcasting Company.

Prêt-à-Porter (1994), Directed by Robert Altman [Film], USA: Miramax Films.

Pretty Woman (1990), Directed by Gary Marshall [Film], USA: Buena Vista Pictures.

Private Lives of Pippa Lee, The (2009), Directed by Rebecca Miller [Film], USA: Screen Media Films.

Privileged (2008–2009), Created by Rina Mimoun, USA: CW Television Network.

Real Women Have Curves (2002), Directed by Patricia Cardoso [Film], USA: Home Box Office.

Rebel without a Cause (1955), Directed by Nicholas Ray [Film], USA: Warner Bros.

Revenge (2011–), Created by Mike Kelley, USA: American Broadcasting Company.

Roberta (1935), Directed by William A. Seiter [Film], USA: RKO Radio Pictures.

Sabrina (1954), Directed by Billy Wilder [Film], USA: Paramount Pictures.

Sabrina the Teenage Witch (1996–2003), Created by Nell Scovell, USA: American Broadcasting Company.

Scream (1996), Directed by Wes Craven [Film], USA: Dimension Films.

Scream 3 (1999), Directed by Wes Craven [Film], USA: Dimension Films.

Seven Year Itch, The (1955), Directed by Billy Wilder [Film], USA: Twentieth Century Fox Film Corporation.

Sex and the City (1998–2004), Created by Darren Star, USA: Home Box Office.

Sex and the City: The Movie (2008), Directed by Michael Patrick King [Film], USA: New Line Cinema.

Sister Act (1992), Directed by Emile Ardolino [Film], USA: Buena Vista Pictures.

Sisterhood of the Travelling Pants, The (2005), Directed by Ken Kwapis [Film], USA: Warner Bros.

Sisterhood of the Travelling Pants 2, The (2008), Directed by Sanaa Hamri [Film], USA: Warner Bros.

Soup, The (2004–), Created by Jay James, USA: E! Entertainment Television.

Star Trek: The Next Generation (1987–1998), Created by Gene Roddenberry, USA: CBS Paramount Domestic Television.

Stolen Holiday (1937), Directed by Michael Curtiz [Film], USA: Warner Bros.

Story of Seabiscuit, The (1949), Directed by David Butler [Film], USA: Warner Bros.

Talented Mr. Ripley, The (1999), Directed by Anthony Minghella [Film], USA: Miramax Films.

That Girl (1966–1971), Created by Sam Denoff and Bill Persky, USA: American Broadcasting Company.

Thoroughly Modern Millie (1967), Directed by George Roy Hill [Film], USA: Universal Pictures.

Twilight Zone, The (1959–1964), Created by Rod Serling, USA: Columbia Broadcasting System.

Ugly Betty (2006–2010), Created by Silvio Horta, USA: American Broadcasting Company.

Untouchables, The (1987), Directed by Brian De Palma [Film], USA: Paramount Pictures.

View, The (1997–), Created by Barbara Walter and Bill Geddie, USA: American Broadcasting Company.

Why Change Your Wife? (1920), Directed by Cecil B. DeMille [Film], USA: Paramount Pictures.

Working Girl (1988), Directed by Mike Nichols [Film], USA: Twentieth Century Fox Film Corporation.

You've Got Mail (1998), Directed by Nora Ephron [Film], USA: Warner Bros.

Ziegfeld Girl (1941), Directed by Robert Z. Leonard, Busby Berkeley [Film], USA: MGM.

INDEX